Letterwriting in Renaissance England

[*superscription*]
For hir Ma*ies*ties affayres

To the R*ight* honorable my very
    good *lord* the *lord* Admirall
    of England.

        post hast
           hast
           hast
       post hast for lief.

[*signature of authorization*]
W Burghley

[*postmaster's timestamp*]
London. 26. Aug
at 9. in the
morninge./.

misspent tyme & lead the rest of my life in such a civill
maner that shall bee bothe pleasinge to god & noe thinge
att all distastfull to yow, ar any of my frendes: tyme past
can hardly be recalled & it is neuer too late to doe well
I knowe Sr it is my duty to honor & obey yow my parents, &
I pray god I may no longer live then to expresse my duty
to yow & my mother: not onely in woord, but allsoe in
deed. Though yor iust displeashure att mee, may bee a motiue
against my submission; yet I beseech yow to pdon this my
bouldnes; ~~—~~ and; the follies of my ill spent tyme, & the
too little acknowledgement, & pformance of my duty, (& humbly
beseeche yow for gods sake) to forgiue & take once againe your
loste sonne to mercy and thincke vppon mee with the eye of pitty and
and not accordinge to my desert. with humble and harty
desier of yowr. and my mothers blessinge I humbly take
leaue & rest.

Yor
euer dutyful
obedient sonn
Lewes Bagot

Letterwriting in Renaissance England

Alan Stewart and Heather Wolfe

This volume has been published in
conjunction with the exhibition
Letterwriting in Renaissance England
presented at The Folger Shakespeare Library®,
Washington, DC, from
November 18, 2004, through April 2, 2005.

Gail Kern Paster
Director

Richard Kuhta
Librarian

Rachel Doggett
Andrew W. Mellon Curator of Books
and Exhibitions

This exhibition and the catalogue have been
funded by The Winton and Carolyn Blount
Exhibition Fund and The Andrew W. Mellon
Publication Fund of The Folger Shakespeare
Library. Crane Paper generously donated the
paper for this publication.

Distributed by
University of Washington Press,
Seattle and London.
ISBN 0-295-98509-7

Photographs by Julie Ainsworth,
except for item 68.

Cover: William Cecil, baron Burghley (1520–1598)
Letter signed, with autograph postscript, to
Charles Howard, 2nd lord Howard of Effingham
(later 1st earl of Nottingham)
The Strand, August 26, 1588
Folger MS X.d.494

Table of Contents

———

Acknowledgments

———

This catalogue, and the exhibition, could not have been completed without the gentle prodding and careful eyes of Rachel Doggett, Andrew W. Mellon Curator of Books and Exhibitions, the fine photography of Julie Ainsworth, Head of Photography, and the conservation prowess of Frank Mowery, Renate Mesmer, Rhea Baier, and Linda Hohneke. Leigh Anne Palmer's editorial assistance and the patience and helpfulness of Betsy Walsh, Head of Reader Services, Georgianna Ziegler, Head of Reference, Erin Blake, Curator of Art, and the Reading Room staff—Rosalind Larry, LuEllen DeHaven, Camille Seerattan, and Harold Batie—were deeply appreciated.

Beyond the walls of the Folger, we are grateful for the design wizardry of Antonio Alcalá and his staff at Studio A. George Way treated us to a wonderful tour of his collection in Staten Island and lent us objects for the exhibition, and Arthur Schwarz of Scarsdale, NY, generously lent two tiny unopened letters from George I. Peter C. Sutton, executive director of the Bruce Museum, in Geenwich, CT, provided an inspiring tour of his exhibition, "Love Letters: Dutch genre paintings in the age of Vermeer."

Finally, we wish to express our gratitude to James Alexander, David Kidwell, and Crane Paper for the generous donation of the paper on which this catalogue is printed.

Alan Stewart
Heather Wolfe

Textual conventions

In producing transcriptions of manuscript letters and other handwritten documents, we have aimed to give the reader as vivid an idea as possible of what they look like, while also attempting to make them readable. Thus, the letters' superscriptions, subscriptions, postscripts, marginal notes, and signatures, have been rendered spatially to the extent that this is possible. The often idiosyncratic spellings (including i/j and u/v graphs), punctuation, and syntax have not been modernized, and lineation has been maintained. We have, however, expanded certain abbreviations that might be confusing to modern readers. Writers of the sixteenth and seventeenth centuries regularly saved time (and paper) by employing contracted forms of words, usually signaled by the use of superscript letters, flourishes, semi-colons, or lines (tildes or tittles) placed above the word. Most of these contractions were standard, and would have been as familiar to Renaissance readers as "Mr." and "Mrs." are today (indeed we have not expanded "M^r" and "M^{rs}"; for the same reason, we have not expanded abbreviations for pounds, shillings, and pence—l for libra, s for solidi, or d for denari). In almost all other cases, we have indicated the expanded letters by using italics and silently lowering the superscriptions. For example,

La:	La*dy* or La*dyship*
L:, Lo, L^p	Lo*rd* or Lo*rdshi*p
Matie	Ma*ie*stie
S^r	S*i*r
w^{ch}	w*hi*ch
wth	w*i*th
y^e	*the*
y^t	*tha*t
yor and y^r	yo*u*r

Several of the letters included in this collection show signs of rethinking and rewriting. In these cases, deletions are indicated by a simple strikethrough of the text (e.g., ~~I have written~~) and additions are signalled by the use of caret symbols (^ ^) at either end of the added text; the added text is also rendered as a superscript. Words or letters in square brackets [ ] have been supplied by the editors.

Except for the reproductions of letters, the majority of images are not actual size. To give the reader a better sense of the variety and range of letter sizes, the headnotes to all letters indicate whether they have been reproduced at 100%, or slightly reduced.

"To the knowing Reader of Familiar Letters"

Love is the life of Frendship, Letters are
The life of Love, the Load-stones that by rare
Attraction make souls meet, and melt, and mix,
As when by fire exalted gold we fix.
They are those wing'd Pestillions that can fly,
From the Anartic to the Artic sky,
The Heralds and swift Harbengers that move
From East to West on Embassies of Love;
They can the Tropics cut, and cross the Line,
And swim from Ganges to the Rhone or Rhine,
From Thames to Tagus, thence to Tyber run,
And terminat their journy with the Sun:

They can the Cabinets of Kings unscrue,
And hardest intricacies of State unclue;
They can the the [*sic*] Tartar tell, what the Mogor
Or the great Turk doth on the Asian shore,
The Knez of them may know, what Prester John
Doth with his Camells in the torrid Zone:
Which made the Indian Inca think they wer
Spirits who in white sheets the Aer did tear.

The luckie Goose sav'd Joves beleagred Hill
Once by her noyse, but oftener by her Quill:
It twice prevented Rome, was not o're-run
By the tough Vandal, and the rough hewn Hun.

Letters can Plots though moulded under ground
Disclose, and their fell complices confound,
Witnes that fiery Pile which would have blown
Up to the Clouds, Prince, People, Peers, and Town,
Tribunalls, Church, and Chappell, and had dride
The Thames, though swelling in her highest pride,
And parboyl'd the poor Fish, which from her Sands
Had been tost'd up to the adjoyning Lands.
Lawyers as Vultures had soar'd up and down.
Prelats like Magpies in the Ayr had flown,
Had not the Eagles Letter brought to light,
That Subterranean horrid Work of night.

Credentiall Letters, States, and Kingdoms tie,
And Monarchs knit in lignes of Amitie;
They are those golden Links that do enchain
Whole Nations, though discinded by the Main;
They are the soul of Trade, they make Commerce,
Expand it self throughout the Univers.

Letters may more than History inclose,
The choicest learning, both for Vers and Prose;
They knowledg can unto our souls display,
By a more gentle, and familiar way,
The highest points of State and Policy,
The most severe parts of Philosophy
May be their subject, and their Themes enrich
As well as privat businesses, in which
Frends use to correspond, and Kindred greet.
Merchants negotiat, the whole World meet.

In Seneca's rich Letters is inshrin'd
What ere the ancient Sages left behind
Tully makes his the secret symptomes tell
Of those distempers which proud Rome befell,
When in her highest flourish she would make
Her Tyber from the Ocean homage take.
Great Antonin the Emperor did gain
more glory by his Letters, than his raign,
His Pen out-lasts his Pike, each golden line
In his Epistles do his name inshrine,
Aurelius by his Letters did the same,
And they in chief immortallize his fame.

Words vanish soon, and vapour into Ayr,
While Letters on Record stand fresh and fair,
And tell our Nephews who to us wer dear,
Who our choice frends, who our familiars were.

The bashfull Lover when his stammering lips
Falter, and fear some unadvised slips,
May boldly court his Mistris with the Quill,
And his hot passions to her Brest instill;
The Pen can furrow a fond Femals heart,
And pierce it more than Cupids feigned dart,
Letters a kind of Magic vertu have,
And like strong Philtres human souls inslave.

Speech is the Index, Letters Ideas are
Of the informing soul, they can declare,
And shew the inward man, as we behold
A face reflecting in a Chrystall mould:
They serve the dead and living, they becom
Attorneys and Administers: In somm,

Letters as Ligaments the World do tie,
Else all commerce and love 'twixt men would die.

———

James Howell, *Epistolae Ho-Elianae* (London, 1650)

Introduction

———

Letters as Ligaments the World do tie,
Else all commerce and love 'twixt men would die.

This is an exhibition about letterwriting—not just the letters themselves, but also the myriad *processes* of letterwriting: the penning, sending, receiving, reading, circulating, copying, and saving of letters. It could be argued that the letter was the single most important genre of the Renaissance: not merely one literary form among many (though it was that too) but the very glue that held society together, the "Ligaments" tying the world, as our opening epigram would have it—the primary form of non-verbal communication for hundreds of years, with the power to inform and influence people over long distances, for better and for worse. Our examples range from the early sixteenth to the early eighteenth centuries, the period in which the Folger Shakespeare Library has its strongest collections, but also the period in which the culture of letterwriting underwent several massive transformations from the rise of the printed book, popularizing the letterwriting manual, to the growth of a reliable postal system.

Letters are as popular today as they have ever been. The edited correspondence of literary, historical, and political figures fills the shelves of the biography sections of bookstores large and small. And we're still in thrall to notions of correct letterwriting. Indeed, it's intriguing to see how letterwriting manuals have evolved surprisingly little over the past four hundred and fifty years. From Erasmus of Rotterdam's 1522 bestseller *De conscribendis epistolis (On the Writing of Letters)*, it's not that great a jump to modern titles such as *Complete Handbook of Model Business Letters, Over 300 Successful Business Letters for all Occasions, Great Personal Letters for Busy People, Complete Book of Effective Personal Letters*, or *How to Write a Love Letter*. Like Erasmus's prototype, these manuals provide "real examples" based on "real situations," guiding the reader through the various parts of the letter, from the address on the envelope to the signature at the bottom, advising on paper, tone, and content—although now they include special sections on e-mail correspondence. Just as in Erasmus's day, you can still hire a "specialist" to write a letter for you, or download customizable templates online from *Instant Love Letter Creator 2.0*.

In recent years, much has been written by historians and literary critics about the theories of letterwriting in the Renaissance, and we glance at that material here. But our focus is on the letters themselves—the pieces of paper written on with ink, sealed with wax, and tied with ribbons, that made their way across Britain (and sometimes beyond) against significant odds, that were read, re-read, given to friends, copied, and finally preserved, ending up in the manuscript collection of the Folger. The text of the letters reveals many things: tenderness, bravado, anxiety, anger, awkwardness, formality, apology. But it is in these letters' very tangibility that we discovered most: in the folds that are now four hundred years old, the grime and fingerprints deposited by the writer and readers and the men who delivered them, the broken seals, the torn ribbons, the ink blots, the maddeningly personalized spelling, the flourishing signatures. It is these material features that we have sought to highlight in the letters that appear here—material features that, as we shall argue, contain and preserve much of the real message of the letters.

Without letters, "all commerce and love 'twixt men would die." In early modern England, letterwriting was the means by which men and women could establish contact, keep in touch, swap news and gossip, forge alliances, undertake commercial business, sue for mercy or for love. Even for prisoners, letterwriting was a basic privilege. Folger MS L.b.658 is a warrant ordering the Lieutenant of the Tower of London to supply one of his prisoners, Sir Thomas Monson, with pen, ink, and paper for writing letters. But this warrant also betrays the dangerous potential of letters: its one stipulation was that the prisoner must account to the Lieutenant for the paper, so that no letters were sent without the authorities' knowledge.

Given their ubiquity in everyday life, it is hardly surprising that letters figure importantly in the drama and literature of the day. Nearly all of Shakespeare's plays use letters as narrative devices, and many scenes begin with an individual reading a letter, alone. The ins and outs of writing, sending, and receiving letters—deceptions and miscommunications because of letters lost, forged, or misdirected, the clichés of love letters, letters being read aloud to a wider audience beyond the recipient —were familiar scenarios in life, and they became familiar scenarios in literature. The conventions of love letters, in particular, became so highly wrought that they gave themselves to parody. In a book called *The Mysteries of Love and Eloquence*, a list of superscriptions and subscriptions for "drolling letters" included: "To the ninth Wonder of the World," "To the Fair Murdress of my Soul," "The Vassal of your severest frowns," "your poor worm, that must of necessity die, if trod upon by the foot of your disdain. . . ."

But the letters in this collection speak for themselves. They are funnier, richer, more bizarre and more moving than anything the fiction of the period has to offer. By understanding the complex conventions of letterwriting, we can bring into focus a more rounded, grittier, and ultimately more convincing picture of everyday life in early modern England.

Tools

IN A WORLD WHERE MUCH OF OUR LONG-DISTANCE CORRESPONDENCE is accomplished by telephone and e-mail, and where most of the letters we exchange are word-processed or typewritten, it is already becoming something of a novelty to return to pen and paper. But in Renaissance England, where all correspondence was handwritten, resorting to "pen and paper" was not quite as simple as it sounds. In order to perform the physical work of penning a letter to be mailed, a writer had to develop a number of skills and assemble—and in some cases create—a range of materials.

The first writing book in English, Jehan de Beau-Chesne's and John Baildon's *A Booke Containing Divers sortes of handes as well the English as French secretarie with the Italian, Roman, Chancelry & court hands. Also th' true & iust proportion of the capitall Romane set forth* (London, 1570?), proved popular enough to be reprinted in 1571, 1602, and 1611, and later to win Beau-Chesne the position of writing master to James VI and I's daughter Princess Elizabeth. The book is explicitly addressed to young learners, with its instructions given in entertaining rhymes—"Rules Made by E.B. For Children to write by." These "Rules" serve as a reminder that a Renaissance writer could not simply pick up a pen and write. All the raw materials of writing had to be prepared: goose feathers needed to be transformed into quill pens and iron gall nuts into ink, while paper needed to be treated so that the ink would not be too easily absorbed. When writing, the writer had to make sure everything was to hand:

> Inke always good store on right hand to stand,
> Browne paper for great haste, or else boxe with sand:
> Dip pen, and shake pen, and touch pen for haire:
> Waxe, quills and pen knife see alwayes ye beare:

Ink-making was a time-consuming process for the writers of the sixteenth and seventeenth centuries. As might be expected, Beau-Chesne and Baildon devote a rhyme to the making of ink:

> To make common ink, of wine take a quart
> Two ounces of gumme let that be a part,
> Fiue ounces of gals, of copres take three,
> Long standing doth make it better to be:
> If wine ye do want, raine water is best,
> And then as much stuffe as aboue at the least:
> If inke be too thicke, put vineger in,
> For water doth make the colour more dimme.

They then go on to specify how "to make Inke in haste," how "to keepe Inke long," and how to concoct a "speciall blacke Inke" (lampblack and gum water make it thicker). Printed household companions often contained pertinent advice on the subject: Thomas Lupton's *A Thousand Notable things, of sundry sortes* (London, 1595?), for example, advises that "If some droppes of Aqua vite, be myxt with wryting ynke, the same ynke wyl neuer be frozen." Virtually every manuscript receipt book that has survived contains, alongside instructions for household essentials like pickling fruit and home cures, a few preferred recipes for making ink.

But ink was not the end of the process. Letters required paper, and paper was an expensive commodity, usually imported from the Continent. Most account books of the period contain multiple entries for paper expenses, whether it was bought in a quire (25 sheets), a ream (20 quires) or in bulk, in a bale (10 reams). To prepare the paper so that the ink would not spread, the young penman would need "stanch graine," concocted from alum and resin, with which to rub the paper or parchment before writing. Then the quill must be well chosen—the authors prefer the third or fourth feather of a goose's wing, or failing that a raven's or a gander's quill. Once the perfect quill was selected, the writer would make the pen with "the clift [cleft] somewhat long, the neb [nib] not too short." He also needed sand (or, if rushed, brown paper) to soak up excess ink on the page after he was done writing, and a pen knife, for frequently paring the nib of the quill so that the writing remained smooth and even.

An inventory of his household taken in August 1556 by Sir William More of Loseley in Surrey reveals the elements required for his writing place, in his private closet: a "little deske to wryte on," "a standyshe [inkstand] of pewter," "a dust boxe [pounce] of bone," "a haere of bone to be made a sele," "a penne of bone to wryte *with*," "a Sele of many Seles," "a penknyf," "a pene of yron," several bookes of paper, one of them bound "in past," "a wrytyng boke of parchment," "a boke to lerne to wryte by," "a slate to wryte in," and scissors (Folger MS L.b.550). The most valuable items by far were the parchment book and the writing slate.

Even with all the materials at hand, the correct bodily posture and the pre-scribed hand position, the aspiring writer had to be aware of the many different ways in which the alphabet could be written, what were known as the various "hands." This was the primary function of Beau-Chesne and Baildon's book and the other writing manuals which followed. Each different hand came with its own history, its own set of expected uses and social signals. Most common in sixteenth-century England was the "secretary" hand, in which most letters and documents were written, a hand that is now unfamiliar to us and difficult to read. Easier to read today is the up-and-coming hand of the sixteenth century, the so-called "italic" hand, primarily associated at the time with women's writing, more socially elite circles (who would write their letters in a secretary hand and sign them in an italic hand, often adding dramatic flourishes to their signatures), and Continental correspondence. Certain professions had their own hands, in which their scribes had to be specially trained—the Court of Chancery, for example, produced a "Chancery hand" that was allegedly so large because Chancery scriveners were paid by the page. In practice, despite the efforts of men like Beau-Chesne and Baildon to prescribe distinct, proper forms, many writers of the sixteenth and seventeenth centuries used a mixture of secretary and italic forms in their letters.

Those whose livelihood depended on good handwriting made huge claims for its efficacy. Martin Billingsley, for example, tutor of Prince Charles (later

Charles I), and author of *The Pens Excellencie or The Secretaries Delighte* (1618), sees a fair hand as the portal to many wonders:

> And what should I say of the Excellency of this Art? Is it not one of the hands by which not only this, but all other common-wealths are upholden? The key which opens a passage to the descrying and finding out of innumerable treasures? The handmaid to memory? The Register and Recorder of all Arts? And the very mouth whereby a man familiarly conferreth with his friend, though the distance of thousands of miles be betwixt them?

———

1

Jehan de Beau-Chesne and John Baildon
A Booke Containing Divers sortes of hands as well the English as French secretarie with the Italian, Roman, Chancelry & court hands. Also the true & just proportio[n] of the capitall Roma[n]e set forth
London: Richard Field, 1602
Folger STC 6450.2

Writing was a two-handed operation. The pen in the right hand needed constantly to be kept in good shape, by a metal penknife—not too soft, not too hard, not too sharp, not too dull—held in the left hand. Beau-Chesne and Baildon provide illustrations of how to hold your pen, and just as important, how not to.

[sig. A2ʳ]   To hold your pen.

> Your thombe on your pen as highest bestow
> The forefinger next, the middle below:
> And holding it thus in most comely wise,
> Your bodie vpright, stoupe not with your head:
> Your breast from the boord, if that ye be wise,
> Lest that ye take hurt, when ye haue well fed.

———

2

Granville family
Manuscript receipt book, late 17th /early 18th century
Folger MS V.a.430

Mary Granville inscribed this receipt book to her daughter: "Mʳˢ Ann Granvills Book which I hope shee will make a better use of then her mother." In the same opening as the recipe for ink are recipes "to make Almond Puddings," "To make the cocke water," and "A Drinke for the Ricketts." The ink recipe has a manicule, or pointing finger symbol, in the margin to signify its importance and to locate it more easily.

To make = Inke = Verie Good

Take a quart of snow or raine water, and a quart of
Beere vinegre, a pound of galls bruised, halfe a
pound of caperis, and 4 ounces of gum bruised; first
mix your water and vinegre together, and putt itt
into an earthen Jug, then put in the galls, stirring
itt 2. or 3 times a day letting it stand 8 or 9 daies,
and then put in your caperas and Gumme. as you
vse it straine itt. &c =

———

3
Nathaniel Rich
Autograph letter signed, to his uncle, Sir Robert Rich
May 12, 1697
Folger MS X.d.451 (187)

The following letter, written in a painstakingly careful round hand, is typical of
many: an apology from a nephew to an uncle for his "bad writing," promising to
continue in his daily efforts to improve.

[superscription]   To
The Right Hon*orable* S*ir* Robert Rich
*Knigh*t and Barron*ett* at Mr Whittakers
In Clapham
These

[letter]   May *the* 12th. 1697

Honored S*i*r:

After my duty presented to you and to my
honored Aunt, These few lines are to acquaint
your Hon*our tha*t I have almost Copyed out another
of *the* Questions and Answers in which I hope
you will find some better writing then in *the*
last which I gave to your Hon*our*, and as soon as
I have done this *tha*t I am now about, I think to
begin another of *the* same if your Hon*our* think
fitt of it, I should have bin very glad to have
seen your Hon*our* and my honored Aunt to day,
but *tha*t I doe take *the* waters I took them yester=
day and I intend to take them to morrow god
willing: pray give my service to m*iste*r & m*istre*ss
Cross, I doe follow my Copying in *the* afternoons
but cannot Cypher in *the* mornings by reason
of my taking of *the* waters but assoon as I

have done taking of them, I will goe every
morning, having no more to add at this time
but begging your honours pardon for troubling
you at this time with my bad writing but
hoping *that* in a short time you will see a great
change for *the* better, so begging your prayers
for me who daily stands in need of them so

I am glad to heer that
your Hon*our* has your health
so well I pray god continue
it to you for health is a
Jewel of great value.

I rest your dutyfull
Nephew & servant to
Comand Till death
Nath*aniel* Rich

———

4
Inkwell (walnut, 4 x 4 cm), 1691
From the collection of George Way, Staten Island

Quills needed to be refilled regularly and replaced often. Made of walnut, this
inkwell has an opening to insert a quill at each corner. One of the openings is for
the "quill in waiting." The base of this hole opens into the central part of the well so
that the quill can fill with ink.

5

Writing box (English oak, 45 x 32.5 cm at base), 1654
From the collection of George Way, Staten Island

Writers would keep their writing supplies stored in these boxes, which were often
outfitted with drawers and other compartments and generally had slanted surfaces
for a more comfortable writing position.

6

Candlestick (brass), ca. 1680
From the collection of George Way, Staten Island

The candlestick was an integral part of letterwriting. Since many rooms were poorly
lit by sunlight, letterwriters required artificial light from candles or fireplaces not
only from dusk onwards, but often for daytime writing as well. This example is
made of brass, with a socketed square base and the typical hollow-stemmed twist
of the Restoration period. Wealthier households could afford longer-burning
beeswax candles, while the middling classes used tallow candles, rendered from
sheep fat. The activity of letterwriting would have been interrupted at regular
intervals, since the wick on a tallow candle required trimming every 15-20 minutes
to prevent it from falling onto unmelted tallow.

7
Seal matrix (silver-lead alloy [?] handle with brass matrix, 4.9 cm long),
17th century
From the collection of George Way, Staten Island

Used to close the outside of a folded letter or to authenticate a legal document,
seals were highly personalized, often containing the initials of the sender or the
family crest or shield of arms. Writers kept desk seals, or seal matrices, and often
had seal or signet rings as well, which were easily portable as jewelry. Individuals
made use of both official and personal seals so that the nature of their business was
evident to the recipient before opening the letter.

The Enimie of Idlenesse:

Teaching the

maner and stile how

*to endite, compose and write all sort
of Epistles and Letters: as well by*
answer, as otherwise.
Deuided iuto foure Bokes, no lesse plesaunt than profitable.

*Set forth in English by William
Fulwood Marchant, &c.*

The Contentes hereof appere in
the Table at the latter ende of
the Booke.

Manuals

THE PRACTICE OF LETTERWRITING IN THE RENAISSANCE gave rise to a sturdy body of theoretical works in Latin explaining what letters were and prescribing how they should be written. It is debatable just how much influence this "epistolography" or epistolary theory had on the actual writing of letters, but it is beyond doubt that most educated men would have been exposed to these texts, since they formed an integral part of a grammar school education.

Theorizing letterwriting was nothing new to the Renaissance. There was a well-established, highly nuanced medieval discipline known as the *ars dictaminis*, whose birth has been traced back at least as far as the late-eleventh-century writings of the monk Alberic of Monte. The *ars dictaminis* understood letterwriting as a rhetorical art, and developed prescriptive, formal models for different genres of letters. Later, humanist scholars added an important element to this tradition with their rediscovery of the letters of the classical writers. In 1345, the Italian poet Petrarch, working in the cathedral library of Verona, stumbled across a manuscript of Cicero's "familiar letters" to Atticus, Quintus, and Brutus, a discovery that reportedly moved him to tears. The familiar letters inspired him in the writing and collecting of his own prose letters, and in developing a new critical theory of letterwriting. In time, the familiar letter became popular with such prominent quattrocento Florentine humanist writers as Giovanni Boccaccio, Coluccio Salutati, Leonardo Bruni, and Poggio Bracciolini, the last two of whom edited collections of their own letters. By the time printing presses started to appear in Europe in the mid-fifteenth century, letterwriting had become a fashionable academic movement, ripe for development.

Foremost among the humanist writers who rose to that challenge was the Dutch scholar Desiderius Erasmus of Rotterdam. In a short piece entitled *Conficiendarum epistolarum formula* (*A formula for the composition of letters*), Erasmus outlined his definition of a letter:

> The letter is variously defined by Latin writers, but with essentially the same meaning. The Greek sophist Libanius defines the letter in this way: "A letter is a conversation between two absent persons." He further defines conversation to mean familiar speech, to have us understand that the letter differs hardly at all from the ordinary speech of everyday conversation. He cautions that it is a great error to use tragic grandiloquence in the composition of letters and to expend all one's intellectual energies in the pursuit of brilliance, profuseness of style, and ostentatious display where there is least need of it. For the style of a letter should be simple and even a bit careless, in the sense of a studied carelessness.

Erasmus understood that, at its best, the familiar letter was a tremendously affecting genre, one that seemed to provide an insight into the relationship between writer and recipient. Letters and letterwriting might be said to have formed his place in history. The complete printed correspondence of Erasmus runs to over three thousand letters, an astonishing number, given the vagaries of archival survival from the period, but less astonishing when we consider the importance Erasmus placed on letterwriting. Like everyone else, Erasmus wrote to his contemporaries, both friends and strangers, in order to forge and consolidate relationships. But he then published many of those letters in print, sometimes altering and manipulating them in order to advertise to the world what appeared to be his network of acquaintances—what a later generation would dub a "republic of letters."

Beyond crafting his personal reputation, letters played a fundamental role in Erasmus's educational program, which was used as the model for several major English grammar schools in the sixteenth century. Study of letters by classical authors was of course a key part of the curriculum, as was the imitation of those letters. The statutes of Rivington School, for example, prescribe for the upper forms

> to be exercised in devising and writing sundry epistles to sundry persons, of sundry matters, as of chiding, exhorting, comforting, counselling, praying, lamenting, some to friends, some to foes, some to strangers; of weighty matters or merry, as shooting, hunting, etc., of adversity, of prosperity, of war and peace, divine and profane, of all sciences and occupations, some long and some short. (J. Whitaker, *Statutes and Charter of Rivington School* (London, 1837), pp. 216–17)

Erasmus himself dictated that any edition of his works "that concern literature and education" should contain four key works, of which the first was *De conscribendis epistolis* ("On the Writing of Letters"), his most sustained work on letterwriting on which Erasmus worked for several years. *De conscribendis* developed from a study aid for some of Erasmus's pupils in Paris, through various different drafts, until it reached its final form of a full-scale textbook in 1522. It was a runaway success and soon established itself as a set text in both Lutheran and Jesuit schools across Europe. Erasmus's lead was followed by other major Continental scholars of the sixteenth century. The Spanish humanist Juan Luis Vives, for example, published his own *De conscribendis epistolis* in 1534, a work more interested in exploring the classical history of the mechanics of letterwriting, especially from the Roman period. Other popular Latin discourses, often published together, include Aurelio Lippo Brandolino's *De ratione scribendi libri tres* (1498), Christoph Hegendorph's *Methodus epistolis conscribendi* (1526), Konrad Celtis' *Methodus conficiendarum epistolarum* (1537), and Georgius Macropedius' *Methodus de conscribendis epistolis* (1543). Towards the end of the century, the Dutch scholar Justus Lipsius produced his *Epistolica institutio*.

Although it is impossible to deny Erasmus's influence on generations of English schoolboys and university undergraduates, it might be fairly asked to what extent Erasmus managed to influence the writing of everyday correspondence. A good number of young Englishmen came away from their education with Erasmus's letterwriting precepts etched in their minds, but there was still a leap to be made from those models, deeply involved in a Latin education, to their possible application in a vernacular English setting.

The first letterwriting manual in English was William Fulwood's *The Enimie of Idlenesse*, which first appeared in 1568, and went through ten editions by 1621. While its dedication to a prominent London merchant, "Master Anthonie Ratcliffe, Master of the worshipfull Companie of the Merchant Tailors of London" (sig. A2ʳ), suggests it was embedded in the commercial concerns of England's capital, the book was in essence a translation, with a few amendments, of a recent edition of a French manual entitled *Le Stile et manière de composer, dicter, et escrire toute sorte d'epistre, ou lettres missiues, tant par response, que autrement* (1566). *The Enimie of Idlenesse* is divided into four books. The first sets forth "the necessarie precepts, which belong to the well composing and inditing of Epistles and Letters" with some examples, while the second prints English translations of letters by scholars drawn from the Italian scholar Angelo Poliziano's *Illustrium virorum epistolae*, one of Erasmus's preferred sources for examples. The third book examines "the manner and forme how to write by answer" matching a letter of a particular kind with its proper response, and the fourth and final book contains some love letters, and a few English verses not found in its French original. Aside from these verses, there is little original in Fulwood's volume: the declared models are from Erasmus's work and various other Latin manuals.

Abraham Fleming's 1576 volume, *A Panoplie of Epistles, Or, a looking Glasse for the vnlearned* was even less concerned with everyday life. Although its title page boasted that it contained "a perfecte plattforme of inditing letters of all sorts, to persons of al estates and degrees, as well our superiours, as also our equals and inferiours," it betrayed that its sources were "the best and the eloquentest Rhetoricians that haue liued in all ages, and haue beene famous in that facultie. Gathered and translated out of Latine into English." The only English names included among the Greek, Latin and Continental authors were two sixteenth-century scholars, Roger Ascham and Walter Haddon, whose contributions were of letters written in Latin.

Perhaps the most influential English text was Angel Day's *The English Secretarie*, first published in 1586. As its title suggests, this manual aimed to be more "English" than the earlier ones despite being clearly modeled on Erasmus. Its focus was on instruction, rather than merely on example, and it pushed the reader to understand the function of the principal rhetorical parts of a letter: the "exordium" ("a beginning or induction to the matter to be written"), the "narratio or propositio" ("wherein is declared or proponed, in the one by plaine tearmes, in the other by inference, or comparsion, the verie substance of the matter whatsoeuer to be handled"), the "confirmatio" ("wherein are amplified or suggested many reasons, for the aggrauating or proof of any matter in qustion" [sic]), and the "peroratio" ("in which after a briefe recapitulation of that which hath beene vrged, the occasions thereof are immediatelie concluded").

The English Secretarie also outlined the four generic divisions of letters—demonstrative, deliberative, judicial, and familiar—and the subdivisions within, hinting at the myriad of purposes that letters necessarily served. For example, demonstrative letters could be "descriptorie," "laudatorie," or "vituperatorie," deliberative letters could be "hortatorie and dehortatorie," "swasorie and disswasorie," "conciliatorie and reconciliatorie," "petitorie," "commendatorie," "consolatorie," "monitorie," "reprehensorie," or "amatorie," judicial letters could be "accusatorie," "excusatorie," "expostulatorie," "purgatorie," "defensorie," "exprobatorie," "deprecatorie," or "inuectiue," while familiar letters were broken down into eight subdivisions: "narratorie," "nunciatorie," "gratulatorie," "remuneratorie," "iocatorie," "obiurgatorie," "mandatorie," and "responsorie." Later editions included not only examples and explanations of these four divisions, but also specialized sections dealing with descriptions of figures, schemes, and tropes, and a discourse on the parts and offices of a secretary.

John Browne's *The Marchants Avizo*, which first appeared in 1589 and went through four editions by 1640, is a different creature altogether. Browne was a prominent figure in the Bristol Society of Merchant Venturers, and his book is drenched in the local color of Bristol mercantile and maritime life. Dedicated to "Maister Thomas Aldworth Marchant of the Citie of Bristowe"—as Bristol was then called—"and to all the Worshipfull companie of the Marchants of the saide Citie" (sig. A2ʳ), *The Marchants Avizo* markets itself very much as a "hands-on" manual designed to facilitate overseas trade for Bristol traders working on the Iberian peninsula. Its supposed readership was the "Sonnes and Servants" of Bristol men for use "when they first send them beyond the Seas, as to *Spayne and Portingale or other Countreyes.*"

The seventeenth century saw the rise of a more utilitarian kind of instruction manual, one that included letterwriting among a range of practical skills that a scholar should learn. These manuals turned away from the sometimes flowery rhetoric of classical models to stress plain writing and pragmatic uses. Following George Snell's *The right teaching of useful knowledg* (1649) came Ralph Johnson's *The Scholars Guide* (1665), E. Young's *The Compleat English Scholar* (1680), and J. Hill's *The Young Secretary's Guide, or, a Speedy Help to Learning* (1680), which went through many editions in both England and America. At the other end of the spectrum emerged rose two distinctive genres of letterbooks: the "secretary" and the "discovered" packet of letters.

————

8

Desiderius Erasmus (d. 1536)
De conscribendis epistolis, quod quidam & me[n]dosum, & mutilum aediderant recognitum ab autore & locupletatu[m], Parabolarum siue. Similium liber ab autore recognitus
Basel: Jo. Froben, 1522
Folger 220-608q

This copy of Erasmus's massively influential book was handed down to various members of the sixteenth-century Shirley family (it is inscribed by George, Thomas, and Henry in both Latin and English). The title and author's name are written on the fore-edge, since books were usually stored with their spines facing inward. Judging from the fine goatskin binding on wooden boards and evidence of brass clasps, the book was a valuable asset to the Shirley library. At the end of the book are two unfinished lists: "A note of all the bokes I have," and "A note of *the* Engleishe bockes *that* I have."

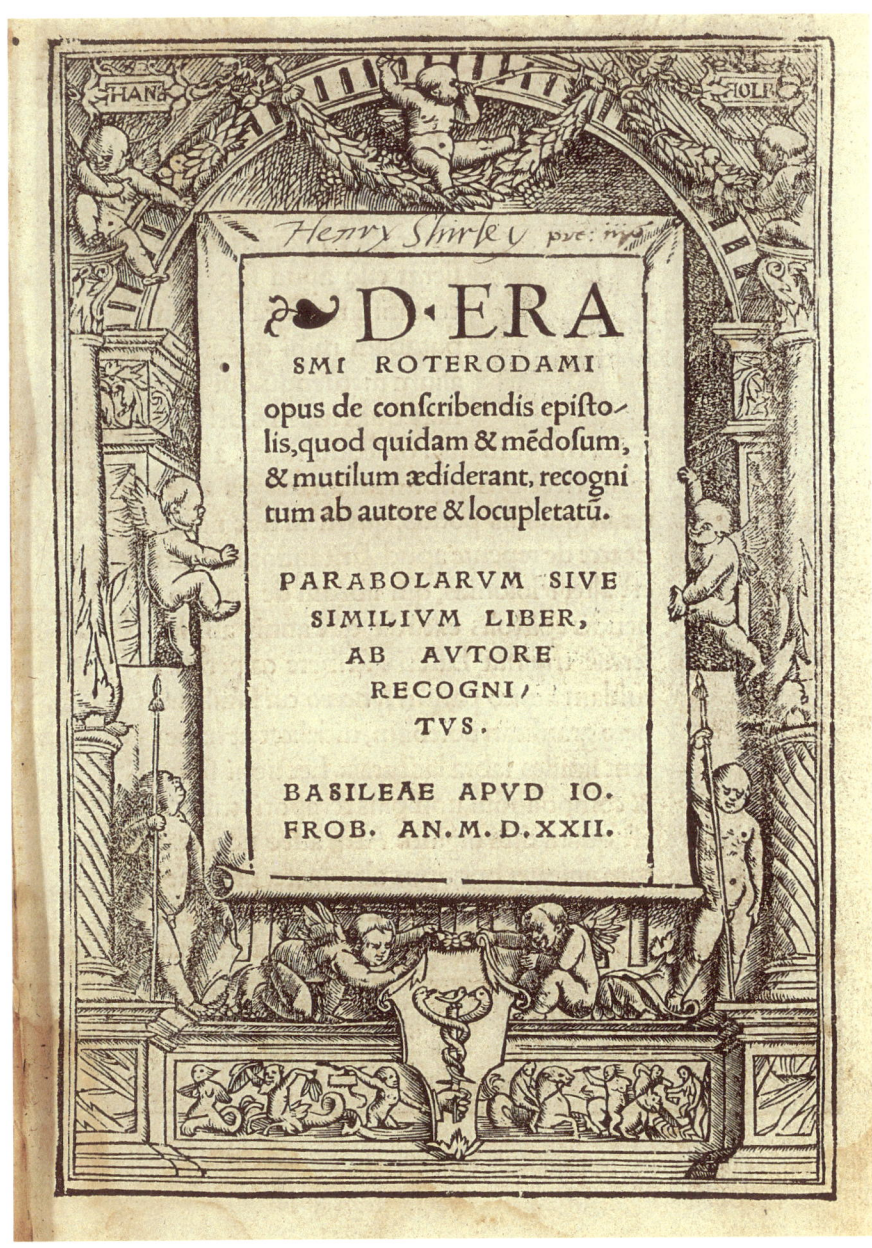

9
William Fulwood
The Enimie of Idlenesse: teaching the maner and stile how to endite, compose and write all sorts of Epistles and Letters: as well by answer, as otherwise. Deuided into foure Bokes, no lesse plesaunt than profitable. Set forth in English by William Fulwood Marchant, &c.
London: Henry Bynneman for Leonard Maylard, 1568
Folger STC 11476

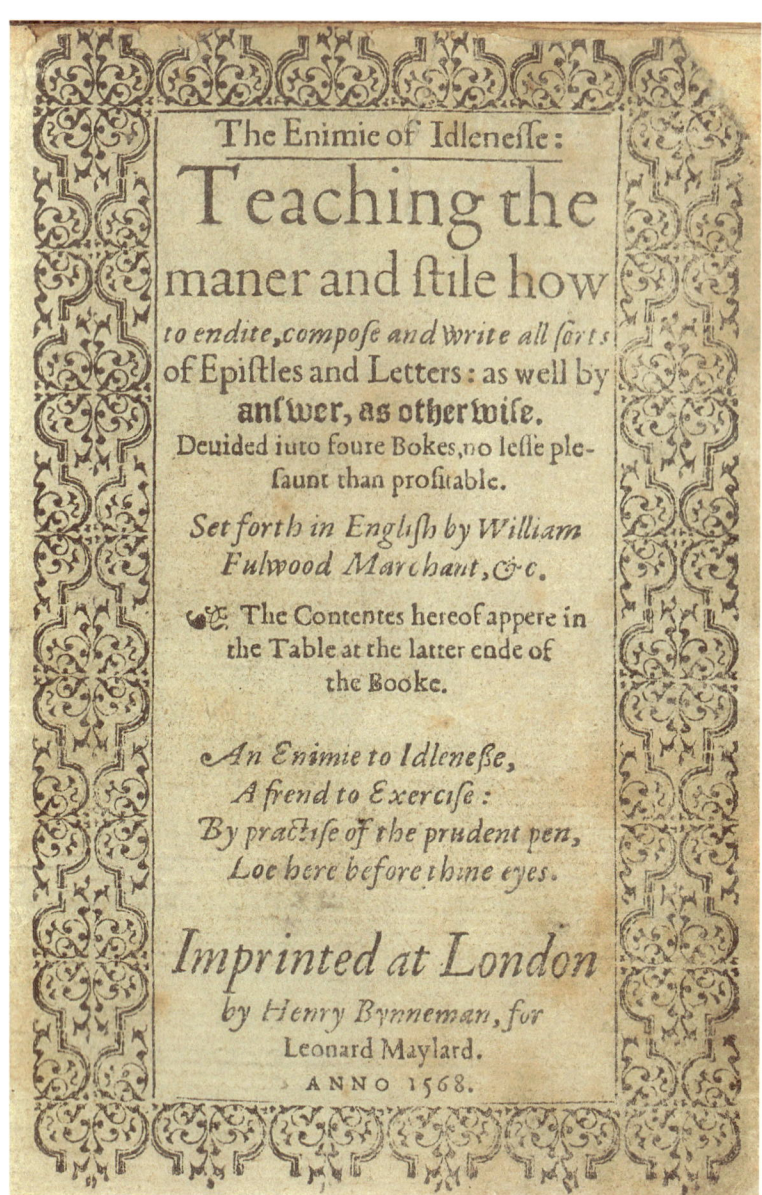

The Enimie of Idleneſſe:
Teaching the maner and ſtile how *to endite, compoſe and write all ſorts* of Epiſtles and Letters: as well by **anſwer, as otherwiſe.** Deuided iuto foure Bokes, no leſſe pleſaunt than profitable.

Set forth in Engliſh by William Fulwood Marchant, &c.

The Contentes hereof appere in the Table at the latter ende of the Booke.

An Enimie to Idleneße, A frend to Exerciſe: By practiſe of the prudent pen, Loe here before thine eyes.

Imprinted at London by *Henry Bynneman, for* Leonard Maylard. ANNO 1568.

The dedicatory verse epistle to the company of the Merchant Taylors of London, in addition to seeking their patronage, testifies to the crucial role of letterwriting in everyday life.

[sig. Aii^r–Aiii^v]

Where vrgent matters of our owne,
    or frends to write vs moue.
As for example when our frende
    in any forren land
Farre distant is, and we desire
    to let him vnderstand
Of this or that, of warres, of peace,
    of strangie newes or else
Of other things that nede requires:
    this work the practise tels,
And shewes by louing letter how
    the mynde shal be discust,

What order, and what Methode eke,
  therein obserue we must.
How to begin, how to procede,
  and how the finall ende
Must ordred be in ech affaire,
  to foe, or else to frende.
So that obseruing of this worke
  in euery point throughout,
A Letter, or Epistle well
  compose we shall no dout.
The vse whereof so nedefull is,
  in vttering of our mynde,
That no wise we may want the same,
  as dayly proofe doth finde.
For why? by letter well we may
  communicate our heart
Unto our frende, though distance farre
  haue vs remou'd apart.
By Letter we may absence make
  euen presence for to be,
And talke with him as face to face
  together we did see.
By letter we may tell our ioy,
  by letter shew our griefe:
By letter from our frende thereof,
  we may receiue reliefe.
By letter what so heart can think,
  or what can head deuise,
To frende, or foe, the same we may
  present before his eyes.
Our steede at home in stable standes,
  our purse also we spare,
When louing letter trots betwene,
  and mynde to mynde declares.
It blabbeth not abrode the hid
  and secrete of our mynde,
To any one, saue vnto him
  to whome we haue assigned.
And looke what so we charge it tell,
  it misseth not a iote:
When messenger by word of mouth
  might hap forget his note,
And either tell somewhat to much,
  or else leaue some vntold:
Therefore the littel Letter well
  to trust we may be bolde.
More might I proue in praise therof,
  but sure it smally needeth:
For very nede it selfe the prose,
  in euery brayne now bredeth. . . .

10

Abraham Fleming (1552?–1607), trans.

A Panoplie of Epistles, Or, a looking glasse for the vnlearned. Conteyning a perfecte plattforme of inditing letters of all sorts, to persons of al estates and degrees, as well our superiours, as also our equalls and inferiours: vsed of the best and the eloquentest rhetoricians that haue liued in all ages, and haue beene famous in that facultie.
Gathered and translated out of Latine into English
London: Ralph Newberie, 1576
Folger STC 11049, c. 2

Drawing on its classical roots, Abraham Fleming's *A Panoplie of Epistles* opens with a charming exchange between a schoolmaster and a very well-informed student on the nature of letterwriting.

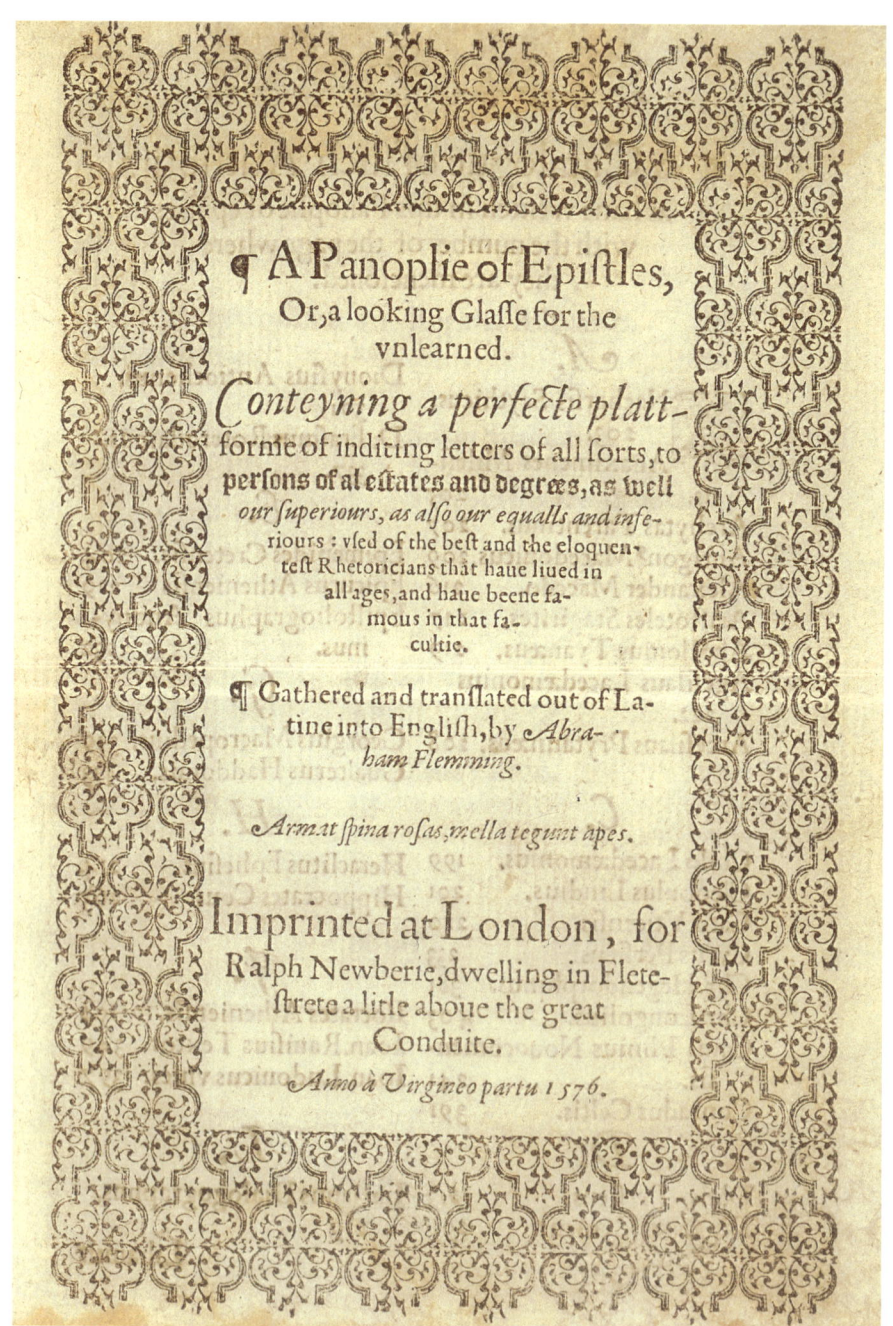

AN EPITOME OF PRECEPTS

whereby the ignoraunt may learne to in-
dite, according to skill and order, reduced
into a Dialogue betweene the
Master and Scholer.

Maister.

What is an Epistle or letter?

Scholer.

An Epistle or letter is a kinde of conference or communication, of one that is
absent, with another that is not present.

Maister.

To what end was it deuised?

Scholer,

That we might conueniently certifie and informe our friendes in their absence,
of all such thinges, as either to them are belonging, or to vs apperteyning.

Maister.

Giue mee the sundrie kindes of Epistles?

Scholer.

Of Epistles, some be demonstratiue, some suasorie, and other some iudiciall.

11

Angel Day (fl. 1575–1595)

The English Secretorie. Wherein is contayned, a perfect method, for the inditing of all
manner of epistles and familiar letters, together with their diuersities, enlarged by
examples vnder their seuerall tytles. In which is layd forth a path-waye, so apt, plaine
and easie, to any learners capacity, as the like whereof hath not at any time heretofore
beene deliuered. Nowe first deuized, and newly published, by Angell Daye.
London: Robert Waldegrave for Richard Jones, 1586
Folger STC 6401

Angel Day's *The English Secretarie* insists that letters should contain a new ABC:
"Aptnes, breuity & comeliness." Despite its Erasmian derivation, this manual makes a
real effort to insist on the importance of letterwriting as a modern, social transaction.

[sig. A1]

Definition
of a letter.

Touching an Epistle, which vsually we terme a letter, no other
definition needeth therof, then that which vse and common
experience hath induced vnto vs. A Letter therefore is that
wherein is expreslye conueied in writing, the intent and meaning
of one man, immediately to passe and be directed to an other,
and for the certaine respects thereof, is termed the messenger
and familiar speeche of the absent: for that all occurrences
whatsoeuer, are thereby as faythfully aduertized, pursued, and
debated, as firmely might fall out in any personall presence or
otherwise to be remembred. . . .

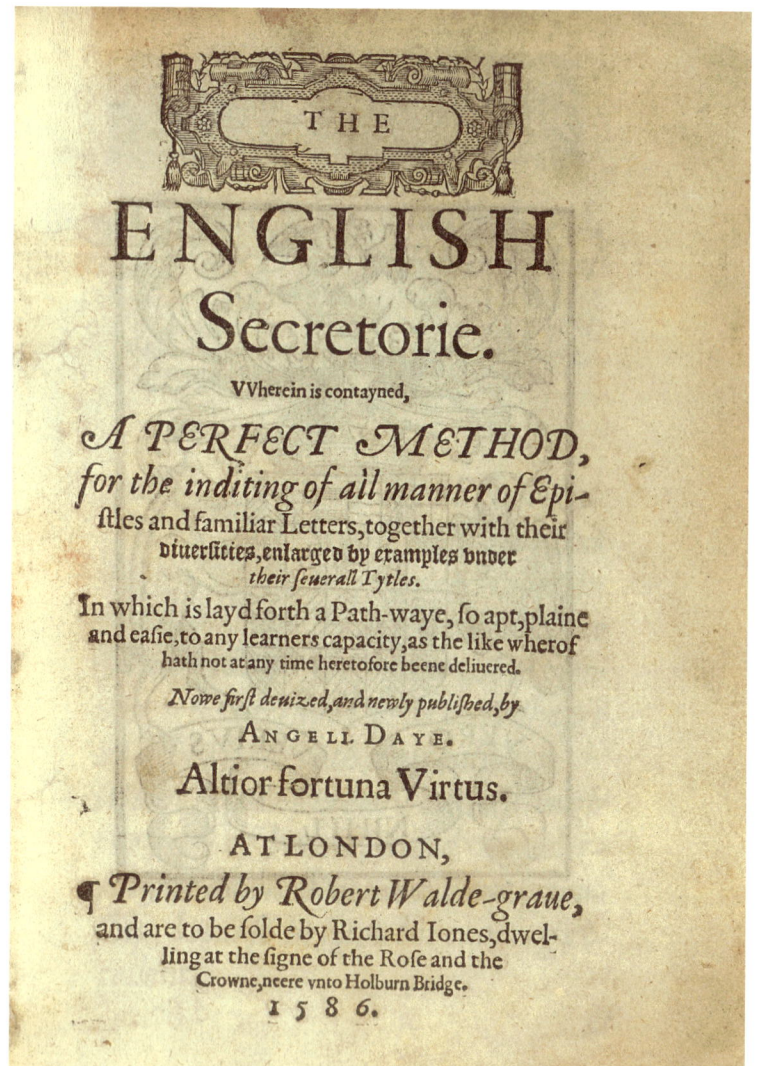

[sig. A2]

What is chiefly to be respected in framing of an Epistle.

Three notes to be obserued in Epistles.

Aptnes, breuity & comelines principally required in letters

Comelines in deliueraunce.

. . . I haue first thought good to draw vnto your consideration, certaine speciall points in this action of all other principally to be regarded. It shall then beseme that for such performance the better to enable him whose forwardnes requireth the same, these three notes in writing of all maner of Epistles be chiefly admitted. ffirst aptnes of wordes & sentences respecting that they be neat and choisly piked, orderly laid downe & cunningly handled, next breuity of speach according in matter & dilation to be framed vpon whatsoeuer occurrent: lastly comelines in deliuerance, concerning the person and cause; wherupon is intended the direction to be framed. These three, as they are seldome in our common vse of writinge, amonge the ignorant at any time pursued, so vnto him that desireth by skilfull obseruation and practize, to become therin more wary and circumspect, are greatlye auaileable to be vsed.

12

John Browne (1526?–1595)

The Merchants Avizo, or Instructions very necessary for their Sonnes and
Servants, when they first send them beyond the Sea, as to Spaine, and Portingale,
or other Countries

London: E.G. for Richard Whitaker, 1640

Folger STC 1051

The Merchants Avizo, apparently based on an actual trading mission of the 1580s, contains a series of letters that show how commerce undertaken by a merchant's factor in Spain and Portugal is to be reported back to the master. In this example the letter is a crucial part of the transaction: not only does it report which commodities make up the cargo, and on which ship, but also the quantities and value of those commodities—and it tells the merchant how he will recognize goods, by reproducing in the margin the merchant's mark which the factor has chosen to use to stamp on each piece of his cargo.

[sig. C3]

A Letter to be sent in that ship where you haue laden goods for
any Merchant.

Emmanuel.

After* my very hearty commendations unto you: I pray for your good health and prosperity, &c. These are certifying you, that I haue laden for your account in the Gabriel of Bristow according to your remembrance, 4. tuns of oile, which is marked with your marke in the* margent. The which doth cost the first pennie 11. Rials and a halfe the Roue, and doth amount unto 75. Duckets, 3. Rials the tunne. More I have laden for you 2. Roues of Cochenele, which cost after 160. Duckets the kintall, and is marked according to the same marke. More 12. Buts of Sack which cost the first peny 15. Dks. the But, marked also with the former. All which goods (God willing) I hope you shal well and safely receive. Heere within inclosed I send you a bill of lading for all your goods, & likewise your account. Thus for this time I take my leave, trusting my selfe very shortly to be at home, for by the grace of God I purpose to come alongst in the *Pleasure*: untill which time I commit you to Almighty God. From S. Lucar the 23 day of December, 1589.

Your assured to my
power, R.A.

* Note that when you write to a Merchant or any other, which is not your Master, or is not a man of worship: then may you well enough begin alwaies your letter after this manner.

13

George Snell (d. 1656)

The right teaching of useful knowledg, to fit scholars for som honest profession; shew-
ing so much skil as anie man needeth (that is not a Teacher) in all knowledges, in one
schole, in a shorter time in a more plain waie, and for much less expens than ever
hath been used, since of old the arts were so taught in the Greek and Romane Empire
London: W. Dugard for John Stephenson, 1649
Folger 152-390q

George Snell's *The right teaching of useful knowledg,* first published over sixty years
after *The English Secretarie,* shows an intensification of Day's insistence on the letter
as an important social transaction. Aimed not at the elite but at "the regent masters
of the rural Schools," the section on letterwriting is predominantly concerned with
the proper etiquette of addressing men of different social rank.

[pp. 102–108] SECT. XXIIII.

The several degrees, and distinct titels of men with whom Scholars must
convers, beeing thus taught and foreknown; now it will bee required that
exemplified epistels, and letters missive should bee here inserted, that by the
whole frame and fashion of them, the learners of this art of secretarie-ship
may bee led by ocular examples; but the interposing of those manie prece-
dential missives, which are needful for to promote this necessarie work,
would make the burden of this business more costly, then the exhausted
Solicitor shall bee abel to bear on to its intended end. Therefore a Centurie of
missive letters, with inchoations, interlocutories, conclusions, subscriptions,
and indorsments accommodated to the most discreet, grave, and prudential
writing of the present age, which are already prepared, beeing laid aside,
these monitions, for the present, shall serv.

1. The regent masters of the rural Schools should often dictate to their
Scholars models, and forms of well penn'd letters to everie degree of persons
afore premised; that upon anie sudden occasion offer'd they taking pen and
paper, may bee abel to dispatch a well-composed letter, to anie person, or
anie rank and qualitie.

2. The Teachinge Masters should caus the learners to inure themselvs to
the most useful phrases and forms of speech, for an Epistolarie stile: for there
may bee a wittie chois made of words and expressions, which will give much
grace and life to Epistolarie writing, where chiefly forms of inchoation, of inter-
locution, of conclusion, of subscription, and of superscription, are to bee noted.

1. Phrases of inchoation; that the Writer may give notice that hee is sensitive of the dignitie of the person to whom his Pen speaketh, and that hee is
apprehensive of his own inferioritie.

2. The Letter-writer should note, and have in store Interlocutorie
forms of speech to bee used now and then in the bodie of letters, importing
duteous respect, unwillingness to bee troubelsom, desire to have his petition
granted, his serious intent to bee thankful, his instant and urgent necessitie,
the great benefit, that the favor prai'd may do him, *&c.*

3. How to conclude letters not insulsly [*sic*] and abruptly, but with
words leading to a mature cessation; and, as the manner now is, with a close
and wittie phrase of transition leading to the Subscription.

4. There must bee special heed taken, that though it must not bee long, yet that the Subscription bee filled with verie affectuous, and vigorous words, expressing all fulness of thanks, of dutie, of honor, of service, and of all other omnimodous observance.

5. That the indorsment and direction bee made, with such cautious, titels, and additions, that nothing bee redundant, nothing deficient.

Hee that can attein abilitie to express neatly and cautiously all sorts of affairs in missive letters, is in a readie waie to bee assumed to anie imploiment of highest importance: Good dexteritie in the skill of a letter-writer, make's a Scholar so qualified, verie readie and abel to use courteous speech, in his common talk.

The skill of writing missives may bee verie much advanced, if everie student of his art, with his book of dictates for missive letters, shal have unwritten paper bound, and therein under certain Common-place-heads, shall write the chief forms, and best materials, out of all well-pen'd letters, that shall com to his hands, this wil greatly enrich, and make copious his epistolarie speech. A scholar well experienced in the art of a good Secretarie, shall bee well prepared for a laudable doing of all civil duties.

maners, according to the pleasure
of the enditer, as may well be perceiued by diuers styles hereafter
folowing.

The second is the Subscription, which must be don according
to the estate of the writer, and the
qualitie of the person to whome
we write : For to our superiors
we must write at the right syde in
the nether ende of the paper, saying : By your most humble and
obedient sonne, or seruant, &c. And
to our equalles we may write towards the midst of the paper saying : By your faithfull frende for
euer. &c. To our inferiors we may
write on high at the left hand say-

The material letter and social signals

BEFORE WE EVEN OPEN A LETTER OR AN E-MAIL, we usually have a fairly good idea about what it contains. Certain material evidence tells us whether it is personal or business-related, whether it is a greeting card, an invitation, a thank you note, a bill, or unsolicited mail. We intuitively set about decoding the external indicators—for example, the postmark, the return address, the handwriting, the quality and size of the envelope (or in case of an e-mail, the subject line)—and whether or not we were anticipating such contact.

In Renaissance England, the clues were also there. In *Twelfth Night*, Malvolio is tricked into thinking a letter is from Olivia, when it is in fact forged by Olivia's gentlewoman: "By my life, this is my lady's hand. . . . And the impressure her Lucrece, with which she uses to seal." And Vincentio observes to the Provost in *Measure for Measure*: "here is the hand and seal of the Duke; you know the character, I doubt not, and the signet is not strange to you." Beyond the style of the handwriting and the image on the seal, the size and quality of the paper, the presence or absence of enclosures, the color of the seal, the form of address, and the signature, would also provide information. For example, if a letter to an earl was addressed "To the right honourable and my singular good Lord" it was from someone lower on the social scale; if it were addressed more informally as "To my very good Lord," it was from an equal. If the signature was located in the lower right corner of the page, then the sender was either writing to a superior or prostrating himself before the recipient in order to ask for forgiveness or assistance. If the seal was black instead of red, a death was being reported or the sender was in mourning.

Because letterwriting was a very goal-oriented activity, manuals devoted page after page to the protocol of such non-textual indicators. In order to maintain or foster personal and professional relationships, a writer had to position him or herself on the page according to a set of well-known social prescriptions. William Fulwood, like other writers and translators of English letterwriting manuals, for example, divides letters into three principal "sorts," and notes the varying and sometimes subtle shifts in humility or familiarity based on a number of additional factors. While the tone and physical layout of a letter depended primarily on whether it was addressed to one's superior, equal, or inferior, the letterwriter also needed to consider whether the recipient was a public or private person, whether he was rich or poor, friend or enemy, well known unto the writer or little known, or whether he enjoyed or disliked reading letters. After covering the rhetorical elements of a well-composed letter, Angel Day's *The English Secretarie* devotes chapters to the four essential parts of a letter: the salutation (or initial greeting); the order of taking leave or farewell; the subscription (the closing line and signature); and the outward direction (or superscription). The neglect or misuse of any of these parts could potentially lead to misunderstanding or offense. A letter from Sir Michael Molynes to William Lambarde points to this danger, which in this case resulted from using a secretary. He writes, "Sir my Lady Wharton hath entreated me to excuse her vnto yow for her ouersight in suffringe her man to seale her lettre directed vnto you before she hadd subscribed hit. . . ." (Folger MS X.d.121 (12)).

Manuals were less prone to comment on the sort of paper one should use or the circumstances under which one should write in one's own hand or leave the writing to a secretary. However, letterwriters were clearly concerned over the bad impression that poor paper or handwriting could make, and usually took special care to reassure their recipients of their good intentions despite outward appearances or circumstances beyond their control. In *The Rules of Civility* (London, 1675), Antoine de Courtin advises that letterwriters show reverence and esteem by using a whole sheet of large paper, even if the entire letter consists of just "six lines," and by enclosing the letter in another paper, on which one should write the superscription, or address (pp. 146, 154). Thomas Blount's *The Academy of Eloquence* (London, 1656) sets the bar a little lower: "For the Hand-writing, if you attain not to perfection, it ought at least to be legible, and the matter fairly written, and truly pointed, with Comma, (,) Colon (:) semicolon (;) period (.) parentheses ( ) Interrogation (?) and Admiration (!) points, as the matter requires. Apostrophe's are now also much in use, which is onely a cutting off a syllable or vowel, for brevity sake; as lov'd, mov'd for loved, moved. . . ." (p. 147).

In satirical writings, bad handwriting was associated especially with the upper classes. For the Spanish humanist Juan Luis Vives, the nobility's illiteracy is a comic butt: as one character complains in his *Lingvæ latinae exercitatio* (Basel, 1539) "[T]he crowd of our nobility do not follow the precept (as to the value of writing), for they think it is a fine and becoming thing not to know how to form their letters. You would say their writing was the scratching of hens, and unless you were warned beforehand whose hand it was, you would never guess." In time, however, bad handwriting became a social embarrassment, and young men were urged to practice their hand rigorously.

While the manuals are silent on the protocols of sealing letters, seals conveyed significant meaning as well. Seals generally consisted of personal arms or family crests, sometimes playfully rendered—the Bacon family, for example, pre-empted thousands of bad pig jokes by using the boar as their seal. A personal seal with embroidery floss underneath it was suggestive of a personal or intimate letter. A black seal represented mourning. If the seal on a letter was *not* the seal of the sender, the recipient would know that the letter had been read and approved by the person whose seal it was—literally, the seal of approval. Seal matrices (small metal molds) and signet rings, also used to seal letters, were clearly valued by their owners. In 1676, John Ogilvy asks in a postscript to the brother of his estranged wife: "If you would procure my old stamp to me or cause seal it on wax *that* I may cause make another by it I will take it as a favore" (Folger MS Add 1273 (131)). Richard Stoneley paid two shillings to get his silver seal repaired in August 1582, while William Petre bought a seal for his wife in December 1597 for four shillings (Folger MSS V.a.459, fol. 73ᵛ; V.a.334, fol. 23ᵛ).

14

Angel Day (fl. 1575–1595)

The English secretorie, or, Methode of writing of epistles and letters: with a declaration of such tropes, figures, and schemes as either vsually, or for ornament sake are therein required. Also the parts and office of a secretorie. Diuided into two bookes. Now newly reuised, and in many parts corrected and amended: by Angel Day

London: Thomas Snodham, [1621]

Folger STC 6407.2

Day instructs his readers to position their signatures according to their relationship to the recipient. If the sender is much lowlier in rank, then his signature should appear at the very bottom of the page.

[p. 15]   And now to the Subscriptions, the diuersities whereof are (as best they may be allotted in sense) to either of these to be placed, forewarned alwayes vnto the vnskilfull herein, that writing to any person of account, by how much the more excellent he is in calling from him in whose behalfe the letter is framed, by so much the lower, shall the subscription thereunto belonging, in any wise be placed.

    And if the state of honour of him to whom the Letter shall be directed doe require so much, the very lowest margent of paper shall doe no more but beare it, so be it the space be seemely for the name, & the roome far enough to comprehend it: which Subscription in all sorts to be handled shall passe in this or the like order or substance.

    Your L. most deuoted and loyally affected. Your Honours most assured in whatsoeuer seruices. Your L. in whatsoeuer to be commanded. The most affectionate vnto your L. of all others. . . .

Subscriptions

Manner and varietie of Subscriptions.

———

15

William Fulwood, trans.

The enimie of idlenesse: teaching the maner and stile how to endite, compose and write all sorts of epistles and letters: as well by answer, as otherwise. Deuided into foure bokes, no lesse plesaunt than profitable. Set forth in English by William Fulwood, marchant

London: Henry Bynneman, for Leonard Maylard, 1568

Folger STC 11476

Fulwood provides rules and examples for "three necessary points": the salutation, the subscription, and the superscription. His advice about subscriptions is much more specific than Day's.

[sig. a7ʳ–a8ᵛ]   Note also that most commonly in Epistles & Letters, there be three necessary points. The first is the salutation of recommendation, which is made in sundrie maners, according to the pleasure of the enditer, as may well be perceiued by diuers styles hereafter folowing.

    The second is the Subscription, which must be don according to the estate of the writer, and the qualitie of the person to whome we write: for to our superiors we must write at the right syde in the nether ende of the paper, saying: By your most humble and obedient sonne, or seruant, &c. And to our equalles we may write towards the midst of the paper saying: By your faithfull frende for euer. &c. To our inferiors we may write on high at the left hand saying: By yours &c.

The third is the Superscription, which must be vpon the back syde, the letter being closed, sealed and packed vp after the finest fashion, whereupon must be written his name to whome the letters shold be addressed, & his dwelling place, (if it be not notoriously knowne) placing therwith the name of his dignitie, Lordship, Office, Nobilitie, Science, or Parentage.

15

of Idlenesse

three necessary points. The first is the salutation of recommendacion, which is made in sundrie maners, accoʒding to the pleasure of the enditer, as may well be perceiued by diuers styles hereafter folowing.

The second is the Subscription, which must be don accoʒding to the estate of the wʒiter, and the qualitie of the person to whome we wʒite : Foʒ to our superioʒs we must wʒite at the right syde in the nether ende of the paper, saying : By your most humble and obedient sonne, oʒ seruant, &c. And to our equalles we may wʒite towards the midst of the paper saying : By your faithfull frende foʒ euer.&c. To our inferioʒs we may wʒite on high at the left hand saying : By yours &c.

The third is the Superscripcion, which

16

Thomas Blount (1618–1679)

The academy of eloquence: containing a compleat English rhetorique, exemplified; common-places, and formula's digested into an easie and methodical way to speak and write fluently, according to the mode of the present times: with letters both amorous and morall, upon emergent occasions. By Tho. Blount Gent. The second edition with additions

London: T.N. for Humphrey Moseley, 1656

Folger B3322

There were no hard and fast rules for the proper address for the various social ranks, but several writers attempted to provide them. Thomas Blount's list of suggestions for superscriptions, the addresses that appeared on the outer blank leaves of letters, is just one example of many.

Superscriptions
FOR
LETTERS,
to be addressed to all sorts of
persons, according to the usage
of the present times.

If to a Duke;

To the most *Noble* (and sometimes)
Excellent or *illustrious Prince.*

And in discourse we stile him *Grace.*

If to a Marquess,

To the *right Noble* or *Right honourable.*

And in discourse his attribute is, *Lordship* or *Honour.*

If to an Earle, Viscount or Baron

To the right honourable.

And to begin a Letter, we, either say,

May it please your Honor or Lordship!

Right honorable!

My Lord!

Which last is used only by Lords to Lords, or
by Gentlemen of some quality, otherwise it is
held too familiar.

17

Examples of superscriptions on letters
Folger MSS X.d.375 (1); X.c.51 (35)

Superscriptions varied greatly in length and style and often strayed from the suggested formulas in letterwriting manuals. Examples at the Folger range from the
hastily-scribbled "ffor your selfe" (autograph letter signed, from Sir John Lenthall
to his cousin, Sir Edmund Warcupp, October 15, 1667, X.d.375 (1)) to the more long-
winded and descriptive: "To the right Worshippfull and my much honored good
Lady the Lady Powell wife to Sir Edward Powell knight and Barronett and one of
his Maiesties Masters of requests, dwellinge at Westminster within the Deanes
yeard nere to the scoolhowse dd [deliver] this I pray" (autograph letter signed,
from Thomas Crompton to Lady Mary Powell, May 1632, X.c.51 (35)).

————

18

Sir George More (1553–1632)
Petitionary letter signed, to James I
December 8, 1612
Folger MS L.b.633

Signed in the lower right-hand corner of the page, Sir George More's petitionary
letter to James I is the model of humility. More had been Treasurer and receiver-
general to Prince Henry, who had died a month earlier. His request to retire to a
more private life was motivated by the observation of his friends that despite his
good service to the king, he had twice been passed over for the Office of the Wards.
Accordingly, he is now "twise wounded in the same pointe, whereof I must confesse the greefe hath touched my harte," and therefore "to cover my shame from the
worldes eie I shall retyre to a place and course of lyfe more private." He does not
want to fall into further disfavor with his request, however, and thus rests "in your
Maiesties hand whether to honour or dishonour as Claye in the hand of the Potter."
The petition was apparently successful, since he was shortly after appointed
Lieutenant of the Tower and then Chancellor of the Order of the Garter.

[superscription]   To the kinge his most excellent Maiestie.

[letter]   Moste gracious Soveraigne

Haveing served your Maiestie ever since your blessed commeing to the Crowne of greate Brittaine
and the late illustrious Prince your noble Sonne about the space of two yeares. I never
durst propose to myself other recompence then a favorable acceptance of my endeavours and
a gracious pardon for my errors. howbeit some my freindes observing in the course of my
service that I had ben not vnfaithfull gave the adventure soone after the death of Sir
George Carewe to moove your Maiestie on my behalf for the Office of the Wardes then
voide for which my name had ben questioned when formerly your Maiestie bestowed that
place. But your Maiestie in your wisdome makeing choise at ether tyme of another
as the worthier, my poore creditt seemed to the world to be twise wounded in the same
pointe, whereof I must confesse the greefe hath touched my harte. ffor although I will

not compare where your Maiestie is pleased to preferre; yet knowing that I haue
laboured all the day in that harvest where many haue receaved theire hyre in full
measure, I trust your Maiestie will not blame me If I hould not vp my head goinge
emptie alone out of the ffield, & sorroweing that I haue not deserved better. This
dreade Soveraigne is my greefe made infinitely greevous with the feare of your
disfavor, and causeth me to hate the light which can never be pleasing to me longer
then the grace of your countenance shall shine vpon me. Wherefore if to cover
my shame from the worldes eie I shall retyre to a place and course of lyfe more
private, I humblie beseech your Maiestie not to ympute it to a mynde discontented
which towardes your Maiestie in me shall never be, neyther yet to a neglecte of your service
which certeinly can not be for your profitt, when with you I shall seeme to haue noe
creditt. But resting in your Maiesties hand whether to honour or dishonour as Claye
in the hand of the Potter. doe with me what you will I will not murmure or
repine. Your many care and Princely vertues, as I shall ever admyre and
thinke them the moste happie which to heare and behould you stand neerest vnto you
So from your royall presence the further I shall be remooved the more it is true) I
shall be greeved: But yet out of a loyall harte ever ready to serve and obey you
I shall for ever pray the Lord of heaven to blesse your Maiestie with many and happie
daies that longe and longe you may stand over vs as the maine flourishing tree
of all our ioy and lyfe in this worlde.   viij^th of december 1612.

Your Maiesties moste humble servant

George More

———

19
Lewes Bagot (1587–1611)
Autograph letter signed, to his father, Walter Bagot
ca. 1610
Folger MS L.a.67
Reproduced at 92%

Apologetic letters from son to father are so common in the period that they almost
form a sub-genre. This is one of the saddest. In 1610, Lewes Bagot wrote to apologize once again for his continued "vncivill kinde of behaviour," promising that this
time he would leave his evil ways. The layout of the letter, with Lewes's signature
crouched in the bottom right-hand corner, captures and emphasizes the extreme
submission of the letter's content. Sadly it was too late, since Lewes died shortly
after. The endorsements on the letter record, in the father's hand, that these were
"Lewes his last letters." A later hand has written, in error, that this letter was to Lewes
Bagot from "Mistress Jane Skipwith," his beloved, presumably because it was stored
with her love letters to him (see items 45–47).

19

Mrs Jane Skipwith to
Lewis Bagott

Lewes his last l^{ter}

1610 &c.

To the wo^{ll}. his good lovinge
father m^r. walter Bagot
att Blithefeild giue
thefe with

L.a.67

Sr

If hetherto I haue spent the beginninge of my tyme in that vnciuill
kinde of behauiour that I haue beene a disparagm.t to my house
& a disgrace to my selfe yet I hope yow will out of your fatherly
loue bee as willinge to forgiue and forgett. as I vnfaynedly
will be most dutifull to yow & by gods grace to amend my
misspent tyme & lead the rest of my life in such a ciuill
manner that shall bee bothe pleasinge to god & noe thinge
att all distastfull to yow, ar any of my frendes: tyme paste
can hardly be recalled & it is neuer too late to doe well
I knowe Sr it is my duty to honor & obaye yow my parents, & I
pray god I may no longer. liue then to expresse my duty
to yow & my mother not onely in woord but allsoe in
deed. though your iust displeasure att mee, may bee a motiue
against my submisshion, yet I beseech yow to pardon this my
bouldnes, ~~and~~ the follies of my ill spent tyme, & the
too little acknowledgement, & performance of my duty, (I humbly
beseeche yow for gods sake) to forgiue & take once againe your
loste sonne to mercy and thincke vppon mee with compassion
and not accordinge to my desert. with humble and harty
desier of yowr and my mothers blessinge I humbly take
leaue & rest.

Yr

Yr ever dutyfull &
obedient sonne
Lewes Bagot

To the woo*rshipfu*ll his good & lovinge
father *Maste*r Wallter Bagot
att Blithefeild giue
these with

[letter]   S*ir*
If hetherto I haue spent the beginni*nge* of my tyme in that vncivill
kinde of behaviour that I haue beene a d[i]sparageme*nt* to my house
& a disgrace to my selfe yet I hope yow will out of your fatherly
love bee as willinge to forgiue and forgett: as I vnfaynedly
will be most dutifull to yow & by gods grace to ame*nd* my
misspent tyme & lead the rest of my life in such a civill
manner that shall bee bothe ple∧ᵃ∧singe to God & noe thinge
att all distastfull to yow, or any of my frend~es~∧ˢ∧: tyme paste
can hardly be recalled & it is neuer too late to doe well:
I knowe S*ir* it is my duty to ho*nn*or & obeye yow my parents, & I
pray God I may no longer live then to expresse my duty
to yow & my mother: not onely in woord, but allsoe in
deed. Though your iust displeasure att mee, may bee a motive
against my submission; yet I beseech yow to p*ardon* this my
bouldnes, ~& xxxxxxxxx~; ∧and∧ the follies of my ill spent tyme, & the
too little acknowledgement, & p*erformance* of my duty, (I hu*m*bly
beseeche yow for Gods sake) to forgiue & take once againe y*our*
loste son*ne* to mercy and thincke vppon mee with ∧the eye of pitty and∧ co*m*passion
and not according to my desert. With humble and harty
desier of yow*r* and my mothers blessinge I humbly take
leaue & rest.

                                        Y*our* euer dutyfull &
                                            obedient sonne
                                            Lewes Bagot

Lewes his last *lett*ers

1610 &c.

M*istre*ss Jane Skipwith to
                            Lewis Bagott. /

20

Angel Day (fl. 1575–1595)
The English Secretorie
London, 1586
Folger STC 6401

Angel Day provides a longer, but similarly groveling version of the son-to-father
apology letter. In the Folger's copy (STC 6401), it is one of the few sample letters in
the volume that has been marked up, indicating that the reader was perhaps studying it in preparation to write a letter of his own. The only other letters in this copy
that have ink blots and other markings are the love letters. As he does with many of
the sample letters, Day annotates this one in the margins with the rhetorical parts
exemplified in each section of the letter.

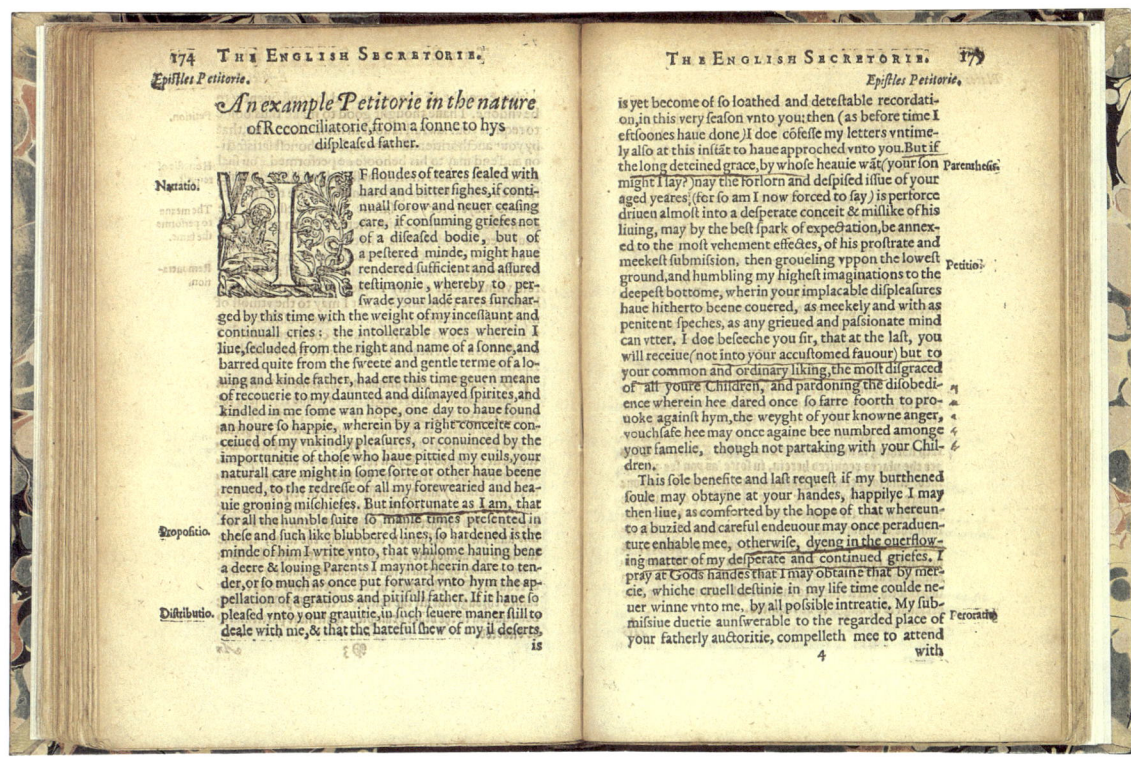

[pp. 174–76]

An example Petitorie in the nature of Reconciliatorie, from a sonne to hys
displeased father.

Narratio. If floudes of teares sealed with hard and bitter sighes, if continuall
sorow and neuer ceasing care, if consuming griefes not of a diseased
bodie, but of a pestered minde, might haue rendered sufficient and
assured testimonie, whereby to perswade your lade*n* eares surcharged
by this time with the weight of my incessaunt and continuall cries: the
intollerable woes wherein I liue, secluded from the right and name of a
sonne, and barred quite from the sweete and gentle terme of a louing
and kinde father, had ere this time geuen meane of recouerie to my
daunted and dismayed spirites, and kindled in me some wan hope, one
day to haue found an houre so happie, wherein by a right conceite

conceiued of my vnkindly pleasures, or conuinced by the importunitie of those who haue pittied my euils, your naturall care might in some sorte or other haue beene renued, to the redresse of all my forewearied and heauie groning mischiefes. But infortunate as I am, that for all the

Propositio. humble suite so manie times presented in these and such like blub-bered lines, so hardened is the minde of him I write vnto, that whileome hauing bene a deere & louing Parents I may not heerin dare to tender, or so much as once put forward vnto hym the appellation of a gratious and pitifull father. If it haue so pleased vnto your grauitite,

Distributio. in such seuere maner still to deale with me, & that the hateful shew of my il deserts, is yet become of so loathed and detestable recordation, in this very season vnto you: then (as before time I estsoones haue done) I doe confesse my letters vntimely also at this instant to haue approched vnto you. But if the long deteined grace, by whose heauie want (your

Parenthesis. son might I say?) nay the forlorn and despised issue of your aged yeares: (for so am I now forced to say) is perforce driuen almost into a desper-ate conceit & mislike of his liuing, may by the best spark of expectation, be annexed to the most vehement effectes, of his prostrate and meekest

Petitio. submission, then groueling vppon the lowest ground, and humbling my highest imaginations to the deepest bottome, wherin your implaca-ble displeasures haue hitherto beene couered, as meekely and with as penitent speches, as any grieued and passionate mind can vtter. I doe beseeche you sir, that at the last, you will receiue (not into your accus-tomed fauour) but to your common and ordinary liking, the most dis-graced of all youre Children, and pardoning the disobedience wherein hee dared once so farre foorth to prouoke against hym, the weyght of your knowne anger, vouchsafe hee may once againe bee numbred amonge your famelie, though not partaking with your Children.

  This sole benefite and last request if my burthened soule may obtayne at your handes, happilye I may then liue, as comforted by the hope of that whereunto a buzied and careful endeuour may once peraduenture enhable mee, otherwise, dyeng in the ouerflowing mat-ter of my desperate and continued griefes, I pray at Gods handes that I may obtaine that by mercie, which cruell destinie in my life time coulde neuer winne vnto me, by all possible intreatie. My submissiue

Peroratio. duetie aunswerable to the regarded place of your fatherly auctoritie, compelleth mee to attend with all humblenesse the resolution of your clemencie, In the hope wherof, resting my decaied and ouerwearied imaginations, I liue till the receite of your knowne liking doe asser-taine, in what sorte may please you to repute me.

The stile of this Epistle is vehement, because the passions of him from whence it came were vehement, and is deducted as you see from the nature of Reconciliatorie, *which aswell for the submissiue and lowest termes it beareth, as also for the vrgent petition therein contayned, I haue rather chosen to place among the* Petitorie. *The part of* Honest *herein deliuered, is passed in woordes meekest and of great obedience, wherein he studieth by all possibilitie to mitigate towards himselfe, the too muche seueritie of his father. The* Exordium *is carried by* Insinuation, *expressing the vehe-ment effectes and surcharged conceites of a minde more than ordinarily greeued. The* Possibilitie *resteth in the father, which commonly by nature is with some more facilitie then estraunged difficultie, entreated towardes his sonne. The Meane to compasse it, is his fatherly instinct, whiche by charged aucthoritie affecteth nothing so much as obedience of his Children. Thus are the places required herein, in sorte as you see performed. And for because within any one title, there is no one thinge affoording matter more plentifull, or with vse more common frequented, then this* Petitorie *kinde, (Insomuche as whatsoeuer containeth any speciall or sole request in the substaunce thereof to bee accomplished, is hereunder concluded) I will force you downe so many examples of all sortes, as that there shall not faile heerein wherewith sufficiently to instruct whatsoeuer in the lyke occasion is or ought to be required.*

———

21

James Howell (1594?–1666)

Epistolæ Ho-Elianæ. Familiar Letters Domestic and Forren; Divided into sundry Sections, Partly Historicall, Politicall, Philosophicall, Vpon Emergent Occasions: By James Howell Esq; One of the Clerks of His late Maiesties most Honorable Privy Councell. The second Edition, enlarged with divers supplements, and the Dates annexed which were wanting in the first, With an Addition of a third volume of new Letters . . .

London: W[illiam] H[unt] for Humphrey Moseley, 1650 (2nd edition)

Folger H3072

James Howell was among the first Englishmen to publish his own letters during his lifetime. The letters, mostly directed to fictitious correspondents, "noblemen," "knights, doctors, esquires, gentlemen and merchants," "with divers others," were written while Howell was a royalist prisoner in London's Fleet prison between 1643 and 1651. He writes that the letters contain "a faithfull relation of the privatest passages that happen'd at Court a good part of King James's reign, and that of His late Majesty." Dedicating the volume in good royalist fashion to "his Majesty" (Charles II, in exile, son of the recently-executed Charles I), Howell articulates the importance of letters: "Letters can tresure up, and transmit matters of State to posterity, with as much Faith, and be as authentic Registers, and safe repositories of Truth, as any Story whatsoever." This letter humorously plays on the constant bugbear of letter-readers: bad handwriting.

[p. 166]

XXX.

To my Cosen I.P. *at Mr.* Conradus.

Cousin,

A Letter of yours was lately deliverd me, I made a shift to read the superscription, but within, I wonderd what language it might be, in which 'twas written, at first I thought 'twas *Hebrew*, or som of her Dialects, and so went from the liver to the heart, from the right hand to the left to read it, but could make nothing of it; then I thought it might be the *Chineses* language, and went to read the words perpendicular, and the lines were so crooked and distorted, that no coherence could be made; *Greek* I perceiv'd it was not, nor

Latin or *English*; So I gave it for mere *gibberish*, and your characters to be rather *Hieroglyphicks* then *Letters*. The best is, you keep your lines at a good distance, like those in Chancery-bills, who as a Clerk said, were made so wide of purpose, because the Clients should have room enough to walk between them without justling one another; yet this widenes had bin excusable if your lines had bin streight, but they were full of odd kind of Undulations and windings; If you can write no otherwise, one may read your thoughts as soon as your characters. It is some excuse for you, that you are but a young beginner, I pray let it appear in your next what a proficient you are, otherwise some blame may light on me that placed you there; Let me receive no more Gibbrish or Hieroglyphicks from you, but legible letters, that I may acquaint your friends accordingly of your good proceedings, So I rest

Westminst. 20 *Sept.*   *Your very loving Cosen,*
         1629.   J. H.

————

22

George Talbot, earl of Shrewsbury (1528?–1590)
Letter signed, to his wife, Elizabeth, countess of Shrewsbury
October 10, 1580
Folger MS X.d.428 (104)

In this letter, the earl of Shrewsbury explains to his wife that, owing to "paine and stifnes" in his writing hand, he is unable to pen the letter himself—presumably he is employing a secretary to do so. His wife Elizabeth, the famous "Bess of Hardwick," may have been secretly grateful for the supposed inconvenience: as other letters show, when his hand is not bothering him, the earl's own handwriting is all but impossible to read (for example, see Folger MS X.d.428 (103)). The letter is sealed with his personal seal of a dog surrounded by the motto of the Order of the Garter, "Honi soit qui mal y pense." The earl had been invested into the Order in 1561.

[superscription]   To my wyef the
Countesse of
Shrewesbury

I pray you send me Acres
so sone as you can for I
maye spare him no longer

[letter]   Wyef I haue receaved y*our* severall *lett*res and am at this
present so trobled w*i*th paine and stifnes in my hand that
I cannot write my self and therefore deferre the
answeringe of the same wh*i*ch I will fully do so sone
as it shall please god to restore the streinth of my
hand that I may write wh*i*ch I hope will be very
shortly   I haue retorned vnto you my L*or*d of Leycesters
*lett*re and praye you when you write againe let his
L*or*dship vnderstand that because I p*er*ceaved by his last

lett*re* vnto me it was doutfull how sone I shulld
obteyne graunte of paiment I haue staied furder
writinge vnto him therin havinge no dout of his *Lordships*
good remembrance & furderance thereof when occasion
might serve And so comitt you to god*es* tuission
This x^th of october 1580

> your faithfull husband
> G Shrewsbury

————

23
Edward Bacon (d. 1618)
Autograph letter signed, to his brother Nathaniel Bacon
Geneva, June 1, [1578]
Folger MS L.d.39

Writing home from Geneva to his brother, Edward Bacon uses the unaccustomed
brevity of his letter to tell his news: "To signifie in what state I am fewe lynes shall
suyffice. I haue had lately a paine in my ryght hand. . . ." This letter, like the earl of
Shrewsbury's letter above, reminds us that the act of writing took a certain amount
of physical strength and stamina—or at least that illness provided a convenient
excuse for not writing.

[superscription]

To his louinge Brother M^r
Nathanall Bacon at
        Styfkey
with   with humble

[letter]

Brother To signifie in what state I am fewe
lynes shall suyffice. I haue had lately a paine
in my ryght hand but am there of almost ryd
I iudge it came of cold so it is gone with
owt other medecyne than warmeth The Spainerd
which parted owt of fflaundres made vs of
Geneva feare but they ar passed withowt doing
vs any hurt the plague being within ther campe
I thancke god I am well & wishe yow the same
When I shal write with lesse troble I will
write a longer ~~troble~~ letter commend me to
my Brothers & Sisters   ffrom Geneva
the first of June.

> Your louing Brother
> Edward Bacon

24

Antoine de Courtin (1622–1685)

The rules of civility; or, Certain ways of deportment observed in France, amongst all persons of quality, upon several occasions. Translated out of French.

London: J. Martyn and John Starkey, 1675 (3rd edition)

Folger C6603A

A translation of Courtin's immensely popular *Nouveau traité de la civilité* (Paris, 1671), this etiquette manual includes chapters on such subjects as "The difference between things decent and indecent, according to Custom," and "Rules to be observed at a Ball," in addition to the chapter below, on letterwriting. A note on the front endleaf states that this copy was purchased secondhand in Edinburgh on August 17, 1695, for a shilling.

[pp. 146–47]

Chapter XVI

Rules to be observed in writing of Letters

To make use of large Paper rather than small, and a whole sheet (though we write but six lines in the first Page) rather than half a one, is no inconsiderable piece of Ceremony, one shewing reverence and esteem, the other familiarity or indifference.

[p. 150]

We are to add the day of the month, the year, and the place from whence we write also; for more respect we put them usually at the bottom of our Letter, on the left hand of our subscription; and indeed to put it at the top when we write to a person of Quality, is something presumptuous.

[p. 153]

No one superscribes a Letter, *For his Dear Wife,* or *Loving Husband,* unless it be one that hath not had ingenuous Education, or have a mind to be laught at. Because the outside of a Letter is to be read by every one that is not concerned in that interest that is between you: nor is it material to him to be informed, that he that writes that Letter is such a Womans Husband.

[p. 154]

It is not amiss likewise, if we take notice, that for greater respect the Letter ought to be inclosed in another Paper, upon which we are to write the Superscription.

———

25

Thomas Dooksie

Letter signed, to Walter Bagot

Leekfrith, March 10, 1611

Folger MS L.a.414

While it was important to observe the protocols of address and the proper layout of a letter, it was also essential to use the right paper. Here Thomas Dooksie's postscript apologizes for the lackluster quality of the paper, although with a pretty feeble excuse: "I must craue pardon for wryting on soe bad paper for I haue lost the key of my desk and can come to noe other."

To the Wor*ship*fu*l*l his good M^r
Walter Bagot Esquyre
at his howse Blythfeeld
     dd

[letter]

Sir
I haue deliu*ere*d and sent forth the warrant*es* all seeme loath
to p*art*e w*ith* monie yet I thinke will lend at the last they
inquyre vearie much what ˄will bee˄ done yf they make deniall
nowe I told them ether to ˄bee˄ bound ouer beefore the Lord*es*
of the privie Councell or els theire answeres to bee
esteemed / and their messingers to come downe M^r B[a]rett
told mee hee hath made meanes vnto Docter Cotton (whoe
heretofore p*ro*missed him a kindnes) but Cannot bee dischardged
but vppon A*ff*udauit that hee is not able to lend the
king soe much excepte hee take it vpon intrest. Thus
remembering my humble service to you and my good
M*ist*ris I rest

Leekefrithe this
x^th of March   y*ou*r loueinge and obedient servant
<u>1611</u>   till death Tho: Dooksie

I must craue pardon for wryting
on soe bad pap*er* for I haue lost
the key of my desk and ˄can˄ come
to noe other /

––––––––

26
Thomas Crompton
Autograph letter signed, to Lady Mary (Vanlore) Powell
[March 14, 1632/33]
Folger MS X.c.51 (39)

Paper was a costly, and often elusive, commodity. Sometimes a writer would have
to eschew normal standards of paper-respect in order to transmit an urgent message. Lady Powell's servant, Thomas Crompton, does just this on a small scrap of
paper roughly one-quarter the size of a standard-sized letter, but prefaces the letter
by acknowledging the "poore peece of paper" it is written upon. In his next letter
to her, he repeats the apology: "I made bould to p*re*sent my dutie to y*ou*r la*dy*shi*p*
in a poore peece of pap*er* w*h*ich I sent towards Lu*n*don on Thursday last . . . for
the w*h*ich I craue pardon, in deed I could gett noe more in all the Towne. . . ."
(Folger MS X.c.51 (40)).

[superscription]　　　　　　　To the right wor*shipfu*ll
　　　　　　　　　　　　　and my much honored good
　　　　　　　　　　　　　lady the Lady Powell

[letter]　　　　　　　　　Maddam.)
　　　　　　　　　　　　　I am bolde to pre*ser*nt this poore peece of pap*er*
　　　　　　　　　　　　　to yo*ur* la*dyshi*ps vew, desiringe yo*ur* la*dyshi*ps patience. I could not
　　　　　　　　　　　　　doe what I did intend to doe but I haue bought
　　　　　　　　　　　　　one gray horse, w*hich* I ride vppon, besids theise two
　　　　　　　　　　　　　bay ones. I haue alsoe sent an honest mans sonn to serue
　　　　　　　　　　　　　my *Maste*r if he like him, but he is rawe and vnskilfull,
　　　　　　　　　　　　　but willinge; I am nowe taken horsse to goe,
　　　　　　　　　　　　　to herefordsheire, where I hope in God / I shall
　　　　　　　　　　　　　here well from yo*ur* La*dyshi*p. (Thus) for want of pay
　　　　　　　　　　　　　maketh me breauiatt the expression of my dutifull
　　　　　　　　　　　　　mind towards my *Maste*r and my La*dy* Vanloore and yo*ur* la*dyshi*p
　　　　　　　　　　　　　humbly takinge my leaue and rest prayinge./

[in left margin]　　　　　　Yo*ur* La*dyshi*ps poore servant tell death.
　　　　　　　　　　　　　Thursday　　　　　　　Tho: Crompton

　　　　　　　　　　　　　─────────

27
John Ogilvy of Balfour
Autograph letter signed, to his brother-in-law, James Rattray, Laird of Craighall
ca. 1675
Folger MS Add 1273 (142)

Even under the most extreme pressures, writers remembered to apologize for any lapse in formality in their letters. This letter was written in great haste by John Ogilvy while his wife lay seriously ill, to request that her brother, the Laird of Craighall, visit her with their mother as a matter of urgency. Ogilvy was forced to use a small piece of paper, folded many times over, and wrote in a rushed untidy hand. Despite all this, he remembered to write a postscript asking that the Laird might "excuse informalitie & little paper" since he was "in heast."

[superscription]　　　　　　　　These
　　　　　　　　　　　　　ffor the Laird of Craighall on heast

[letter]　　　　　　　　　　Loving brother
　　　　　　　　　　　　　You did promise to me to bring out the Lady yo*ur* mother your sister is
　　　　　　　　　　　　　verrie daingaurously sick in traveling & is most disyrous that you may
　　　　　　　　　　　　　come alongst w*ith th*e Lady so expecting to see you on heast I am
　　　　　　　　　　　　　　　　　　Sir
　　　　　　　　　　　　　　　　　Your affectionatt brother
　　　　　　　　　　　　　　　　　　and humble serv*ant*
　　　　　　　　　　　　　　　　　　　Jo: Ogilvy

pray ye mak hast for shee is
verrie disyrous to see you I disyr
ye may ~~suffer~~ ∧lett∧ *your* servant Allex: Cattenoch
come to me with the bearrer

[postscript on
address leaf] excuse informalitie &
littel paper being in heast

[endorsement] Ogilvie begging
Laird C. to come
& see his wife
who was ill

...

Anne Anne
                        Anne bacon
.... Anne   .... Anne bacon
                    Anne Anne bacon
          Anne
                        ny nne bacoy

...

Secretaries

READING LETTERS WRITTEN IN THE SIXTEENTH and seventeenth centuries often gives us a sense of immediacy and personality missing from other archival documents. After all, are not letters, as Erasmus and so many others repeatedly pointed out, just a conversation between absent friends? It comes as a shock to realize that many of these highly personal familiar letters involve a third party—a secretary. A recent survey of sixteenth-century letters written by women found that at least a quarter of them were physically penned, and possibly authored, by someone acting as a secretary, and there is good reason to believe that the figures would be similar in a survey for all letters written. Scribes of all kinds were an integral part of letterwriting in the Renaissance. Men and women who were either completely illiterate or did not know how to write would enjoin friends or family, or else pay professional, itinerant scribes to pen letters for them, to be signed with the "mark" or signature of the sender.

However, it was the permanent personal secretary, resident in his master's household, who aroused the most attention. For the secretary, as the etymology of his name suggests, was often privy to his master's most intimate secrets. The secretary was therefore a man in which infinite trust had to be placed and who had the power to use or abuse that trust. A secretary worked very closely with his master, to the extent that it is by no means clear who is responsible for a particular document. The intimate practices of master and secretary are all too often lost to posterity, but we can catch a glimpse of one working relationship, in the testimony of the earl of Essex's secretary, Henry Cuffe. Cuffe recalled the composition of one tract recording a military expedition. First, he received "his *Lordships* Large [i.e. general] enstructions" for the tract. Then Cuffe "penned very truly" a first draft, drawing on "my owne knowledge" of events, plus "sundry *p*articulers of moment" that Essex provided. "And after I had penned it as plainely as I might alteringe little or nothinge of his owne drawght, I caused his Lordship to *p*eruse it on[c]e againe and to adde extremam manu*m* [the finishing touches, literally the final hand] w*h*ich he hathe donne, as you may *p*erceve by the enterlyneinge" (Lambeth Palace Library, London, MS 658, fol. 88).

Monarchs very rarely wrote entire letters in their own hands. Especially in international correspondence with fellow sovereigns, English kings and queens almost always employed a highly educated secretary to pen official documents. Except in a few notable cases, secretaries were generally self-effacing, their pens silently articulating the thoughts of their employers. Letters *to* monarchs were almost exclusively in secretarial hands as well, as a show of respect, although those in the inner circles of the monarch more commonly wrote in their own hands.

The importance of the secretary is perhaps best witnessed by the creation of the post of "secretary of state" or "principal secretary," the right-hand man to the sovereign, and the nominal head of the privy council, an official group of the monarch's most trusted advisers. Quite often during the early modern period, the burden was so great that two secretaries occupied the post simultaneously. Many of the most prominent politicians of the Tudor period were principal secretaries, including Thomas Cromwell, the architect of the English Reformation; Sir Francis Walsingham and William Cecil, later lord Burghley, Elizabeth's most senior and trusted advisers; and Burghley's son Sir Robert Cecil, who served both Elizabeth I and James I as Secretary of State.

A second, later definition of "secretary" was a manual devised to train budding secretaries, or others with occasional secretarial or letterwriting duties, how to write and act according to the dignity of their position. Angel Day's *The English Secretarie* was an early English example, followed in 1616 by Thomas Gainsford's *The Secretaries Studie*. However, this wide-ranging genre soon became more tailored to entertainment than practical training, its content often more akin to the subject-matter of prose romances and foretelling the popularity of epistolary novels in the eigteenth century. From the archives of the Stationers' Company we know that in 1636, a volume was planned entitled *Love's Secretary, or A Cabinett of choice and curious letters complementall and occasionall*, although the book (if it was ever printed) seems not to have survived. Over the next few years, however, French models of book secretaries dominated the English market. The star of the scene was Jean-Louis Guez de Balzac, who authored some twenty-seven letter collections: these were the key influence on Jean Puget de la Serre's *Le Secretaire de la Cour* (1628), which provided some of the raw materials for *The Academy of Complements* by "Philomusus;" and *Le secretaire à la Mode* (1640), which was promptly translated by John Massinger as *The Secretary in Fashion*. Another French import, Jacques du Bosc's *Nouveau recueil de lettres des dames de ce temps: Auec leurs responses* (Paris, 1635), was englished by Jerome Hainhofer as *The Secretarie of Ladies*; however, those women seeking instruction in letterwriting were better served by *The Female Secretary*, published in 1671 by Henry Care.

Towards the end of the seventeenth century, mirroring a general trend in letterwriting manuals, more practical, less class-bound secretaries began to appear. In 1687, John Hill published his *The Young Secretary's Guide, Or A Speedy Help to Learning*. The first half predictably enough contained "The true method of *writing letters* upon any subject; whether business or otherwise: fitted to all capacities, in the most smooth and obliging style; with about 200 examples never before published. As also instructions how properly to *entitle, subscribe, or direct a letter* to any person of what quality soever, together with full directions for *true pointing*; and many other notable things." Rather than the usual fare of love letters, the second half was devoted to the more technical secretarial business of legal procedure and business documentation. *The Young Secretary's Guide* was followed by T. Goodman's *The Experienced Secretary, Or, Citizen's and Countryman's Companion* (1699); and a section on letterwriting found its way into William Mather's 1737 edition of *The Young Man's Companion*. With their focus on the realities of English life, these volumes moved away from the influence of the French letter-collections, and could be said to have paved the way for the highly localized epistolary novels of eighteenth-century England.

28
Jean Puget de la Serre (ca. 1600–1655)
Il segretario di Corte, o le Maniere di scriuere alla Modernae
Venice, 1661
Folger 176-713.1

This frontispiece engraving depicts a typically intimate working arrange-
ment: the master reads and dictates, while the secretary writes.

29
Angel Day (fl. 1575–1595)
The English Secretary, or Methode of Writing of Epistles and Letters: with a
Declaration of such Tropes, Figures, and Schemes, as either vsually or for ornament
sake are therein required
London: by P.S. for Cuthbert Burbie, 1599
Folger STC 6404, c.2

As promised in the first edition of the *English Secretarie*, Day included an extra section, "Of the parts, place, and Office of a secretorie," in all following editions. Interestingly, in endeavoring to describe the strange position occupied by the secretary in relation to his master, Day turned to an architectural metaphor—a secretary was like a closet, the small lockable room where a lord or lady would undertake his or her private study or devotions: in a culture where even a bedchamber granted no privacy, the closet was "the most secrete place in the house, appropriate vnto our owne priuate studies." The secretary, it follows, is also a "most secrete place," and "a reposement [repository] of secrets." In the Folger copy of the third edition, a reader has included a manuscript index of rhetorical tropes on the facing page to this section.

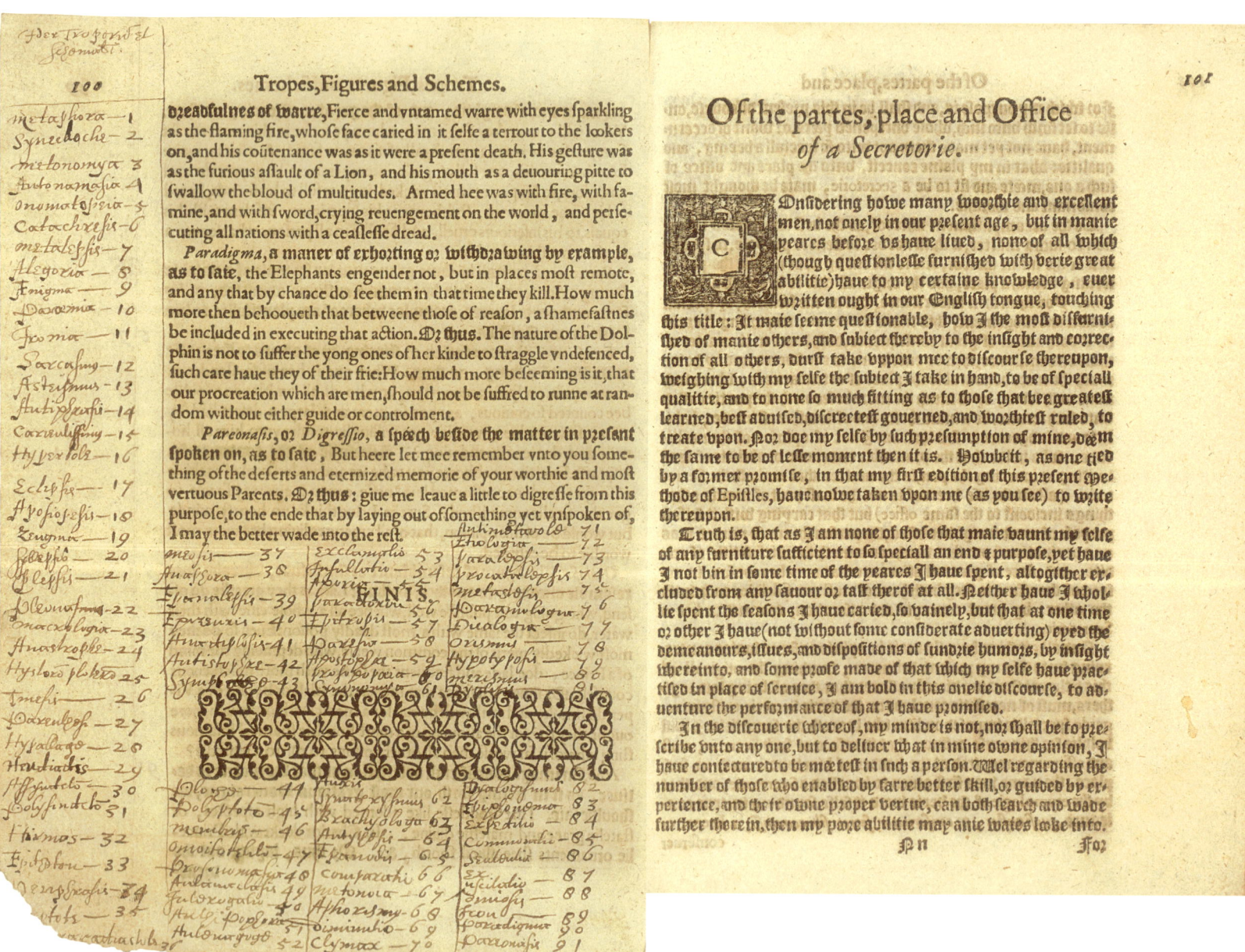

[pp. 102–103]

So then am I not of opinion of the multitude, who holde that the praiseable endeuour or abilitie of well writing or ordering the pen, is the matter that maketh the *Secretorie*, (albeit the vse heereof is not the least part of manie other things incident to the same *office*) but that carying with it selfe a purpose of much weightier effect, the person thereunto named was as a deriuatiue from that which containeth the chiefest title of credite, and place of greatest assurance that may be reposed, in respect of the affinitie they both haue of *trust* and *fidelitie*, each with the other, by great conceyte and discretion, tearmed to bee a *Secretorie*. . . .

By this reason, we do call the most secrete place in the house, appropriate vnto our owne priuate studies, and wherein wee repose and deliberate by deepe consideration of all our waightiest affaires, a *Closet*. . . .

It hath beene alreadie before alledged, that by the verie *etimologie* of the worde it selfe, both *Name* and *Office* in one, doe conclude vppon *secrecie:* If so, then in respect of the *couertnes, safetie* and *assurance* in him reposed, and not otherwise, the partie seruing in such place may be called a *Secretorie*. The *Closet* in euerie house, as it is a reposement of *secrets*, so is it onelie (as I saide before) at the owners, and no others commaundement: The *Secretorie*, as hee is a *keeper and conseruer of secrets*, so is hee by his Lorde or Maister, and by none other to bee directed. To a *Closet*, there belongeth properlie, a *doore*, a *locke*, and a *key*: to a *Secretorie*, there appertaineth incidentlie, *Honestie, Care,* and *Fidelitie*.

———

30
Elizabeth I (1533–1603)
Letter signed, to Philip II of Spain, in Latin, written by Roger Ascham, her Latin secretary
Greenwich, February 17, 1565/6
Folger MS X.d.138 (2)
Reproduced at 82%

Relations between Elizabeth of England and Philip II of Spain were always very delicate, but the official correspondence between them is a model of decorum. This letter negotiating for the release of English prisoners in Spain was written by Roger Ascham, who served as Latin secretary to both Queen Mary and Queen Elizabeth. His duties with the latter ranged from this kind of penmanship to teaching Elizabeth to write a good italic hand, and to read Greek—which experience provided anecdotal materials for his popular educational handbook, *The Scholemaster*, first published in 1570. Against the image of the anonymous, secret secretary, Ascham does not disappear from view. Indeed, he takes the opportunity to signal his presence very publicly (and internationally) by signing the letter himself, on the last leaf. The letter is endorsed in Spanish by a secretary, followed by the Spanish Queen Isabella's rather unpractised signature.

Serenißimo et Potentißimo Principi,
D. Philippo, Hispaniarum, vtri-
usq̃ Siciliæ, Hierusalem et cæt.
Regi Xcat. Fratri, Con
sanguineo, & Amico nr̃o char.mo

A Su M.d

La Reyna de Ynglaterra etc.by del Febo
1566

Sobre La restitucion a subditos
de las naos y hazienda de te-
nidas en Gibraltar
Para q̃ se embiaxe cierta justi-
mento en sellarlo con el
sello del Almirante etc
de Ynglaterra

Ysabel

et vra bona gratia, Authoritate, et expresso iussu, Naues nrorum minus iam diu
detenta, vna cum bonis vniuersis, proprijs Dominis tandem restituuntur. Et
quo iustius statuatur istic de tota istharum rerum ratione, mandauimus, vt fieret
Instrumentum pub.cum Sigillo magni Admiraldi nri Angliæ confirmatum: in quo,
certa nomina Dominorum cuiusq nauis, et rata portio bonorum cuiusq Domini,
vere et iuste explicarentur.

Speramus ig.r hanc rem, breui, vra bona gratia, ita plene confectum iri, ut in tam
iusta causa, nec nri posthac nobis supplices esse, nec nos in eorum gratiam scri-
bere, amplius, opus, simus habitura. Si pari enim casu, Hispanici Negociatores vlli
in Anglia vrgerentur, æquo non ferremus animo, nec vllo pateremur modo, vt ipsi
de vlla vel æquitatis vel humanitatis parte, sibi apud nros denegata, iure con-
queri potuerint.

Itaq plane pollicemur nris, cum semel hæc integra causa ad plenam V.ræ S.tis noti-
am peruenerit, non diu se expectaturos, quin iustissima æquitatis ratione, omnia
eorum negocia, primo quóque tempore, facile et fœliciter illis expedita sint fu-
tura. DEUS C.am Ser.tem in omni florenti fœlicitate diu-
tissime conseruet incolumem. Ex Regia nra, Grenouici, XVII die
February. An.o Dni. M.o D.o LXV.o Regni v.ri nri VII.o

Serenitatis Vestræ bona soror
Consanguinea

Elizabeth R

R   Aschamus.

31
James I, king of England (1566–1625)
Letter in secretarial hand, with autograph postscript and sign manual, to George
Keith, fifth earl marischal of Scotland (1553?–1623)
Hampton, October 3, 1604
Folger MS Add 1270

One of the convenient side effects of the convention that letters by sovereigns were
usually written by a secretary was that the king could make a personal and emphatic
point simply by adding a marginal note or a postscript in his own hand. George
Keith, the earl marischal of Scotland, had been one of James's leading Scottish
councillors for over two decades, but in recent years he had been repeatedly cen-
sured for failing to turn up to Privy Council meetings. In 1604, the parliament of
Perth called on Keith to act on the commission to co-operate with the English
commissioners regarding James's pet project, the union of England and Scotland,
but Keith again failed to rise to the occasion. This letter, as so many, was written for
James I by one of his secretaries, but the king decided not only to sign the letter, but
to add his own autograph postscript reiterating the letter's central message, in
terms that were decidedly less polite than those employed in the body of the letter.
Here we can see quite clearly the advantages of having a secretary pen most of the
letter—James's intervention is rendered all the more vivid, blunt and effective.

[superscription]

To our right trusty and welbeloued
cowsen and counsellour The earle
Marshall of our kingdome of Scotland.
in all possible haste.

[letter]

James R:

[James' handwriting]
I can not nou admitte
any excuse of youre
absence quhaire ye
are to serue youre
king & youre cun=
trey in so godly &
honorable an earande.

Right trusty and welbeloued cowsen and counsellour wee
wee greete yow hartely well / hauing by your seruant
directed hether vnto vs for excusing your absence signi=
fied our mynde wee haue thought good of new to putte
yow in rememberaunce especiallie of our pleasour, that as
yee will do vs acceptable seruice, yee faill not to keepe
the prefirid dyet / for as the mater to be entreated
toucheth vs in honour by setling the peace and perpetuall
tranquility of this whole Ilande, so it toucheth yow
and euery particulare subiect, but you almost more then
any other being in office and place aboue manie. Therefor
wee will admitte no pretense of excuse and wee thinke
the number of the nobility whose helpe and concurrence
should be in so great a mater almost ouer few when yee
shalbe all here. And if the paynes and chardges of
an erand so deere to vs and so important to all youre
welfares, may deterre one of your ranke, wee may thinke
the great paines and trauelles taken by vs for yow all
not so worthilie bestowed as wee did expecte / Soo looking
assuredlie that all excuses sette aparte ye will addresse

your selfe hether in as quiet and sober maner as yee
thinke good (seeing yee will haue so many peeces of your
own frendship who will keepe company with yow) wee bid
yow hartely farewell / from our honour of Hampton the
third of October 1604.

E. Marshall:

a letter from King
James the 6th To the
Earle Marischall
the 3^d of October
1604

————

32
Anne (Gresham) Bacon (d. 1595)
Draft letters in the hand of her husband, Nathaniel Bacon, to her mother and
mother-in-law, with practice signatures
ca. early June, 1573
Folger MS L.d.21
Reproduced at 90%

Anne (Gresham) Bacon was born the illegitimate daughter of Elizabethan London's
foremost merchant, Sir Thomas Gresham, by a Mistress Dutton, one of Gresham's
household servants; Mistress Dutton had been married off by her master to
Thomas Dutton, one of Gresham's factors working in Antwerp and Hamburg.
Acknowledged from birth by her biological father, Anne brought a considerable
fortune to her marriage, in summer 1569, to Nathaniel Bacon, the second son of the
Lord Keeper Sir Nicholas Bacon. But while the money was good, Anne's education
left much to be desired, and her husband had to help his new wife in her epistolary
endeavors. Drafts of two routine letters that were to be sent from Anne, one
addressed to "Madame," presumably her mother-in-law Lady Bacon, and one to
"Mother Dutton," her mother, are in the hand of her husband Nathaniel—although
it is not clear whether he in fact composed the letters, or acted as a scribe for his
wife's dictation. In the middle of the page, Anne Bacon's multiple attempts at
forming her signature are visible.

Madame. I vnderstand by Davie your servaunt, how your
Ladyship is in good health, whereof I am very glad, &
praie God long to continewe the same. I vnderstand
also by him, how your Ladyship loked at his lat cominge
from hence to haue received some lettre from me. It is a
thinge left vndone the oftener, not for that ther wanteth
any good will to writ, but only because ther hap=
peneth seldome occasion wherof to writ. How well
I haue speade sins my beinge with childe for my health,
I dout not but your Ladyship & my father heareth

L.d.21

Madame I vnderstand by Daþie yor servaunt, how yor
La: is in good health, wherof I am very glad &
praie God long to continewe ye same. I vnderstand
also by him, how yor La: loked at his laſt comynge
from hence to have receiued some lre from me. It is be
thinge left vndone I offices, not for yt ther wanteth
any good will to writ, but only becauſe ther hap-
peneth seldome occaſion wherof to writ. And well
I have speade sins my beinge at thilke for my health,
I dout not but yor La: & my father heareth
from time to time by wch meanes lres. My
huſbande mindeth nowe in these three weakes to have
me from hence to waepen & ther I am to remaine
& wait for my deliuery, of wch I make accompt
about by weake 6 after Wichsones. & thus deſiringe
yor La: to take in good part these fewe lines, wth humble remembrance of my dutie to your La: & my father I take my leave

Anne   Anne bacon
        Anne   Anne bacon
  H   Anne   Anne Anne bacon
                      ij nne bacoy

Mr of Sutton, it is so longe sins I wrot vnto you, so I am
nowe halfe aſhamed to writ, & yet rather becauſe I have oft
hard from you, & you neuer have harde from me. for I receiued
diuers tokens from you, & I hartely thanke you for them.
I vnderstand by my huſband, how carfully you did enquire
for me at his beinge at London. I see therby yor dawghter
is not by you forgotten, though she be out of yor sight.
I am even nowe vpon my setinge of Mounteth & goinge
to waepen to houſe of my brother wodhouse ther to waet
vntill I be deliuered. God graunt me well to do, I wisſh my
fortune were so good as to have you ther. I am sure yow
ſhould be welcome thither. I hope yow will praie for yor
dawghter, thongh yow be not wth yet. & thus I leave
wishinge to yow, as a dawghter ſhould wishe vnto her
mother. I praie yow comend me to my father yor huſband.

ij   nne

from time to time by Mr Stringars le*tt*res. My
husbande mindeth w*i*th in these three weakes to haue
me from hens to waxam, & ther I am to remaine
& wait for my delivery, of w*hi*ch I make accompt
about vij weakes after Midsomer. & thus desiringe
yo*u*r La*dyship* to take in good part these fewe lines, with hum=
ble remembrance of my dutie ∧both to yo*u*r La*dyship* & my father∧ I take my leave.

Mot*h*er Dutton, it is so longe sins I wrot vnto yow, as I am
nowe half ashamed to writ, & *th*e rather because I haue oft
hard from yow, & yow never hard againe from me. for I received
divers tokens from yow, & I hartely thanke yow for them.
I vnderstand by my husband, how carfully yow did enquire
for me at his beinge at London. I see therby yo*u*r dawghter
is not by yow forgotten, though she be out of yo*u*r sight.
I am ever nowe vpon my levinge of Norwitch & goinge
to waxam a house of my brother woodhouse ther to wait
vntill I be delivered. God graunt me well to do. I wish ∧with all my hart∧ my
fortune were so good as to haue you ther. I am suer, yow
shold be wellcome thether. I hope yow will praie for yo*u*r
dawghter, though yow be not w*i*th her. & thus I leave
wishinge to yow, as a dawghter sholde wishe vnto her
mother. I praie yow co*m*mend me to my fat*h*er yo*u*r husband.

33
Nathaniel Bacon (1547–1622)
Draft letter, to Lady Anne Heydon, in the hand of his secretary Martin Man, with
autograph corrections
ca. December 1591–July 1593
Folger MS L.d.69

In this letter, Nathaniel Bacon protests to Lady Anne Heydon that he has done
nothing to provoke her son against Lady Anne and her husband. It is not the letter
that was sent to Lady Anne, but a draft in Bacon's secretary's hand with Bacon's
amendments, which were presumably written into the copy as it was finally sent.
The lines of the letter are widely spaced, to allow Bacon's comments and corrections to be interlined. Some of these are minor clarifications, some ensure a
smoother style, while others are more significant rethinkings of the matter in hand.

Maddame, Synce yo*u*r last going out of norff*olk* Mr Leedys ~~hath made~~ ∧did mak∧ offer to
deliuer vnto me a message from you, wherof I refused to take knowledge
unles he did set *the* same downe in wrighting ~~vnder his hande~~ ∧*that* th*er* might be no mistaking∧. And though
I might haue aunswered a message w*i*th a message, yet to avoide *the* harme
that oftentimes groweth ~~therbie~~ in miscariadge, I am content to signifye
my aunswer by this my le*tt*re. you haue prayed Mr Leedys (as yt seemeth)

to tell me that you heare, I am an especiall Stirrer & adviser of your

soonne Mr *Christ*ofer heidon against you & his fath*er*, w*hi*ch you take verie

vnkyndlie at my handes, wishing me to consider, what an vnkynde

griefe yt would be vnto mee, yf anie of myne should so p*r*ovoke my

self, And th*er*fore you desire that I would desist to giue countenau*n*ce

or mayntenau*n*ce anie furth*er* vnto yo*ur* soonne, And I will take knowledge

of no more then this, bicause no more is set downe. ffor aunswer

hervnto I deny not, but y*our* soon*n*e hath acquaynted me w*i*th some p*r*ocedin*ges* betwen

his father & him, and hath asked my advice touching *the* same,

that he might *the* better governe him self in dew respect toward you &

his father, And yet not giue over his right in that, w*hi*ch is dew

vnto him, and w*hi*ch is unduely sought (as he deliuereth) to be taken from

him & his, And herin I haue p*er*formed that duetye, w*hi*ch I did holde my

selfe tyed vnto. for as it was wisedome in yo*ur* soonne not to relye vpon

his owne iudgm*en*t onely, but to heare other mens for confyrming

~~his conscience~~ ∧him∧ what was best to be don, So was it *the* parte of me & others

not to reiect yo*ur* soonne in so honest a request, And asmuch would

I haue don for yo*ur* husband & you, If I had ben required. To saie that

[fol. 1^v] I am a stirrer of yo*ur* soonne against you & ∧or∧ his father, therin am I

wronged by him or her whosoeuer thei be that saie so, And if you

or anie other can charge me therw*i*th, spare not to publishe yt to my

shame, ∧And∧ I crave no favo*ur* therin of you or anie p*er*son elles, And I know

that yo*ur* soonne will both now & her*a*fter iustefye me therin. for yo*ur*

vnkynde taking of this at my hand*es* yt is no new thinge for you to take

∧a∧ thin*ges* vnkyndly from me without cause ~~And though~~ ∧And I marveile *that* you,∧ I might

∧who haue these many yeares shewed me so litle kindnes,∧

manie waies herunto replye, ~~yet~~ ∧but∧ I ~~will passe yt over as I~~ ∧should so cumber you ~~to the rest~~∧

∧will nowe challendg me for unkindnes.∧ ~~haue don afore this tyme~~ you drawe a ∧~~worldly~~∧ ~~reason from *the* fleshe in~~

by putting me in mynde of myne owne children: ~~whome~~ ∧wherevnto I saie∧ yf I shall

vniustly p*r*ovoke ∧them or be vnkind to them∧, yt maie be that God ∧who often punisheth one sin*n*e with an other∧

will ~~punishe *the* same by their~~

~~vnkyndnes towardes me~~ ∧also punish me by p*r*ovokinge them against me or by th*er* vnkindnes towards me∧. but

∧what is this to *the* purpose seing∧ I am not able to charge yo*ur* soonne w*i*th anie

vnkynde vsage eith*er* ~~of~~ ∧towardes∧ you or his father, ∧& yf you be able to charg him w*i*th any, I will not

iustefie him in it∧. ~~for~~ to charge him w*i*th vnkyndnes

bicause he will not yealde to do whatsoeuer you & his father will haue

him do, is farre from reason, ∧for∧ howsoeuer he oweth a great dutie both

vnto his fath*er* & vnto you, he oweth also a duetye vnto his wief and

familye, w*hi*ch may not in respect of his oth*er* duetye be left unregard[ed].

wheras in *the* ende you praie me to desist in geving countenau*n*ce or

maytenau*n*ce to yo*ur* soonne: The countenau*n*ce or mayntenau*n*ce w*hi*ch he can

anie waes receive from me is verie small, And yf vnder thes word*es*

you meane to haue me leave his companye or otherwise that he

maie not comu*n*icate his mynde vnto me in anie honest cause or sorte

[fol. 2^r] ~~which maie~~ ∧yea though it∧ concerne you or yo*ur* husband, I vtterley refuse to satisfye

yo*ur* request herin. for as I will not be ∧so∧ tyed ~~so~~ vnto yo*ur* soonne, as

to leave you or S*ir* Willia*m* in anie iust cause, wherin I am able to

pleasure you, yf yt shall seeme good vnto you at anie tyme to vse me,

so will I not reiect yo*ur* soonne at *the* instaunce of you or anie other,

so longe as yt shall please him to vse me, as one gentleman

maie & ought to vse another. for I am *per*suaded that yo*ur* soonne

both doth & will beare a good harte toward*es the* churche of God

& *the* welfare of his contrey And ~~I hope that he taketh profytt~~ ∧ therfore so mutch *the* more∧

∧~~he~~ is ∧he∧ to be esteemed of by me & others ∧~~by thes troubles wherwith yt hath pleased God to exercise him~~

~~I might wright more, but these maie suffice to this~~

~~message.~~ Thus wisshing both you Madame & S*ir*

will*ia*m plentie of the grace of God for *the* better

guiding you in these many trobles wher*with* it

hath pleased God to exercise you, I take

my leave.

[endorsement]   Letter to my

La: Haydon

———

34

Robert Cecil, earl of Salisbury (1563–1612)

The State and Dignitie of a Secretarie of Estates Place, with the Care and Perill Thereof

London, 1642

Folger S387

Sir Robert Cecil became Principal Secretary in 1596, occupying that position under both Elizabeth and James, two notoriously difficult masters. As a result, Cecil clearly had his reservations about the post, and set down his thoughts in a tract that was published only posthumously in 1642. In it he points out that the secretary is an exception to the other officers of state, since his appointment derives not from a patent, but from a "Confidence and singular affection" invested in him by his master, an affection that Cecil represents as like "the mutuall affections of two lovers." This intimate relationship not only makes the secretary vulnerable to the vagaries of royal favor, but also the object of envy to his fellow councillors.

[sig. A3ʳ–A4ʳ]   All Officers and Councellors of Princes have a prescribed Authoritie by Patent, by Custome or by oath, the Secretary onely excepted, but to the Secretary out of a Confidence and singular affection there is a libertie to negotiate at discretion at home and abroad with friends and enemies in all matters of speech and intelligence. . . .

Their fellow Councellors envy them because they have most easie and free access to Princes, and wheresoever a Prince hath cause to delay or deny to search or punish, none so soone beare so much burthen.

Kings are advised to observe these things in a Secretary.

First that he be created by himself, and of his owne raising.

Secondly that he match not in a factious familie.

And lastly that he have reasonable capacitie, and convenient abilitie. . . .

As long as any matter of what weight soever is handled only between the Prince and the Secretary: Those Councells are compared to the mutuall affections of two lovers, undiscovered to their friends.

When it commeth to be disputed in Councel, it is like the conference of Parents and solemnization of Marriage, the first matter, the second Order, and indeed the one the act, the other the Publication.

35

M. de la Serre (ca. 1600–1665)

*The secretary in fashion: or, A compendious and refined way of expression in all manner of letters. Composed in French by P. S*ʳ *de la Serre, historiographer of France. And translated into English, by John Massinger*

London: J[ohn] B[eale] and S[tephen] B[ulkley] for Godfrey Emerson, 1640

Folger STC 20491

In his letter to the reader, the translator Massinger attacks some of his book-secretary predecessors, as well as the other current vogue in letter collections, the supposedly intercepted packet of letters. Although one might well dispute the contention that de la Serre's work outclasses his peers so utterly, *The Secretary in Fashion* went through two further, enlarged editions in 1654 and 1673, testifying to its longterm popularity.

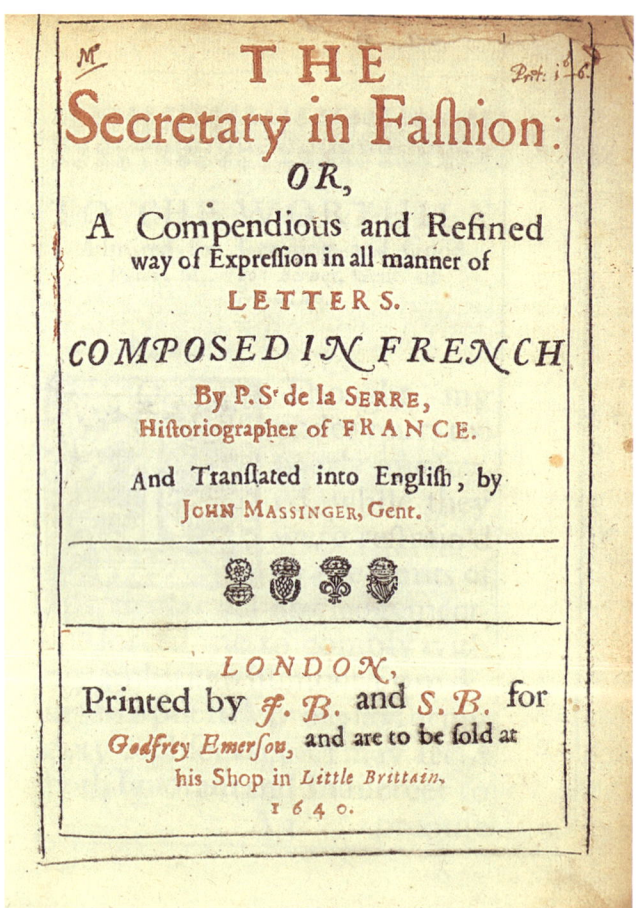

[sig. A2ʳ–A3ʳ]   The Translator to the Reader.

> . . . I see thee already blear-eyed with reading *Monsieur Balzaac*, and the *Packet of Letters*; forgive mee good Reader, I aske thee most humbly Mercy, and with much Resentment call backe my former Imprecation, since I per-ceive thee already exposed to a more rigorous Pennance, than that which my Charity would have suffered my Justice to impose upon thee: For what mis-cheif could I have imagined . . . equall to the Malice of this which thou hast already incurred? in the one thou learnest nothing but to speake Baudy with

a good Grace, in the other nothing but to blow a horne; Here thou suckest in the Principles of Atheisme, there of Ignorance; Here thou art instructed to Preach in an Epistle, there to Court thy Friend in a Sermon: This stuffs thy Memory with Stolne French, that with English not worth the Stealing: The one Commands thee to Violate the Laws of all Ancient Rhetorique, the other to observe none. The one will give thee Rules how to speak *Balzaac*, (or) badly, the other like a Post (*id est*) nothing at all.

The Consideration of this (Loving, Kind, Courteous Reader) . . . did even force my Spirit to reclaime the Idolatrous from adoring that Malicious Idoll the *English Secretary*, that Image which *Nebuchadnezzar the King had set up*, the *Post* with a *Packet of Letters*, and that most abhominable *Baal*, *Balzaac*: by divulging this Peece of Excellent Workmanship, (which the Gods them-selves did hammer and frame in the Head of *Monsieur La Serre*;) by letting this Bird of Paradise fly out of her Cage, that she might recreate Mortality with the Charmes of her Voyce, and resuscitate the Intombed Spirits of Men, from that Leaden sleep which the former *Tarantulaes* had throwne them into.

———

36

Jacques du Bosc [Monsieur du Bosque] (d. 1660)
The Secretary of Ladies. Or, A new collection of Letters and Answers, composed by Moderne Ladies and Gentlewomen . . . translated out of French by I.H.
[Jerome Hainhofer]
London: Tho. Cotes for William Hope, 1638
Folger STC 7267

Another French import came from Jacques du Bosc, the proto-feminist author of *L'honnête femme*, translated into English as *The Compleat Woman*. In 1638, Jerome Hainhofer translated du Bosc's *Nouveau recueil de lettres des dames de ce temps: Auec leurs responses* (Paris, 1635) as The *Secretary of Ladies*, subtitled "A new collec-tion of Letters and Answers, composed by Moderne Ladies and Gentlewomen" which aims "to vindicate the honour of dames, and to make it appeare that Letters are not the peculiar heritage of one sexe." The Reader is advised that "if there bee any who cannot yet consent that Gentlewomen should write, I assure my selfe this book will convert them; where they shall finde so many things of worth, they shall bee compeld to renounce their ignorance or envy." Rather than provide models for composition, these letters animate a conversation between two women, one socially superior to the other. Pairs of letters are matched on given topics—so the first letter, "She prayes her to returne to Paris, and bring her in dislike with the Country," is paired with one that "Answers, that besides the losse of their conversation, she is vext with that of the Country: and that she will never make vew of solitude while she can hope the honour of their company." As the two women work their way through common topics of conversation—life in Paris versus country life, men and their inconstancy, love, marriage, and social etiqutte—there emerges an intense, and perhaps inappropriate relationship between them, where the socially superior woman rebukes the other for her overly ardent expressions of love.

An advertisement to the Reader, by a friend of the Collector.

Be not astonisht to see this Collection come out in print, hee that hath tane
the paines, to make it had reason to thin[k that] after you had read the letters
of so many ingenious men, you would take it well to see these offers of
women. There is no colour to say it ill becomes their sexe: for if it be not
amisse that they are able to make a complement, you must not thinke it
strange that they can write one. Tis the principall subject of these Letters,
which are not confused nor shufled together, as many others which the vulgar
esteeme good. They are not treatises, nor orations; they are no deepe discourses wherein there is nothing smels of a Letter, but Sir your servant. But it
is not needfull, to witnesse these good, that I make others appeare ill. I will
onely say that if there bee any who cannot yet consent that Gentlewomen
should write, I assure my selfe this book will convert them; where they shall
finde so many things of worth, they shall bee compeld to renounce their
ignorance or envy, for by one of these names I must call the cause of their
error, which I would farther oppose if these Ladies had need of my Apology
but they defend themselves better by neglect, than those dreames deserve.
And I will content my selfe to say, that if this age hath seene many that write
with approbation of all the world upon the most important matters,
Religion, and morality, wee need not make it such a marvell that they can
[mak]e good letters, seeing they can ma[ke] good bookes. But it is time to
finish this advertisement; and I vow I am to blame to detaine the reader from
the booke it selfe, where he shall receive much more satisfaction, than I am
able to promise.

Essex and his secretaries: a case study

By the 1590s, it was *de rigueur* for a top-ranking politician to have not just one, but a cohort of secretaries. Queen Elizabeth's last, doomed favorite Robert Devereux, second earl of Essex, set up his secretariat with great care and deliberation. In 1585, he appointed Thomas Smith, a fellow of Christ Church, Oxford, and university orator, to be his secretary. Smith was joined three years later by Edward Reynoldes, also an Oxford academic, who became Essex's closest secretary. When in 1595, Smith was elevated to become clerk to the Privy Council, Essex replaced him with Henry Wotton, a well-traveled Oxford graduate. Completing the team were Henry Cuffe, who had been regius professor of Greek at Oxford and a fellow of Merton College (Essex matched Cuffe's Oxford salary) and the solitary Cambridge representative, William Temple, a fellow of King's College. In addition to these paid employees, Essex was also supported in quasi-secretarial duties by friends such as Anthony and Francis Bacon. Essex in turn was a kind of secretary for Elizabeth: he once complained to Francis Bacon late one evening that "I am oppressed with [a] multitude of letters that are come, of which I must give the queen some accompte to morowe morninge." Many of the papers from Essex's secretariat have survived, allowing us a glimpse into a world where the line dividing the master from the secretary often disappears altogether—sometimes with devastating effects.

37
Robert Devereux, 2nd earl of Essex (1566–1601)
Autograph letter signed, to his mother, Lettice (Knollys) Devereux Dudley Blount, countess of Leicester
Lees, September 1, [after 1588]
Folger MS Add 1038

Essex was notorious for his terrible handwriting, and many of his correspondents must have been grateful to receive a letter penned by one of his secretaries. But on one occasion, the system backfired. His mother declared herself "greeued" (aggrieved) with a letter bearing his signature that allegedly was insulting to her. Although Essex remonstrated that he hadn't signed any letter that referred to her, she insisted that he had, and ultimately he had to climb down and apologize. In his defense, he claimed that "amongst the infinite letters which are offred to me to signe" it was possible that "I might signe some such ere [before] I knew whatt yt was."

[superscription]   To my noble and most honored
                                            mother the Countesse of
                                                  Leycester.

[letter]   Madam.
                          I am glad to take this occasion of writinge both to present
                          my seruice to your ladyship and to excuse the signing of the letter
                          which your ladyship found your self greeued with. Because your ladyship doth
                          so constantly affirme my hand was to yt I will beleeue
                          yt. though I protest I know nott thatt my hand was
                          sett to any letter thatt did concerne eit[h]er your ladyship or
                          any towards you butt amongst the infinite letters which
                          are offred to me to signe I might signe some
                          such ere I knew whatt yt was. and yet I am
                          sure ther was neuer any in thatt place thatt was
                          more scrupulous or thatt did refuse more. for in
                          those causes whether I haue nott the bond of duty
                          and affection to the I am hardly drawne to preiudice
                          any. And therefore I hope your ladyship will be satisfied
                          for thatt error. I will nott trouble your ladyship with
                          the newes of our palsy troublesome world. which hath
                          made me a greatt deall both honester and thriftier
                          then euer I was or shold haue bene els. I do
                          send your ladyship many wishes of whose happinesses you
                          most desire and rest

                                        your ladyships most affectionate and
                                             most obedient son.
                       I desire to be commended to my
                       fayre mayde and to Sir Christopher Blunt.
                                                          Essex.

                       Lees this first of September

                       ————

                       38
                       Robert Devereux, 2nd earl of Essex (1566–1601)
                       Letter signed, to Roger Manners, earl of Rutland, with autograph postscript
                       St. Albans, October 16, [1595?]
                       Folger MS Add 1039

                       Sometime in 1595, a series of three letters ostensibly authored and signed by Essex
                       was sent to the young earl of Rutland, who was about to embark on a tour of the
                       Continent. The first letter contained "generalities"; the second was more "particular"
                       and devoted to the "course of studie" Rutland should adopt, while the third letter
                       was a last-minute pep talk, answering the young man's request for "some advice
                       nowe at the verie instant of your goinge." After running through what Rutland
                       should do, the letter appears to draw to a close—and then, in a different hand,

Essex's own, the earl explains how the letter came to be penned: "This was written yesternight att St Albans butt so ill written as I was fayne to use my mans hand to copy yt out. Excuse the hasty writing and my indisposition after my iorney which keepes me from correcting yt. More leysure may bring forth a worke of more price. though this as all thatt I direct unto you is full of affection and accompanyned with my best wishes." Critics and editors have spilled a good deal of ink pondering the implications of this postscript. Does this mean that Essex himself composed and penned the original letter, only to realise that in his handwriting it was too "ill written" to be sent out? Or is this postscript merely a ploy to make it look as if Essex composed the letter? Is the reference to "St. Albans" an indication that in fact the author may have been Essex's friend Francis Bacon, whose family estate of Gorhambury was near St. Albans?

[superscription]

To the right honorable
my verye good lord &
Cousen the Earle of
Rutland

[letter]

My lord. Since you haue required of me some advice
nowe at the verie instant of your goinge, I must not
refuse you, thoughe my want of leisure and health will
make that which you receave from me little worth. My
first letter to your lordship did contayne generalities: my second
was particular, to direct you in course of studie: and this
shall onlie tell you what are the notes I would wish
you to gather in your travail, which being but a posting
nightes worke after everie bodie is gone to bed, I desire
may be private to your self, and may serve to awake you in
some thinges, though it cannot instruct you in all. /
When your lordship comes into any Countrey, I would wish you
to observe the nature of the climate, and temperature
of the ayre: for so you shall both iudge of the healthful=
nes of the place, and may haue some inducement to gesse
at the disposicion of the people. Also to marke the
condicion of the soile, whether it be fertile, or barren,
Mountaynous or even, full of woodes or champion, and to
note the principall rivers, their begynninges & course, the
streightes and passages that do sever one province or piece
of province from another, and what theire length or bredth
is: the circuite and the Diameter or length of the Countrey:
howe it is peopled and inhabited: what are the commodities
with which it aboundes, and which it ventes: and of the
other side what it wantes: and drawes to it from forrain
partes. What portes it hath, what shipping, and
howe their trafficke lyes: howe the people are armed,
and trained, what fortified Townes or Castells, what
revenewe, what arsenall: what Alliances, and what
known enemies the state hath. for these thinges will
leade you to knowe whither any Countrie be ritch or poore,
stronge or weake. But aboue all thinges I would

haue you vnderstand the manner of governement of the
place where you are. where the Souueraintye is, in one,
as in a Monarchie, in a fewe, or in the people: or if
it be mixt, to which of these formes it most inclines. /
Next what ministers of State and subalternat governors,
as Counsaile and Magistrates: Thirdlie by what lawes
or Customes it is governed: and lastlie what is the
execucion of iustice in peace, and their discipline in

[verso]

warr. If your lordship will tell me that these thinges will
be to manie to remember: I aunswere, that I had
rather you trusted your note booke then your memorie. /
If you obiect that some of these thinges being martiall,
and others pointes of State, you shall not be able to
collect them, nor iudge of them: I must aske you, whither
you would not get a pylote on a strange coast, & guyde
in an vnknown way? And so if where you come, you
seeke after these thinges, you shall assoone fynd directors
to guyde you to them, as to any matters of sport or
vanitie. The first thing your lordship must seeke in all this
course, is industrie. for as greate difference is betwixt
it and idlenes, or betwixt an actiue sprightfull man, and
a slothfull, as betwixt a lyving man, and a dead. The
second is to dirrect that industrie to good thinges. for els the
more you do, the more yll you do, and the faster you goe,
the farther you go owt of the way. The last is that
you be rather endevoringe to do well, then believing you do
well. for besides that all self conceyted young men do growe
infinitelie vayne, when once owt of opinion that they are
wise, or good inoughe they hold themselues pleased with
them selues, they fall more backward in a monneth, then they
growe forward in a yeare.   This was written yester=   [Essex's hand]
night att Saint Albans butt so ill written as I was
fayne to use my mans hand to copy yt out.
Excuse the hasty writing and my indisposition
after my iorney which keepes me from correcting yt.
More leysure may bring forth a worke of more
price. though this as all thatt I direct unto
you is full of affection and accompanyned with my
best wishes. from

                              your lordships most affectionate
                              cosin and now frend

                              Essex

this 16th of October

[endorsement]   The Earle of Essex to thEarle
                              of Rutland then in his
                              trauail.

39
State letters of 1533–ca. 1630, including copies of "framed letters" between Anthony
Bacon and Robert Deveraux, earl of Essex (1600)
copied ca. 1650
Folger MS V.a.239

We know that Francis Bacon quite often drafted letters for Essex, sometimes of a
quite personal nature, as with several pieces designed to be sent to Elizabeth. But perhaps the most bizarre ghostwriting happened in 1600, when Essex was out of favor
with the queen and Bacon came up with a plan for rehabilitating his patron. He
drafted what appeared to be an exchange of letters between Essex and his own
brother Anthony Bacon, one of the earl's closest advisers to whom Essex might be
expected to write candidly. In the first letter, which runs to ten pages in this manuscript, "Mr. Anthony Bacon" urges the earl not to listen to those supposed friends
who would have his court career dead and buried, but rather to consider the evidence
as it stands (a method that tellingly prefigures Bacon's empirical scientific methods).
In his reply, "Essex" thanks "Anthony" for his kind words, but argues that the queen's
inability to forestall rumor and his ruin points to the victory of his enemies, who
have gained ground in his absence. The letters were not published until 1657, but in
the meantime, multiple copies circulated—there are least ten known extant copies
of the correspondence, of which the Folger holds three (in V.b.234, V.a.239, V.b.132).
In all the copies, they are clearly marked as "confected" correspondence.

[pp. 316–19]

Two letters framed the one as from
Mr Anthony Bacon to the Earle of Essex;
th'other as the Earles answere thervnto
deliuered with the aduise of M^r. Anthony
Bacon, and the priuitie of the Earle to bee
shewed the Queene vppon some ffitt
occasion as a meane to worke her
Maiestie to receaue the Earle againe
to fauour and attendance. /

My singuler good lord this standing att a stay
doth make mee in my love toward*es* your Lo*rdshi*pp iealous;
least yow doe somewhat; or omitt somewhat, that amounteth
to a new errour; ffor I suppose of all former matters
there is a full expiation; wherein for any thinge
which your lo*rdshi*pp doth, I for my p*ar*te (who am remote)
cannot cast or devise wherein any errour should bee,
except in one point which I dare not censure nor
disswade; which is, that as the Prophett saith in
this affliction yow looke vpp ad manum frutientem
and soe make your peace w*i*th god; and yet I have
heard it noted, that my Lord of Leicester who
could never gett to bee taken for a saint yet
in the Queenes disfavour, waxed seeminge re=
ligious, w*h*ich may bee thought by some; & vsed by
others, as a case resembling yours; if men doe

not see, or will not see the difference betweene
your two disposicions; but to bee plaine with your
Lordshipp my feare rather is, because I heare howe
some of your good, and wise friendes not vnpracti=
sed in the court; and supposing themselves
not to bee vnseene in that deepe and vnscrutable
center of the court, which is her Maiesties minde
doe not only toll the bell; but even ring out
peales; as if your ffortune were dead, and
buried; and as if there were noe possibillitie
of recovering her Maiesties favour, and as if the best
of your condicion were to live a private & retyred
life out of want; out of perill, and out of manifest
disgrace, and soe in this perswasion of theirs
include a perswasion to your Lordshipps wardes; to frame
and accomodate your Actions and mynde
to that end; I feare (I say) that this
vntymely dispaire may in tyme bring forth
a iust despaire; by causing your Lordshipp to
slacken and breake off your wise loyall and
seasonable endeavour, and industrie for
reintegration to her Maiesties favour, In
comparison whereof all other circumstan=
ces are but as Atomi; or rather as vacuum
without any substance att all; against this opinion
it may please your Lordshipp to consider of these
reasons which I haue collected, and to make
Judgement of them; neither out of the
Melancholly of your present fortune
nor out of the infusion of that which cometh
to yow by others relation; which is subiect
to much tincture; but ex rebus ipsis, out
of the nature of the persons, and actions
themselves; as the truest and lesse deceiving
grounded of opinion. . . .

39

40

Sir Francis Bacon (1561–1626)

Sir Francis Bacon his apologie, in certaine imputations concerning the late Earle of
Essex. Written to the right Honorable his very good Lord, the Earle of Deuonshire,
Lord Lieutenant of Ireland

London: [Richard Field] for Felix Norton, 1604

Folger STC 1111, c.1

Bacon always maintained that these letters served no purpose beyond enhancing Essex's standing with Elizabeth, and that Essex not only commissioned them but was instrumental in circulating them. However, at Essex's final trial in February 1601, following his aborted rebellion against the queen, Essex struck back at Bacon, now his prosecutor. When Bacon urged him "to confess, not to justify," the earl replied:

> To answer Mr. Bacon's speech at once, I say thus much; and call Mr. Bacon against Mr. Bacon. You are then to know that Mr. Francis Bacon hath written two letters, the one of which hath been artificially framed in my name, after he had framed that other in Mr. Anthony Bacon's name to provoke me. In the latter of these two, he lays down the grounds of my discontentment and the reasons I pretend against mine enemies . . . For then Mr. Bacon joined with me in mine opinion, and pointed out those to be mine enemies and to hold me in disgrace with her Majesty, whom he seems now to clear of such mind towards me; and therefore I leave the truth of what I say and he opposeth unto your Lordships' indifferent considerations. (*The Letters and the Life of Francis Bacon*, ed. James Spedding (London, 1862), vol. 2, pp. 226–7)

Bacon replied, "Those letters, if they were here, would not blush to be seen for anything contained in them. I have spent more time in vain in studying how to make the earl a good servant to the Queen, than I have done in anything else." Essex was found guilty of treason and executed, but it was not the end of the story. Bacon was still on the defensive in 1604, when he published an *Apologie* attempting to explain his actions vis-à-vis Essex, whose reputation had been rehabilitated after the accession of James I.

[pp. 60–62]   . . . And not to trouble your Lordship with many other particulars like vnto these, it was at the selfe same time that I did draw with my Lords priuitie, and by his appointment, two letters, the one written as from my brother, the other as an answer returned from my Lord, both to be by me in secret maner shewed to the Queene, which it pleased my Lord very strangely to mention at the barre: the scope of which were but to represent and picture foorth vnto her Maiesty my Lords mind to be such, as I knew her Maiestie wold fainest haue had it, which letters whosoeuer shall see, (for they cannot now be retracted or altered, being by reason of my brothers, or his Lordships seruants deliuerie, long since comen into diuerse hands) let him iudge, specially if he knew the Queene, and do remember those times, whether they were not the labours of one that sought to bring the Queene about for my Lord of *Essex* his good.

Yeates Sculp

Oenone

Love and friendship

MOST SURVIVING LETTERS FROM EARLY MODERN ENGLAND concern themselves either with affairs of state or financial and legal matters. Amongst this dry paperwork, however, one occasionally encounters a letter that strays from prescribed social conventions and feigned informality to reveal love, anger, frustration, a playful sense of humor, or an irrepressible urge to gossip or converse. As John Donne reminds us in a verse letter to his friend Sir Henry Wotton: "more than kisses, letters mingle Soules, / For thus friends absent speak" (Donne, *Poems* (London, 1635), p. 135). Letters such as these take us closer to natural conversation than any other kind of written document.

While Angel Day writes confidently about every other category of letters in *The English Secretarie*, he begins to waver when he gets to the last section of his book, "epistles amatorie." The vast and unfamiliar terrain seems to overwhelm him:

> . . . whereof because the humours of all sortes with loue possessed, are so infinite and so great an vncertaintie in them remaineth, as that perchance cuen in ye verie writing of his letter, the louer himself is somtimes scarce certain of his own intended purpose therein, the lesse must of necessitie be the precepts of the same, for that in some of them wee require and entreate in others expostulate the matters and occasions falling in the necke therof, other times complaine, another while fawne and speake faire, then purge or cleare an accusation supposed agaynst vs. Finallie, innumerable are the deuises wherewith the reynes of loue are conducted. But in as much as I haue heretofore giuen vnto all other titles their seuerall precepts, I will somwhat also in this place speake to the purpose thereof. . .(London, 1599, pp. 142-43)

Other manuals from this period treat love letters with similar circumspection. Like Day, William Fulwood concludes his manual, *The Enimie of Idlenese*, with six love letters in prose and six in verse, but unlike in his other chapters, provides no instructions. Nicholas Breton's collection of letters, *Poste with a Packet of Mad Letters*, contains love letters (and their replies) intermingled with letters of every other ilk, including stiflingly boring but potentially useful ones such as "A Letter to a friend for dispatch of businesse" and "A kinde Letter of a Creditor for money."

It is questionable whether letterwriting manuals, etiquette manuals, "female secretaries," and collections of familiar letters and love letters were popular because of their entertainment value or for the potential usefulness of their exemplary letters. Dire consequences, or at least major embarrassment, could ensue if one were discovered to have copied love letters directly from one of these books. In *Merry Wives of Windsor*, Falstaff's plans to seduce Mistress Page and Mistress Ford with love letters in order to get at their husbands' money backfires when they discover that their letters are identical, and that he probably "hath a thousand of these letters, writ with blank space for different names (sure, more!); and these are of the second edition. He will print them, out of doubt; for he cares not what he puts into the press". In *Divers Crabtree Lectures* (London, 1639), John Taylor tells the story of "two young Virgins talking of their Sweethearts and Sueters," who ridicule a man who presented one of them "with a Coppy of Verses, and many Letters of Complements in writing, which . . . he intreated me to accept of them, for they were of his owne invention. And when I had perused them, I remember'd that I had read them in Print, for hee stole them out of divers bookes of Complements" (pp. 202–203). At the same time, the Folger copy of Vincent de Voiture's *Letters of Affaires of Love and Courtship* (1657) was clearly read with an eye for imitation, as it is underlined throughout and contains many manuscript notes (Folger V683). And the examples of love letters in the Folger's copy of Angel Day's *The English Secretarie* (London, 1599) are spattered with ink stains and underlinings (STC 6404, c.2).

———

41
Robert Dudley, earl of Leicester (1532?–1588)
Autograph letter signed, to Elizabeth I
Tilbury, [August 3, 1588]
Folger MS Add 1006
Reproduced at 85%

Leicester was the queen's most intimate favorite, their friendship enduring until his death, just one month after he wrote this letter from the royal camp at Tilbury. One of Elizabeth's pet names for Leicester was her "Eyes," and to signal their intimacy he twice adds eyebrows over the word "moost" and subscribes the letter with a pair of eyes before his signature. Although the letter ostensibly reports the readiness of the Queen's army to defend England against the Spanish Armada, his tender appelations for her—"your mōōst swete maiesty," "my mōōst dere Lady"—make the letter both official *and* familiar. He sealed the letter with his personal coat of arms—a bear and ragged staff badge within the garter—over lime-green embroidery floss ties.

[superscription]

To *the* Queens most excell*en*te
M*ai*esty

[letter]

I am loth my most dear La*dy* to trowble you
you w*ith* out some Juste cause, wh*ich* at this tyme
god be thanked here ys none touching y*our* army
here but all thing*es* as well as quyett & as
forwardly bent to y*our* s*er*vyce as any soldyers
or subiect*es* in *the* world ca*n* be. but yet
I may not forgett vppo*n* my knees to yeld
to y*our* mōōst swete ma*ie*sty, all humble & dutyful
thank*es* for y*our* great comfort I rec*eive* euer fro*m*
y*our* owen swete self.   I am sorry that
I ca*n* wryte y*our* ma*ie*sty no newes, yet most
gladd *tha*t I may hold vp my hand*es* to god

I am lothe my most dere La. to trowble yo[u]
y[i]s w[i]t[h]out some great cause, w[i]th al let me [thank]
god to be thancked here y[i]s nowe nothyng y[a]t ar[?]
here but all thinges as well as yo[u]rsellf & as
forwardly And he y[a]t shyw[e]s as any soldio[r]
or subiect as yo[u] would cā be. but y[a]t
I may not forgett yo[u]r my humble to yo[u]
y[a]t moost sw[ee]te m[i]s, all humble & dutyfull
thancks for yo[u]r gr[e]at comfort I vow and so
y[i]s owny swete self.   I am sory that
I cā wryte y[i]s not no newes, yet most
gladd y[a]t I may hold by my hand to god.
for yo[u] and i shall wache so t[h]at y betuarde[?]
yo[u], for he he aduers no greu[s], he f[igh]t[e]th
for yo[u] & yo[u]r enimyes fall before yo[u].

felt all good prayse & glory Reyned y[i]s
[...]esses, & lose and gratious lā, my overcome[?]
he greatly y[i]s agaynst his enymes & yo[u].
the romagate [...] yo bseed y[i]s camp here
& euen now by my L. [...] of ou[r] word & w[...]
stumpe[?] auytord & they w[ith] also grea[?] to vew y[i]s
people w[i]th ou ar so[u]ndly to be sene as any in
crystendome I think. may yo[u] se y[ou]se [...] feylid
& surely so pu[n]ishment must follow, I see
wryt[e]ly so my all of so of the offend[er]s w[i]th ar to
many at such a tone, I god euermore p[re]serve
my moost dere La o. that she may to y[i]s about y[i]s
his people & country and o peace as she may begun
f[rom]. an so g[re]t fro Tylbury t[h]is saturday

                    by y[i] most faythfull & most
                        obedient w[i]th
                            R Leycester

To yo'r 9 — most assured

Lecester. Tilburie.

for *the* mercyfull dealing he vseth towarde
you, for by the newes we heare, he fighteth
for y*ou* & yo*ur* enymyes fall before you.
Lett all honor prayse & glory be geue*n* him
therfore; & loose not, gratious La*dy* any occasion
he geueth y*ou* agenst his enymyes & yo*ur*s.
This ronnagate hath p*er*used yo*ur* Camp here
& eue*n* now ys my L*ord* ~~& master~~ of ormo*n*d & M*aste*r
Stannopp aryved & they be also going to vew yo*ur*
people w*hich* ar as semely to be sene as any in
Crystendom I think. may yo*ur* hors holde fyled
& surely so*m* punyshment must follow, I haue
wrytten to my ll*ords* of so*m* of the offenders w*hich* ar to
many at such a time, / god euer more preserve
my mōōst dere La*dy*, that she may to *the* co*m*fort of
his people & Church end in peace as she hath begoun
Amen. in so*m* hast fro*m* Tylbury this Saturday

by yo*ur* most fathfull & most
obedient ˜˙ ˜˙

R. Leycester

———

42
Sir John Ferrers (ca. 1580–1633?)
Autograph letter signed, to "Good knight*es*" (including Sir Walter Ferrers)
Warwick, July 30, 1604
Folger MS L.e.675
Reproduced at 93%

Ferrers, as Surveyor of Needwood Forest, teases his cousin, Sir Walter, for the many
blots in the account book relating to timber sales, and includes an ink fingerprint
blot to accentuate the joke, asking for "his leave" to "be merry" with him. He also
commiserates with his cousin about being "cheated out of the league" at the dawn of
the newly established peace between Catholic Spain and Protestant England, explaining that it was because Walter never did penance for his venial sins or received abso-
lution from his confessor (the Treaty of London was signed at Somerset House
in the following month).

Good knight*es*   although you had greate pleasure in servinge
yo*ur* owne warrant*es* duringe the parlement, wher
the ofter you shotte the better you were lyked,
itt is much differinge w*ith* vs heare in needwoode
who are restrayned of our ffees, yett havinge notis
by my kynd frend m*r* warde have provided you
a bocke & doe wysh my selffe att the eatinge
of him, the pease is concluded w*ith* spayne &
I am sory that you my good Cosen Sir Walter,

Good knight although you had private pleasure in soundinge your owne warrant duringe the parlement, when the offer you sette the better you now lyked it is much difference to ϕ as I have in neadlewood who are restrained of our flock, yett fearinge notice by my ... friend in ... so ... provided you a barke & doe ... my ... att the outinge of him, the prease is recommended to ϕ spare & I am sory that you my good cosen doe matter did perceive for you buriall ... nether ... to ... of obstinacie by good ... matters, my ... is now perfecte, although in ... you had made many ... att your cominge from London, I hope you will rede your poore frend ... to be more ... ϕ you, who is ... devoted to your lordes. & ... my hartie commendations to you bothe I wish you well assured: A: Harris.

... the ... of ...
July 1604

are [cheated] outte of the leage, ffor that you never
did penans for your veniall offences, nether hope to
receve of obsolution by your gostly ffather, my boke
is now perfecte, although in yours you had made many
[ink fingerprint] bloottes att your comminge from London, I hope
you will geve your poore frend leve to be merry
with you, who is much devoted to your loves,
& so with my hertie commendations to you both
I rest your well assurred:

Jo: fferrers:

warwicke this xxxth of
July 1604 /

————

43

Lady Anne (Bacon) Townshend (1573–1622)
Autograph letter signed, to her son, Sir Roger Townshend
August 8, 1619
Folger MS L.d.595
Reproduced at 100%

Anne Townshend writes like a prattling, but endearing mother in this letter to her
baronet son, whom she refers to as "Hodge." Leaping from subject to subject—a
storm, her sleep, smallpox, fishing—and then apologizing for her "scribbling," she
also breaks an important rule by revealing familial ties in the superscription.
Antoine de Courtin's *The rules of civility* states that "No one superscribes a Letter,
For his Dear Wife, or *Loving Husband*, unless it be one that hath not had ingenuous
Education, or have a mind to be laught at." The letter is sealed with the Townshend
arms, a chevron ermine between three scallops argent.

[superscription]

To hir very Louinge sunn
Sir Roger Townshende at
Rainum geue these –

[letter]

My deare Hodge I would most gladly heere how you doo after this great
storme, I slepte but a littell this last night, yet the Lord of his mear[c]y
be praised we are all well. the smale Poxke is in ouer towne god
I beseech him deliuer vs from them? They saye Mrs Norgat and hir
daughter died both this last weeke of the Smale Poxke: There is
a very fearfull burning feaver *tha*t goeth mutch a bout, sutch a one as
had there can be no greater I think (god for ever mark me thankful
for his great mearcy therein). O shall I tell you news
I am casting my flues I have mutch a doo with them I have no
fish but *tha*t I put in and Eales as yet? I wish I could gitt
sum body to tyl my flockes before harvist be done. So in hast I pray
god for ever bleasse the and keape the and send vs all a
ioyfull meetinge. I rest ever

your most Louinge mother
Ann Towneshende

have you not hard from your sister latly? is
Mr Jhon [Popes] come downe.
I wish you might reade my scriblinge?

This .8. day of August 1619

43

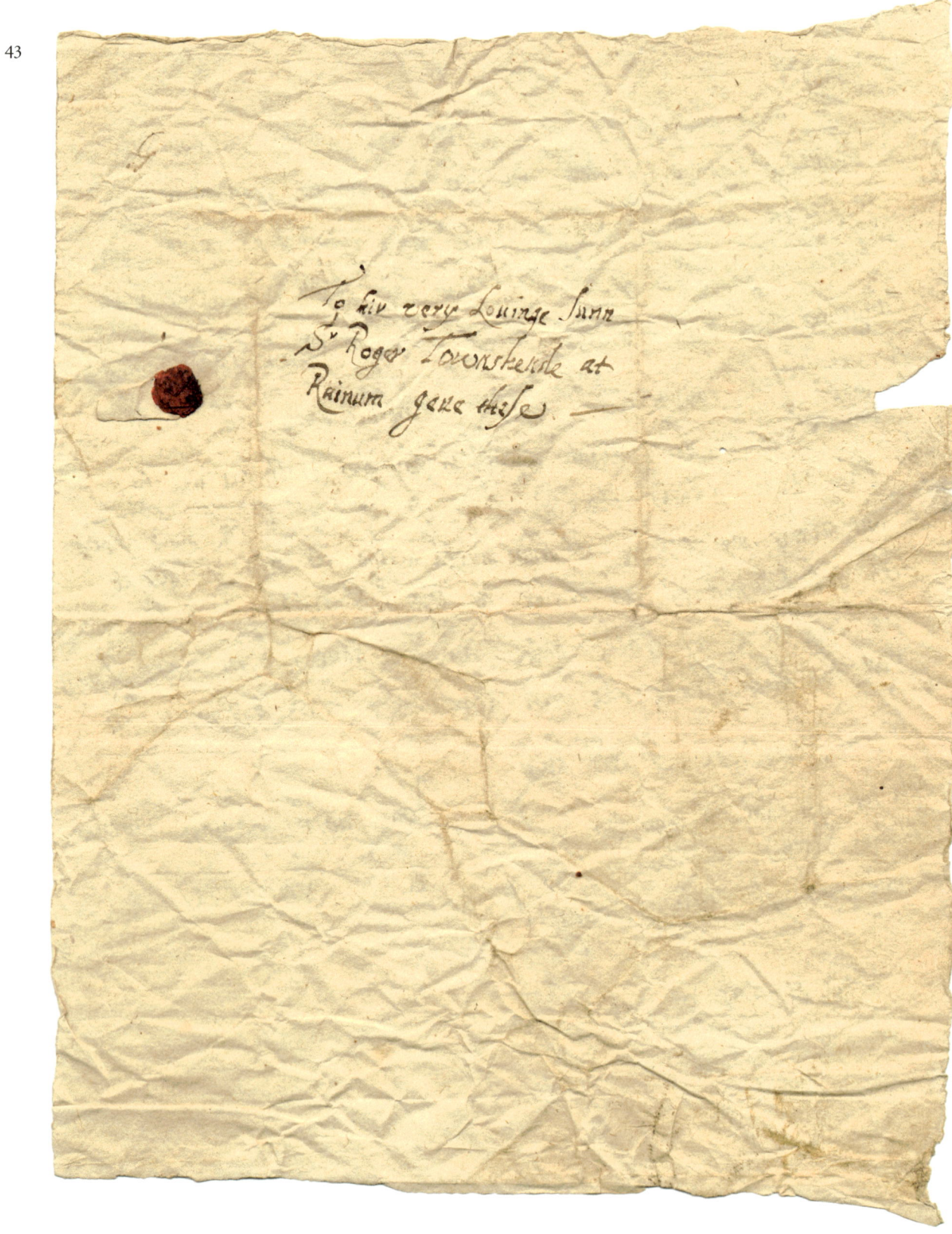

To his very Louinge Sunn
Sr Roger Townshende at
Rainum geue these

Ld. 595

My deere Hodg, I would most gladly heare how you doo after this great
storme, I slepte but a litell this last night, yet the Lord of his mercy
be praysed we ar all well, the Smale Pocke is in over towne god
I beseach him deliver vs fro them. Sage Mrs Norgat and hir
daughter died both this last weeke of the sd Smale Pocke. There is
a very fearfull buriing feaver y goeth much a bowt, sutch as one as
had, there can be no greater I think, god for ever make me thankfull
for this great mercy therein. O we shall I tell yow newes
I am caring my fflax I have much a doo to them I have no
fish but y I put in and Eales as yet. I wish I could gitt
a lode to tell vp flocke before harvist be done. So in hast I pray
god for ever blesse the and keepe the and send vs all a
Ioyfull meetinge. I rest ever

have yow not hard fro yor sister lady, is
Mr Eden stays in towne.
I wish yow might meale my spittinge.

Your most Louinge mother
Ann Towneshende

this 8 day of August 1619

44

Sir William St. Loe

Autograph letter signed, to lady Elizabeth St. Loe, later countess of Shrewsbury,
at Chatsworth

London, October 24, [ca. 1560]

Folger MS X.d.428 (77)

In this letter, the third of Bess of Hardwick's four husbands, Sir William St. Loe,
addresses her by the name of her beloved country estate in Derbyshire, "My honest
swete Chatesworth." He provides a litany of husbandly complaints, advice, and
news—his linens are too coarse, his teeth ache, the horses and the "loitering" horse-
keeper at Chatsworth need to be looked after, and the queen has upbraided him for
his long absence, responding to his excuses by saying "so be it" and not allowing
him to kiss her hand.

[superscription]
     To my loving Wyff att
     Chatesworth geve these
     wyth spede. /

[letter]
     My honest swete Chatesworth I lyke the ∧wekelye∧ pryce off my ~~sys~~
     hyred cowrse stvff so evyll thatt upon thvrsdaye nextt I wyll
     send ytt home agayne att whyche daye the weke endyth
     I praye yow cawse soche stvff as Mowsall left packt in a schete
     to be browght hythar by the nextt caryar   there be hand
     towels and other thyngs thearein thatt I mvst occvpye when
     I ∧schall lye∧ att Whyte hawll ~~scholl lye~~ my man hath neyther schvrtt
     nor eynye other thyng to schyft them vntyll thatt cvm./
     trvst non off yowre men to ryde eynye yowre howsyd horsys bvtt
     onelye Ihames cromp or Wyllyam marchyngton bvtt neyther
     of them wythowte good cawse serve spedelye to be doen
     for nags there be enow abowte the howse to serve other
     pvrposys. / One hand*esf*vll off otes to everye one off the geldyngs
     att a wateryng wylbe svffysyent so they be not laboryd
     yow mvst cawse svm to oversee the horskepar for thatt
     he ys verye well learnyd in loyteryng. / the qven hath
     fownde greatt fawt wyth my long absens sayeng sche
     wolde talck wyth me farder and ~~that sevs sche sa s~~ that
     sche wolde well chyde me, wherevnto I anseryd
     thatt when her hyghnes vnderstode the trawth and the
     cawse sche wolde nott be offendyd wherevnto sche sayed
     verye well syr very well sowbeytt ~~had~~ ∧hand∧ off hers dyd
     I nott kysse. / the lorde kepar hath promysed me fayth
     fvllye to be att boeth dayes heryng and that yff eyther
     lawe or consyens be on my syde I schall have ytt to my
     contentasyon. / vawghan ys cvm vnto towne bvtt nott yett
     bagott. / stevyns and we schall go there on frydaye nextt
     at whyche tye hys brother wylbe here who hath dysbvrsed
     sevyn hvnderyed off the xij. hvnderyed pownds. / I
     have had exstreme payne in my teeth sythens sondaye
     dynar. / thvs wyth akeng teeth I ∧end∧ prayeing the lyveng

to preserve the and all thyen ~~from~~ ∧Wryten att∧ london ageynst
my wyll ~~wy yff~~ where I am yff other wayes owre mattars
myght well be endyd.   xxxxxxxxxxxx thys xxiiij^th off
october./

                yowre ∧loving husband∧ wyth a kend hartt vntyll
                we mete

yff yow thynck good lease
yowre fysshyng in dove vnto
agard we ar the losers by
svferryng hytt as we have doen.   Wyllyam Seyntlo

————

45

John Ogilvy of Balfour
Autograph letter signed, to his brother-in-law, James Rattray, Laird of Craighall
Blackstone, September 22, 1674
Folger MS Add 1273 (120)
Reproduced at 90%

This is one of a series of letters from Ogilvy to the Laird of Craighall about Ogilvy's
estranged wife. It is simmering with indignation at his wife's slight of returning his
letter unsealed, which irked him so much that he had rather have given "the whole
arm with the hand that wrote it" than have had her read it. He continues: "while
I breath this life and while there is blood in my veins she shall never see my hand
write nor have any kindness from me for I find it all truth that is spoken of her, &
I suppose the worst is not yet known" (modernized). He apologizes for his "passionate digression," and then vows to burn anything of his that she tries to return to
him. They were eventually reconciled (see item 27).

[superscription]   These
        ffor the Laird of Craighall
           Younger

[letter]   Loving brother
I acknouledge my selfe verrie much oblidged to you for your kindnesses and
I most say extraordinarie civilities in this straitie I am in, and you may be
confident *tha*t I shall not be uanting to resent them to the utmost limits of
my pouer, as for this slight your sister hath given me in restoring my
letter unsealed, it is not unlyk the former I gott my selfe in that cheap
peltoune uhen your father & she both tourned ther baks on me uhen I
I come to disyre ∧them∧ to come in from the raine; but before your sister had
sein the fondnesse of my respect contained in my letter I rather have given
the uhole arme u*ith* the hand *tha*t urote it & uhile I breath this life and
uhile ther is blood in my veins shee shall never see my hand urite nor
have any kindnesse from me for I find it all truth *tha*t is spoken of
her, & I suppose the uorst is not yett knouen; but shou her I shall be
once alyk u*ith* her ere it be long, & oun her in this cause uho uill I
shall spend fortune & life ere she gett her uill of my estate

Loving brother

I acknowledge my selfe verrie much obledged to you for your kindnesses and
I most say extraordinarie civilities in this straitie I am in, and you may be
confident yt I shall not be wanting to resent them to the utmost limets of
my power, as for this slight your sister hath given me in restoring my
letter unsealed, it is not unlyk the former I gott my selfe in that cheap
poltoune when your father & she both turned ther baks on me when I
                    X them
I come to disyre x to come in from the raine; but before your sister had
slein the fondnesse of my respect contained in my letter I rather have given
the whole arme ut the hand yt wrote it & while I breath this life and
while ther is blood in my veins shee shall never see my hand write nor
have any kindnesse from me for I find it all truth yt is spoken of
her, & I suppose the vorst is not yett knowen; but shou her I shall be
once alyk ut her ere it be long, & own her in this cause who will I
shall spend fortune & life ere she gett her will of my estate
after this slight she hath given me & lett her gallant it out as
fast as she pleaseth she shall find opposition to what she intends
pray ye pardon my passionatt disressions for I assure you all
the slights she can give me shall not make me alter my affextions
to you so long as ye doo not directly own her against me as others
doo, trouble not to ask these bonds from her nor any thing shee
hath of mine for I will burn it all as soone as I shall have it
in my offer if it be sent by her, and so lett her doo her vorst, and
all yt will own her in this cause I doo not valow on straw so I am

Blakstoune the 22 of Septbr   your verrie affec'att brother
                                             and servant,
      1671

lett your sister see this letter and
ere it be long I shall send her on ut
and broader seal on it if I will

9/14

Brother
send my chaquer
my violl and ane
great gallos bridle
of mine to ffleyt to
yt at Crockats wt the
ffirst occasions

Those
ffor the Laird of Craighall
Younger

16.. no..
Craighall
to
Craighall

MS HD 1272

after this slight she hath given me & lett her gallant it out as
fast as she pleaseth she shall find oppositione to uhat she intends
pray ye pardon my passionatt digressione for I assure you all
the slights she can give me shall not make me alter my affectione
to you so long as ye doe not directly oun her against me as others
doe, trouble not to ask these bonds from her nor any thing she
hath of mine for I uill burn it all as soone as I shall have it
in my offer if it be sent by her, and so lett her doe her uorst, and
all yt uill oun her in this cause I doe not valou or stoae So I am

Your verrie affe<i>cion</i>att brother
and servant,

Blakstoune the 22^d of Sep<i>tem</i>ber

1674

Jo: Ogilvy

lett your sister see this letter and
ere it be long I shall send her on u<i>ith</i>
ane broder seal on it if I live

[postscript on address leaf]

brother
send my chaquer
my violl and anie
great gallos bridle
of mine to Alyt to
Pat<i>rick</i> Crockats at the
first occasions

[endorsement]

1676.
Ogilvie to Craighall
abusing his wife
Craighals sister

46, 47, 48
Jane Skipwith
Autograph letters signed, to Lewes Bagot
March 24, April 14, April 16 (ca. 1610)
Folger MSS L.a.851, 852, 853
L.a. 852 reproduced at 100%

In an inexperienced but carefully written italic hand, Jane Skipwith writes this series of three letters to her cousin over a three-week period. Each is closed with her personal seal stamped over embroidery floss (mustard, light blue, and red) and folded into a tiny packet. In the postscript to the first letter, she writes: "I haue sent you a lettel bockes of marmilet to brecke your fast with all." In the second letter she refers wryly to his father's attempts to marry him to an honorable woman with a large dowry (honor "dothe goe fare with most men nowe dayes"), adding that she "writ not this out of any mistrust I haue of your loue," and in the third, written just two days after the second one, she frets that the carrier has arrived without a letter

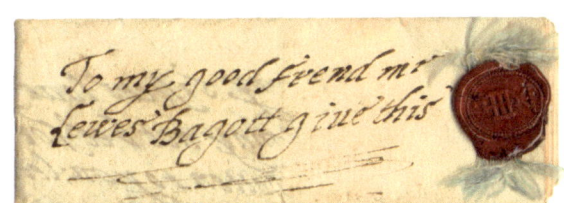

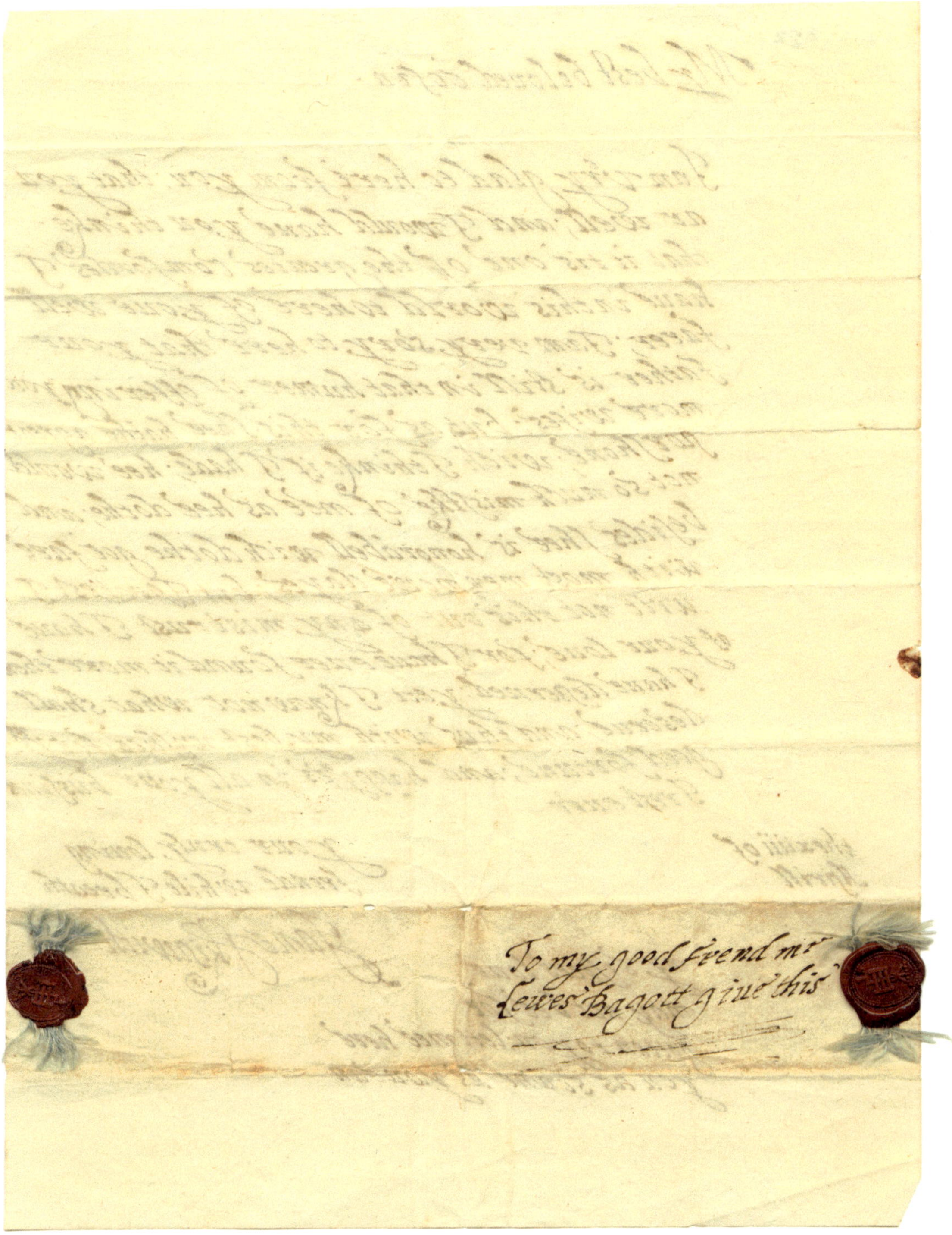

L.a. 852

My best beloved cosin.

I am very glad to here from you that you
ar well, and I would haue you thinke
that it tis one of the greates comfordes I
haue in this world to here of youe well
faree, I am very sory to here that your
father is still in that humer of offering you
more wifes; but as for this shee hathe a great
porshone, wich I thinke if I hade, hee would
not so much mislike of mee as hee dothe, and
besides shee is honorabell wich dothe goe farre
with most men nowe dayes; but I protest I
writ not this out of any mistrust I haue
of your loue; for I haue euer found it more then
I haue deserued; yett I know not what shall
deserue, and thus with my best wishes for y^r
good fortune, and happyes in all your busines
I rest euer

the xiiii of
Aprill

your truly louing
frende while I breath

Jane Skipwith

my sisters loue
may not bee for
gotten to you; lett mee here
you as soone as you can

from him, "and if you knewe but how wellcome you[r] letters are to mee: you would not bee soe sparing of them." Lewes died the following year.

[superscription]   To my good frend m^r
Lewes Bagott giue this

[letter]   My best beloued cosin.

I am v$_\wedge$e$_\wedge$ry glad to here from you, that you
ar well, and I would haue you thinke
that it tis one of the greates[t] comfordes I
haue in this world to here of your well
farer; I am very sory to here that your
father is still in that humer of offering you
more wifes; but as for this; shee hathe a greate
porshone; wich I thinke if I hade; hee would
not so much missl[i]ke of mee as hee dothe; and
besides shee is honorabell wich dothe goe fare
with most men nowe dayes; but I protest I
writ not this out of any mistrust I haue
of your loue; for I haue euer found it more then
I haue desserued; yett I know not what shall
deserue; and thus with my best wishes; for your
good fortune; and happy$_\wedge$n$_\wedge$es in all your bussines
I rest euer –

the xiiii of   your truly louing
Aprill   frende whilc I breath

                              Jane Skipwith
my sisters loue
may not bee for
gotten to you; lett mee here
you as soune as you can

————

49
Mary Hatton
Autograph letter signed, to Randolph Helsby
Quistiebirch in Hatton, March 27, 1655
Folger MS X.d.493 (6)
Reproduced at 100%

Evidence of the courtship between Mary Hatton and Randolph Helsby begins with a letter from Mary on September 10, 1653. The Folger has five letters from Mary to Randolph, all but one written during the two years before they married in 1655. They reveal a romantic and opinionated mind, as she opines on the worthlessness of romance novels and plans for their upcoming nuptials. The last letter in the series, which she signs "Your affectionate & obedient wife whilst Mary Helsby," is dated April 4, 1668.

These
ffor Mr Randolphe Maisby
att ye North gate streete
in
Chester.

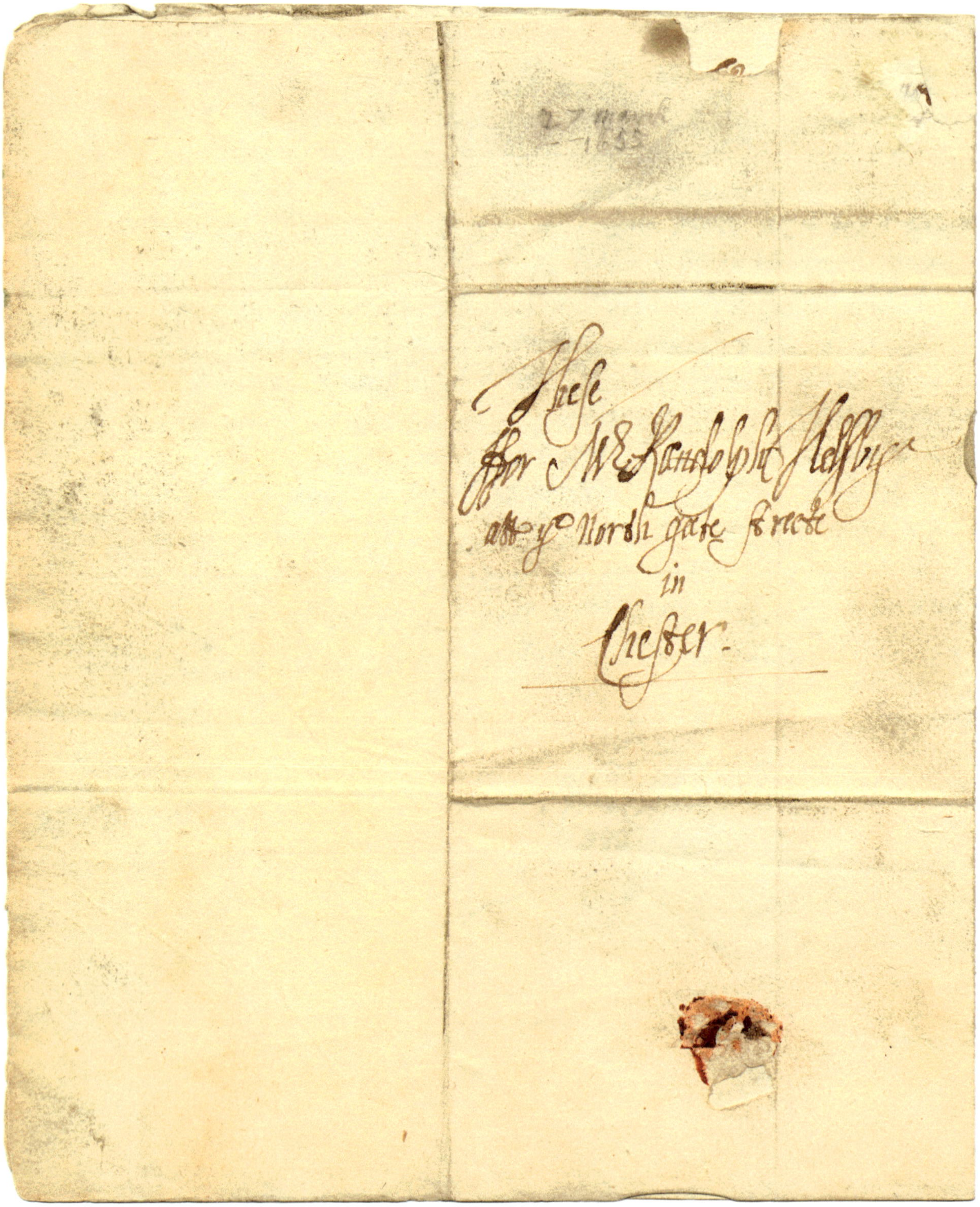

My deareste

I shall ev̄ account myselfe (scarcely
need you write so anxious) the happiest of women wheres
we shall dwell or abide prey then be content. Do you
nott remember when wee met now soe long agoe in ye great
plac̄ Inne at Stanemore when my pillyon girth brake and
when we walked togeth̄ ov̄ ye pastures to the cottage
engarlanded wth wie & honey suckle & in the middest of
a gardene bloomeing wth flow̄s hedḡd rownd for infulnes
& content tis there I would fain dwell wth you for euer &
euer But tis follie for me to write thus as so many
haue spk̄d I could almost weep with pleasure at the
thought of dwelling there wrapt in the peace of each
others loue untill that last daye of our marriage when
as sheldons nxt shall haue departed Brooke or Banke
ye more House or Nsienedtey or Heppyton what
doth it matter which tis true the best house is not
allwayes the best placed Mis aunts pearle that she
gaue to my dear moth̄ will serue well enough wth
the beautiful laces of mis gerards Ieam so busie in
makeing readie all my garnishments that Ihaue but
had little time to rest as Icannot now spare you more
for many lett̄s but Idid read abed after we nd
from thester upon that wild windie day. Ido not
me thinkes approue of stories of romaunce are so alike
that they seem as if I had read ye same one hundred
times besides that how vain it is (for him which
writt it) to make ye yong gentle women run awaie
wth a sweet hearte (her yonge of manie years)
when all were agreed upon ye matche Ieue onely
his more sober wrekle tis all as olde as Nesslys towre
but this and this is in deede some thing veny grestle &

neuer as such a youthe could make itt If you haue not
read itt I would aduise you sadly if by my commendations
you would waste a candell out itt I had rather do
some thing of more use than he that writt it by turning
my wheel without a stop till some other had read throu
itt in my stead but it hath litle bits in itt that surely
he could not with carefullness & practise be without
much commendation. I do scorne & disdaine these tripling
pass times & nought else can Ilearne from manie of
them there is so much more prettynes in yor poetries that
I shall keep itt with all ye rest but why do you tell
me that hath so smale a portion that I am soe uery rich
there yor similiter stoppeth but when we are married
you can then say in very truth that Ishall be rich
beyond all earthly riches with that affecon you will
giue to me much longer than I can remaine

Quiticld the
in Royston ye
27th of March
1655 .

Sr
yor ffreind
Mary Hatton :

These
ffor Mr Randolph Helsbye
att *the* North gate Streete
in
Chester.

My deareste/
     I shall eu*er* account myselfe (scarcely
need you write so anxious) the happiest of women where*soeue*r
we shall dwell or abide, prey then be content. Do you
not remember when wee met now soe long agoe in *the* great
old Inne at Stanemore, when my pillyon girth broke and
when we walked togeth*er* ou*er the* pastures to the cottage
engarlanded w*ith* iuie & honey suckle & in the middest of
a gardene bloomeing w*ith* flow*er*es. If twere for ioyfulness
& contente tis there I would fain dwell w*ith* you for euer &
euer/ But tis follie for me to write thus (as so manye
haue talked) or I could allmost weep with pleasure at the
thought of dwelling there wrapt in the peace of each
others loue untill that last daye of our marriage when
as shaddows wee shall haue departed / Brook or Banke
the mote House or Aluandley or Happsford what
doth it matter which tis true the best house is not
allways the best placed / My aunts pearl*es* that she
gaue to my dear moth*er* will fitt well enough with
the beautyful laces of m*ist*res gerards/ I am so bussy in
making ready all my garnishments that I haue but
had little time to read & I cannot now spare you more
for many lett*er*s butt I did read abed after we rid
from Chester upon that wild windie day / I do not
methinks approue of stories of romaunce all so alike
that they seem as if I had read *the* same one hundred
times / besides that how vain it was (for him which
writt it) to make *the* yong gentle woman run awaie
with a sweet hearte (her young*er* of manie years)
when all were agreed upon *the* matche saue only
his more sober unckle / tis all as olde as Helsby towre
but this / and this is in deede some thing very freshe &

newe as such a youthe could make itt / If you haue not
read itt I would aduise you sadly if by my commendations
you could waste a candell ou*er* itt / I had rather do
some thing of more use than he that writ it by turning
my wheel without a stop till some other had read throu
itt in my stead / but it hath little bits in it that shewe
he could not with carefullness & practise be without
much commendation / I do scorne & disdaine these trifling
pass times & nought else can I learne from manie of
them There is so much more prettyness in y*our* poetrie that
I shall keep itt w*ith* all *the* rest ./. but why do you tell
me that hath so small a portion that I am so very rich

there yo*ur* similiter stoppeth / but when we are married
you can then say in very truth that I shal be rich
beyond all earthly riches w*ith* that affec∧^ti^∧on you will
giue to me much longer than I can remaine

Quistib*irche*	*Sir*
in Hatton *the*	yo*ur* ffreind
27th of March	Mary Hatton:
1655.	

———

50
Randolph Helsby
Autograph letter signed, to Mary Hatton
The Strand, July 2, 1654
Folger MS X.d.493 (10)

Survival of both sides of a correspondence in their original form is rare. The Folger
has two letters from Randolph to Mary, from December 1653 and July 1654. The one
below is written from the Strand. After confessing to her that "Yo*ur* sweete lett*er* is
all I haue att pr*e*sente of muche comforte," Randolph reports on the latest fashions
(making a passing reference to "Lord Oliver" ‹Cromwel)›) and describes in great
detail a musical boat ride on the Thames. The frequency of their correspondence is
evident: a letter from Mary dated thirteen days later (and endorsed by him "July 15
54") mentions letters she had received from him that noon, and her delight at
receiving "the beauteous ∧^rose^∧ w*hich* methought I could see enclaspt by a little
thin hande w*hich* tenderlie did place itt in mine. It smelleth sweetely of yo*ur* good-
nesse & shall be placed in my breaste & in my haire till it withereth / but your loue
shall neu*er* ende saue with the hande that gaue it / nor euer shall mine for you."

[superscription]

ffor the verie virtuous good Ladye the
M*ist*ris Mary Hatton
att
Walthamstowe
in
Essexe
These   pr*e*sent.

[letter]   My Mad*a*me./
                    Itt reioyceth me greatly that you
are tarrying again att Walthamstowe &
shall faile not to do as you list whilest you be
there: I praye you make my love as you will
to my ladye & tell her my bad foote is much
too painefull to truste to stirrope for some daies.
Yo*ur* sweete lett*er* is all I haue att pr*e*sente of
muche comforte. I haue slepte *the* bett*er* for
kneweing howe near you tarry to me & truste me
I shalbe nearer to you ere long/: M^r^. Boothe came

to me one daie this weeke with muche complain
ing*es*: I am yet angered euerie daie w*i*th sights
& men who by looke & acte & speeche on one
partie or *the* oth*er* seem as they dwelled (I hope
butt tarrie) in an enemyes countrie: I wish not &
in deede am fearfull to drawe on some of
them. My hande is shackld by *the* contynued
remembrance of you & *the* knoweing of what muste
come forthe of them that shewe all out for
like warmeness. Thus my deareste mistris you
neede little fear I shall yet abide & grinne
so long as I tarrie here/. Althings on a time
were tis true dreery enough, but *the* towne
could not go in sackeclothe & ashes foreue*r*
(w*hi*ch my lo*r*d Oliuer verily knoweth): I doubted
alwayes if *the* fashion could last long after
*th*e apparell was worne bare enough for
stubborne folke to see *the* nakidnesses of
many of them that once did weare itt /
I was with much companie *the* last weeke

[verso]

on *the* Themes Wee had good voyces & singinge
of maddrigalls & oth*er*s all *the* waye to Hampton
& backe againe Itt was very pretty to heare
& in especiall *the* sweetlie loud notes of *the* greate
beautys in th*e* Companie to witt M*istr*is Cicelie Wynne
& her couzen Doll, My ladye Powell allso
hath a good voyce, but lord how itt broke
awaie from all curbe & time/ yett she
wente [flowndring] aboute bravelie to *the* verie
last : I did wish you had been there: the
daye was especiall fine & you would have
ioyed ouer it But how sillily young M^r
Brearton gott made upon Doll? I thinke that
a brace or two of his like would make a good
playe to be called *the* Beddlambes & Belle
Dames: It was pretty ∧enough∧ to watch how doll worked
her eyes, now full of drollerie when he came round
aboute her, & then how she drops them prettily &
here & there cast them aside till he was smill all
ou*er* fantastickly & went nigh stumbling into her
lapp, & she I could [sweare] not caring one groate
for his paines: Thinke you of Megg Laurence there
with her feete, ∧(sutch feete∧ like Chris Dixons in *the* shewe
from Leedes) all ways in *the* way of *the* companies eyes,
& all for *the* wanting of an elle more of gowne. But
there there be not many women so greatly to my
likeing allbeit twould be more to ill if you had her
to learne her a little of yo*ur* graces, ffor I verily see
fewer euerie day that could & would. Then we
all got out at Charing & tooke coache to *th*e Parkes

& thence to M*ist*res Wynnes & suppd & sinfullie dancd
late, & soe home to bedd. I shalbee gladder then
all when I can come to you att Walthamstowe
& still remaine eu*er*   Mad*a*me
                                                    yours only
                                   Rand: Helsbye
ffrom *the* Strande
        this 2^d of Julij 1654//

2^d July 1654.
                                   Randolph:

————

51
Lydia Dugard (1650–1675)
Autograph letters signed, to Samuel Dugard
February 6, 1669
Folger MS X.d.477 (17)
Reproduced at 100%

Lydia and Samuel Dugard were first cousins, and they were in love. A series of thirty-
one letters from Lydia, the daughter of the printer and headmaster William Dugard,
to Samuel, a fellow at Trinity College, Oxford, describe her daily life and feelings in
striking detail. Because of their close familial ties they tried to conduct their relationship in secrecy, although in this letter Lydia reports that after being questioned
by her mother's closest friend, "I confes'd some of the truth. I am not sorry I did
so." As their correspondence swelled, Lydia began intertwining Samuel's first initial
with her own in "their" signature. In 1672, Samuel defied university regulations for-
bidding fellows to marry; when he was discovered shortly thereafter, he was forced
to resign. Lydia died in childbirth three years later.

[letter]   Feb: 6. 1669
              Dear Cousin

              How glad I am to hear of your better health you may easily guise, when
              I shall tell you how much tis wish't for and desired by mee, how like you I grow when
              I am told the contrary, and how apt I am to fear the worst when ~~there~~ to others
              thinking there is so litle ground of fears that should some know perhaps they'd
              smile and say my thoughts were too much taken up, and it was ~~care~~ ^needles^ to be so much
              consern'd for anothers wellfare. but sure you won't be one of those, won't blame
              me for that which your self is the cause of. till the cause be removed the effects
              will continue, and till you sease to bee what you are (which I beleive will never
              be) I cant allter or grow weary of loving one whose deserts call for the greatest respect
              and whose affection I should be ungratfull too did I not answer with the like.
              but I begin to chek my self for writing so truly, and taking such a liberty as
              will cost me a blush when I think you are reading it. it is a fault (for some would
              call it so, if you dont,) I ~~am~~ often run in to, which I somtimes blame my self for,
              but which I the lese unwillingly allow my self in because (if I have not forgot)

Feb: 6. 1669.

Dear Cousin

How glad I am to hear of your better health you may easily guise, when
I shall tell you how much tis wish't for and desired by mee, how like you I grow when
I am told the contrary, and how apt I am to fear the worst when there to others
thinking there is so little ground of fears that should some know, perhaps they'd
smile and say my thoughts were too much taken up, and it was needles to be so much
concern'd for another's welfare. but sure you won't be one of those, won't blame
me for that which your self is the cause of. till the cause be removed the effects
will continue, and till you sease to bee what you are (which I beleive will never
be) I cant alter or grow weary of loving one whose deserts call for the greatest respect
and whose affection I should be ungrateful too did I not answer with the like.
but I begin to chek my self for writing so freely, and taking such a liberty as
will cost me a blush when I think you are reading it. it is a fault (for some would
call it so, if you don't) I am often run it to, which I somtimes blame my self for,
but which I the lese unwitingly allow my self in because (if I have not forgot)
I speak with lese confidence and more fear by word of mouth then in paper.
if you dislike it, tell me, and I'le promise to be guilty of it no more. I did not think
such reports would have bin spread abroad from our Whitford Journy. a year
or two since it would have troubled me much, but now since I am so used to
hear people talk of you and mee, I matter it but litle and can hear all they say.
a Gentelwoman at London hearing my uncle had two sons said she beleiv'd one
of them would not allwayes call me cousin. she told me she wish'd me very well
and bid me be well advised, and not rashly dispose of my self. with abundence
more of good counsell. she urged me so much and beg'd me so earnestly to tell
her the trath, that at last, ~~being tired with her importunity~~ since she was
my mothers great freind, since she lov'd me almost from my cradle, since I
realy beleive shee'd be faithfull, and sine I was tired with her importunity I
confes'd some of the trath. I am not sorry I did so. if I had bin silent she would
have thought (it may be) I was inveagle, and should undervalue my self. but when
I told her what you was, she changed her advice and cautions into approbation
and said she liked it a great deal better then if I had lov'd some young
gallant though he had a good estate. sure that report will be fresh again
at easter when we go a second time into worcester shire. My uncle intends
you shall acompany him to grafton, and spend some of that litle time you

have left in seeing what we should have seen in the summer. all wish to
see and hear you, and expect a sermon when you come. I thank you for that which
you have presented me with. it realy deserves thanks as well for its own as the
~~Authors~~ sake. it is such a one as might be expected from you, and such a one as canot
but take with all, My Uncle would fain have seen it but I neither shew'd it him
nor told him what it was. I should have done both had not you forbid me. ~~who~~
cousin Anna salutes you but, is half angry at your long silene. her distemper God
be thanked be wears away apace and she is returning to her formor mirth and
livelyness. Aunt is still at warwick with Cousin Spooner who is very weak and
in a consumption. My Sister presents her service to you. she sent me latly the
most passionat sorrowfull letter that ever I receaved from her. wherein she tels
me her dear Mr S. has bin at deaths dore, and though beyond expectation he is
recoverd yet she fears her troubles are of the same length with her life. she
and I have a great desire to see each other. shee'd fain impart her griefs to me at
large that I might simpathize with her and comfort her. I intreated my Uncle to
let me goe to Coventry but he as he constantly does denig'd me so that I must contenit
my self (but with much ado) with writing to her. if it wold be as noy trouble I
would request you to give her a line or too, and enclose it in your next to
mee. shee'l take it exceeding kindly, and you'l at once oblidg her and (Dear Cousin)

your faithful

Lydia Dugard.

I should have written to Mrs Milbourn as you desired
me but that her son came hither and spared me the
labor. Mr Frankland told her that which you wrote
conserning him. I supose she would gladly have him
at that Coledg but he is so weakly that he is all=
together unfit for a scoller in that regard.

I speak with lese confidence and more feare by word of mouth then in paper.
if you dislike it, tell me, and Ile promise to be guilty of it no more. I did not think
such reports would have bin spread abroad from our Whitford Journy. a year
or two since it would have troubled me much, but now since I am so used to
hear people talk of you and mee, I matter ∧it∧ but litle and can hear all they say.
a Gentalwoman at London hearing my Uncle had two sons said she beleivd one
of them would not allwayes call me cousin. she told me she wish'd me very well
and bid me to be well advised, and not rashly dispose of my self. with abundence
more of good counsell, she urged me so much and beg'd me so earnestly to tell
her the truth, that at last, ~~being tired with her importunity~~ since she was
my Mothers great freind, since she lov'd me almost from my cradle, since I
realy beleivd sheed be faithfull, and sinc I was tired with her importunity I
confes'd some of the truth. I am not sorry I did so. if I had bin silent she would
have thought (it may be) I was inveagld, and should undervalue my self. but when
I told her what you was. she changed her advice and cautions into approbacion
and said she liked it a great deal better then if I had lov'd some young
gallant though he had a good estate. sure that report ∧you spake of∧ will be fresh agein

[verso]

at easter when we go a secund time into worsester shire. My Uncle intends
you shall acompany him to graffton and spend some of that litle time you
have left in seeing what we should have seen in the summer. all wish to
see and hear you and expect a sermon when you come. I thank you for that which
you have presented mee with. it realy deserves thanks as well for its own as the
~~senders~~ ∧augthers∧ sake. it is such a one as might be expected from you, and such a one as cant
but take with all. My Uncle would fain have seen it but I neither shew'd it him
nor told him what it was. I should have done both had not you forbid me. ~~all~~
cousin Anna saluts you but, is half angry at your long silenc. her distemper God
be thanked ~~be~~ wears away a pace and she is returning to her former mirth and
livlyness. Aunt is still at warwick with Cousin spooner who is very weak and
in a consumption. My sister presents her service to you. she sent me latly the
most pasionat sorrowfull letter that ever I reseaved from her. wherein she tels
me her dear Master R has bin at deaths dore, and though beyond expectation he is
recoverd yet she fears her troubles are of the same length with her life. she
and I have a great desire to ∧see∧ each other. sheed fain impart her greifs to me at
large that I might simpathise with her and comfort her. I intreated my Uncle to
let me goe to Coventry but he as ∧he∧ constantly does denig'd me. so that I must contents
my self (but with much ado) with writing to her. if it wold ∧not∧ be ~~to~~ trouble I
would request you to give her a line or too, and enclose it in your next to
mee. sheel take it exeeding kindly, and youl at once oblidg her and (Dear Cousin)

your faithfull

Lydia DuGard.

I should have writen to Mrs Melbourn as you desired
me but that her son came hether and spared me the
labor. M^r frankland told her that which you wrote
conserning him. I supose she would gladly have him
at that Coledg but he is so weakly that he is all=
together unfit for a scoller in that regard.

52

[Samuel Dugard] (1645?–1697)

*The marriages of cousin germans, vindicated from the censure of unlawfullnesse,
and inexpediency. Being a letter written to his much Honour'd T.D.*

Oxford: Henry Hall for Thomas Bowman, 1673

Folger D2459

In 1673 Samuel Dugard, a fellow at Trinity College, Oxford, published a letter out-
lining the reasons why marriage between cousins was valid. No doubt troubled by
the social taboos against this kind of marriage, he took matters into his own hands
by trying to enlighten the general public. Although the argument is presented
hypothetically, he alludes to his personal interest in "The Epistle to the Reader."

[sigs A4ʳ–A5ᵛ]

And though I expect to be no lesse Censur'd by some, for pleading for these
Marriages then if I my self were a person engaged in them, yet if I can here
and there prevail with a few to lay aside prejudice, and correct a mistake so
generally receiv'd, I shall think it a good reward for these small Pains I have
taken. But, if I may make a wish more then Ordinary for this Paper, I would
Choose one place peculiarly for its good acceptance, and that upon the
account of two Persons, whose Credit and Interest is not less dear to me then
mine own; and though their Loves are not so slight as that a Censure can
shake them; nor they so ill persuaded of the lawfulnesse of such Marriage, as
that they will think any affliction they may undergoe with others, or apart by
themselves to be a scourge for their Wedlock as unlawfull, yet they will find
the more Friends if this Pamphlet be well accepted.

———

53

Anon.

*Cupids messenger. Or, a trusty friend stored with sundry sorts of serious, witty,
pleasant, amorous, and delightfull letters. Newly written.*

London: Miles Flesher, [1638]

Folger STC 6122.3

Cupids messenger, an anonymous collection of fictional letters, came out in numerous
editions. While the woodcut title page hints at its primary subject, the book also
includes other categories of letters that could be read both for entertainment and
for assistance in writing one's own letters. On either side of the two below are letters
"To his friend falne to pouertie" and "A Letter from a Chapman in the Country to
a Tradesman in London." Each letter ends with a different set of initials, and sometimes a placename and a date, although the date changes from edition to edition.

[sig. E3–E4]

A Letter of a Gentlewoman to a Gentleman with
whom she fell in loue.

*If euer I could wish my selfe vnborne (most worthy sir) or my well being taken
from mee, I call truth and my sometimes modesty to witnesse, it is now: not that
I haue found you, but that I am forced thus to seeke you. Call to minde (faire,
and I hope virtuous Sir) some horrid and violent women, taken with the loue of*

their owne fathers, as was Mirah: or incestuously pursuing their nearest brother, as was Biblis: so my affection will appeare more modest, and my suite more pardonable: I dearely loue you, (and in so saying me thinkes the gods blush to heare me,) who in the strictest lawes of desire are most worthy to bee loued, whose vertues might inflame a Nunne, and excellentest qualities take the most retired: If I haue (as I know to well I haue) contrarie to the nature and custome of Virgins, ouer-shot my selfe in my violent passions, pardon her that had rather die then make it knowne, yet chuseth rather to make it knowne. Then not enioy you so desired, and farre more worthy to be desired. If you were acquainted what afflictions I suffer in my discouery, yet fearing all will not serue, you will, I hope, rather incline to pittie, than disdaine: little will the death of a silly mayden auaile the triumph of your beautie, and the ouerthrow of my credit lesse benefit your virtue. Raise me from the one by your loue, & assure me from the other by your secresie: whilest I will euer remaine a most constant votaresse of all your perfections, blessing the parents that left behinde them such an issue.

Althorp. May 22. Never lesse her owne.

R.D.

His Answer.

How happie may I thinke my selfe (sweetest of creatures, & beautifullest of women) that hauing bound my selfe in the search and pursuite of a iewell, haue it now offered & giuen into my hands, farre aboue my expectation; farre tran-scending my hopes; I accept it as louingly as you freely bestow it, and will account it no lesse deare and pretious, then if much time and long labour had beene the purchase of it, esteeming it a blessing thrown vpon me, by the appointement of the highest, and sutable to my happy desires. Nor shall I need to load my memory with those horrid examples, to giue your loue a freer & wel-comer passage into the very depth of my loue and choisest desires: to loue we were made, and by loue we are made: they onely are without being that haue not the heauenly tast and enioying of it. I onely deny those excellencies which you lay to my vnguilty charge, it was the reflection of your owne worth (stricken from me) which hath Narcissus *like so inamoured you, it was your owne image, showne in my eies, which hath thus captiuated you: which since you like in so dim and dull a mirror. I will cherish, and make much of it only for your sake, that you may the perfectlier see your selfe, and the more loue me: for your loue, take all I am; for my secresie, I will not breathe it to my selfe how I attaine this happinesse, but liuing and dying, rest the true honourer and admirer of your worth and vertue,*

Yours more than his owne.

H. H.

————

54

E[dward] P[hillips] (1630–1696?)

The mysteries of love & eloquence, or, the arts of wooing and complementing; as they are manag'd in the Spring Garden, Hide Park, the New Exchange, and other eminent places. A work, in which are drawn to the life, the deportments of the most accomplisht persons, the mode of their courtly entertainments, treatments of their ladies at balls, their accustom'd sports, drolles and fancies, the witchcrafts of their perswasive lan-guage, in their approaches, or other more secret dispatches. To compleat the young practioners of love and courtship, these following conducing helps are chiefly insisted on. Addresses, and set forms of expressions for imitation; poems, pleasant songs, letters, proverbs, riddles, jeasts, posies, devices, a la mode pastimes, a dictionary for the mak-ing of rimes, four hundred and fifty delightful questions, with their several answers. . . .
London: printed for N. Brooks, 1658
Folger P2066

The mysteries of love & eloquence is one example of an increasingly popular genre in the second half of the seventeenth century—the courtship manual, which contained songs, poems, letters, and complements geared towards men and women alike. As the passage below shows, not all of its entries were meant to be taken seriously.

[pp. 142–43] Superscription for the *Drolling-Letters.*

To the most gracious Queen of my Soul.
To the most illustrious Princess of my Heart.
To the Countess Dowager of my Affections.
To the Lady of my Conceptions.
To the Baroness of my Words and Actions.
To the spring Garden of all pleasure and delight.
To the Peerles Paragon of Exquisite Formosity.
To the thief of my heart and Affections.
To the Empress of my thoughts.
To the Lady, and Mistress of my thoughts and service.
To the Lilly white-hands of my Angelical Mistress, These present.
To the Compleat Mirour of Beauty and Perfection.
To the ninth Wonder of the World.
To the most Accomplish[ed] Work of Nature, and the Astonishment of all Eyes.
To the Fair Murdress of my Soul.
To the Rose of pure Delight.
To the Choise Nutmeg of Sweetest Consolation.
To the Most Flourishing Bud of Honour.
To His Most Sacred Angel, Mistress *&c.*
To Her who is Day without Night, a Sun full of Shade, a Shade full of
    Light, Mistress, *&c.*
To the Atlas of her best Thoughts and Affections, Her Dearly beloved
    M. L. Broom-man in
            SOUTHWARK.
      These.

Subscriptions.

MAdam,
    Your Gally, Gally, Gally-Slave.
Madam,
    Your Always burning Salamander.
Madam,
    Your continual Martyr.
Madam,
    Your poor Worm, that must of necessity die, if trod upon by the
    foot of your disdain.
Madam,
    Your Captive, willingly fetter'd in the Chains of your beauty.
Madam,
    The Vassal of your Severest Frowns.
Madam,
    The Most Loyal Subject to Your Imperial Power.

55

Ovid's epistles, translated by several hands
London: J. T. for R. Wild, 1688 (4th edition)
Folger O663

John Dryden observes in the introduction to this translation of Ovid's "heroicall epistles" that "they are generally granted to be the most perfect piece of Ovid, and that the Style of them is tenderly Passionate and Courtly." Primarily written in the voices of forsaken women, most letters in this edition are illustrated with engravings. In this one, Paris's first wife, the nymph Oenone, writes him a letter on the back of Cupid, after learning that Paris has deserted her for Helen of Troy.

John Donne's marriage letters: a case study

Today John Donne is best known first as one of the English language's greatest poets, and second as a famed divine, but in the seventeenth century he was also celebrated as a letter-writer. Remarkably, over two hundred letters written by Donne were published within the thirty years after his death. Given Donne's background, the letterwriting is unsurprising, for like many of his educated contemporaries, he spent time working as a secretary—to the top-ranking legal official in England, the Lord Keeper of the Great Seal, Sir Thomas Egerton. It was while working for Egerton that Donne fell in love, and fell into a scandal that threatened to wreck his life. The scandal also prompted him to write a flurry of letters that were not among those published in the seventeenth century and that are among the Folger's most prized possessions.

In late 1597, John Donne entered the service of Sir Thomas Egerton. He had become friendly with Egerton's son, also named Thomas, when they both served in the English forces' mission to the Azores islands earlier in the year; when young Thomas died while fighting in Ireland in 1599, Donne was given the honor of bearing his sword at the funeral. Sir Thomas was happy to employ the witty, competent young lawyer as his personal secretary, and took him into his household at York House, on the Strand in Westminster. There Donne met the niece of Sir Thomas's wife, a young woman—then only thirteen, half his age—named Anne More, the youngest daughter of Sir George More of Loseley in Surrey. It seems that they fell in love, only to be parted when Lady Egerton died in January 1600 and Anne was recalled to her father's country estate. The two were reunited when Anne returned to Westminster with her father for the parliament of late 1601, in which both Sir George and Donne served as MPs. In December of that year, John Donne and Anne More were secretly married, with Donne's "chamber fellow" from Lincoln's Inn, Christopher Brooke, giving the bride away and acting as witness, and Christopher's younger clergyman brother Samuel, a friend of Donne's from Cambridge, presiding over the service.

Donne knew that Sir George would not approve of the marriage. The Mores were landed gentry, while Donne was the son of a London ironmonger, forced to work for his living. Worse, Donne had a certain reputation as a womanizer, and it was rumored that he shared his family's tendency towards Roman Catholicism. On February 2, 1602, unable or unwilling to face Sir George in person, Donne did what any good secretary would do—he broke the news in a letter (Folger MS L.b.526), apparently carried to Sir George by Henry Percy, the Catholic earl of Northumberland. If Donne had the slightest hope that the letter would win over his new father-in-law, he was sadly mistaken. As his early biographer Isaak Walton wrote, "This news was to Sir George so immeasurably unwelcome, and so transported him as though his passion of anger and consideration might exceed theirs of love and error." Not only did the angry father separate John and Anne, he also persuaded Sir Thomas Egerton to dismiss Donne from his service, and had Donne and the Brooke brothers thrown into prison. According to popular legend, Donne characteristically turned misfortune into a punning quip: "*John Donne, Anne Donne, Un-done*."

Incarcerated in London's Fleet Prison shortly after his initial confessional letter, cut off from his employer, his wife, and his father-in-law, Donne once again resorted to letters, petitioning Sir George on February 11 for his release and reconciliation, although he knew that whatever he wrote was unlikely to be welcome: "The inward accusations in my conscience, that I have offended *you* beyond any ability of redeeming yt by me, and the feeling of my Lord's heavy displeasure following yt, forceth me to wright, though I know my fault make my *letters* very ungracious to yow." Seeking to "disculpe" himself, Donne denied rumors that he had had a "contemptuous and despightfull purpose" towards More himself, and lamented that his fall had been "so headlong, that being thus push*ed*, I shall soone be at bottome, for yt pleaseth God, from whom I acknowledge the punishm*ent* to be iust, to accompany my other ylls, with so much sicknes as I haue no refuge, but that of Mercy." He promised that "all my endevors, and the whole course of my lyfe shalbe bent, to make my selfe worthy of ~~her~~ ₍your₎ fauor and her Loue, whose peace of Conscience, and quiett, I know must be much wounded and violenced, if y*our* displeasure sever vs" (Folger MS L.b.527). On February 12, when Sir George refused to have anything to do with the matter, Donne appealed to his erstwhile employer, Sir Thomas Egerton, protesting "how farr my intentions were from doing dishonor to y*our* Lo*rdshi*ps house; and how vnable I ame to escape vtter and present Destruction, if y*our* Lo*rdshi*p iudge onely the Effect and Deede." His services to Egerton "had alwayes so much honesty, as that onely this hath staynd them," and he begged Egerton "to lessen that Correction, w*hi*ch y*our* iust wisdome hath destind for me; and so to pitty my sicknes, and other Misery, as shall best agree with y*our* honorable disposition," signing himself "Yo*ur* Lo*rdshi*ps most deiected and poorest servant" (Folger MS L.b.528).

Only a day later, events had moved on, and Sir George had secured Donne's release from prison. Donne wrote to give him "vnfeyned thanks" for "this mild change of Imprisonm*ent*" and to ask him to disregard previous rumors that he had "deceiud some gentlewomen before, and that of louing a Corrupt Religion." He also asked "that by some kind and comfortable message yow would be pleasd to giue some ease of the afflictions w*hi*ch I know y*our* Daughter in her Mind suffers; and that (if it be not against y*our* other purposes) I may with y*our* leaue wright to her, for withowt y*our* leaue I wyll neuer attempt anything concerning her." He was "unchangeably resolud to bend all my Courses to make me fitt for her" (Folger MS L.b.529).

Although Donne was out of prison, he was under effective house arrest, unable to speak to, or even to write to, his wife. On March 1, he wrote again to Sir George, lamenting that "this storme hath shakd me at roote in my Lords [Egerton's] fauor, wher I was well planted," and worrying that "those yll reports w*hi*ch Malice hath raysd of me, may have trobled" Anne. Now, "though I be not hedlongly destroyd, I languish, and rust dangerously," unable to seek employment elsewhere, unsure that his friends will help him further, and in debt, thanks to the forty pounds his imprisonment has cost. He asked for Sir George's help in rehabilitating him with Egerton, and reiterated his request to write to his wife (Folger MS L.b.532).

On the same day he wrote to Egerton with similar sentiments: the commissioners will pardon him, and Sir George has agreed to sue Egerton for his "restoringe." However, although

All these Irons are knocd of; yett I perish in as heavy fetters, as euer, whilst I languish under y*our* Lo*rdshi*ps Anger. How soone my History is dispatchd? I was carefully and honestly bred; enioyd an indifferent fortune; I had (and I had understandinge enough to valew yt) the sweetnes and security of a freedome, and indepen[den]cy; withowt markinge owt to my hopes any place of profitt, I had a desire to be your Lordships servant; by the fauor which your good sonns loue to me, obteind, I was 4 years your Lordships Secretary, not dishonest, nor gredy. The sicknes of which I dyed, ys, that I begonne in your Lordships house, *th*is Loue. Wher I shalbe buried I know not. It ys late now, for me (but *that* necessity, as yt hath continually an Autumne and a wytheringe, so yt hath euer a springe, and must put forthe) to beginne that Course, which some years past, I purposd, to trauaile; though I could now do yt, not much disaduantadgeably. But I haue some bridle vpon me now, more then then, by my Marriadge of this gentlewoman: in prouiding for whom, I can and wyll show myself very honest, though not so fortunate.

Donne realized that what had happened had tainted him for life:

To seek preferment here with any but your Lordship were a Madnes. Euery great Man to whom I shall address any such suite, wyll silently dispute the Case, and say, Would my Lord Keeper so disgraciously haue imprisond him, and flung him away, if he had not donne some other great fault, of which wee hear not? So that to the burden of my true weaknesses, I shall haue this Addicion, of a very preiudiciall suspicion, that I ame worse, then I hope your Lordship dothe think me, or would that the world should thinke.

His only option is to "turn back to your Lordship, who knows, that Redemtion was no less worke then creation." Employing the rhetorical trope of *anaphora* for added emphasis, he concludes the letter with a series of repeated phrases and a final emotional appeal: "I know my fault so well. . . . I know your Lordships disposicion so well . . . . I know myne own Necessity, owt of which I humbly beg, that your Lordship wyll so much entender your hart towards me, as to giue me leaue to come into your presence. Affliction, Misery, and Destruction are not therc; and euery where els, wher I ame, they are." Donne uses the remaining space on the page to further express his absolute humility, by breaking his subscription into four lines: "Your Lordships / most poore and / most penitent / seruant," and signing his name in the bottom right corner (Folger MS L.b.533).

His poetic pleas fell on deaf ears. Although the young couple found a home in the house of Anne's cousin Sir Francis Wolley, and in time managed to reconcile with Anne's father, Egerton sadly refused to reinstate his secretary. As a result, Donne spent the next thirteen years without proper employment, and without a dowry, often relying on the generosity of friends and relatives to support him, Anne, and their growing family. The marriage lasted until 1617 when Anne died in childbed after giving birth to her twelfth child. Donne was devastated, and never remarried. He promised his seven surviving children that they would never have a stepmother; according to Walton, "burying with his tears all his earthly joys in his most dear deserving wife's grave, [Donne] betook himself to a most retired and solitary life."

To the right wor: S^{r}
George More Kt.

Sr

       If a very respective feare of yor displeasure, and a
doubt, that my L: whom J know owt of yor worthines to loue yor much,
would be so compassionate wth yow, as to add his anger to yors did not
so much increase my sicknes, as that J cannot stir J had taken the
boldnes, to haue donne the Office of this Letter by waytng vpon yow
my self: To haue giuen yow truthe and clearnes of this matter
between yor Daughter and me; and to show to yor plainly the limits
of or fault, by wch J know yor wisdome wyll proportion the punishmnt.
So long since, as at her being at yorkhouse this had foundacion: and so
much then of promise and Contract built vpon yt as wthowt violence
to Conscience might not be shaken. At her lyeng in town this last
parliamt, J found meanes to see her twice or thrice: we both knew
the obligacions that lay vpon vs, and wee adventurd eqally, and about
three weeks before Christmas we married. And as at the doinge, there
were not vsd aboue fyue persons, of wch J protest to yow by my saluation
there was not one that had any dependence or relation to yow so in all the
passage of it, did J forbear to vse any such person, who by furtheringe
of yt might violate any trust or duty towards yow. The reasons why
J did not foreacquaint yow wth it, (to deale wth the same plaines that J
haue vsd) were these. J knew my present estate lesse then fitt for her; J
knew, (yet J knew not why) that J stood not right in yor opinion; J
knew that to haue giuen any intimacion of yt had been to impossibilitate
the whole mattr. And then hauing those honest purposes in or harts and those
fetters in or Consciences me thinks we should be pardoned, if or fault be but
this, that wee did not by fore-reuealinge of yt, consent to or hindrance
and torment. Sr, J acknowledge my fault to be so great, as J dare scarse
offer any other prayer to yow in myne own behalf, then this to beleeue this
truthe, that J neythr had dishonest end nor meanes. But for her
whom J tender much more, then my fortunes or Lyfe (els J would J might
neythr ioy in this Lyfe, nor enioy the next) J humbly beg of yow, that she
may not, to her danger, feele the terror of yor sodaine anger. J know
this Letter shall find yow full of passion: but J know no passion can
alter yor reason and wisdome; to wch J adventure to comend these
perticulers; That yt ys irremediably donne; That if yow incense
my L, yow destroy her and me; That yt is easye to giue vs happines; And
that my Endevors and industrie, if it please yow to prosper them, may
soone make me somewhat worthyer of her. If any take the

advantage of yor displeasure against me, and fill yow wth ill
thoughts of me, my Comfort is that yow know that fayth and
thanks are due to them onely, that speak when theyr informa=
cions might do good: wch now yt cannot work towards any party.
For my Excuse I can say nothing except I knew what were
sayd to yow.   Sr I haue truly told yow this Mattr, and
I humbly besseche yow so to deale in yt, as the perswasions of
Nature, reason, wisdome, and Christianity shall informe yow,
And to accept the vowes of one whom yow may now rayse or
scatter, wch are, that as all my Loue ys directed vnchange=
ably vpon her, so all my Labors shall concurr to her con=
tentment, and th show my humble Obedience to yor selfe.

From my Lodgnge by ye
Sauoy. 2° Februa: iboi

                                    Yors in all duty and
                                        humblenes

                                            J: Donne

56
John Donne (1572–1631)
Autograph letter signed, to Sir George More
The Savoy, February 2, 1601/2
Folger MS L.b.526
Reproduced at 98%

[superscription]
To the right wor*shipfull* S*i*r
    George More k*nigh*t.

[letter]
S*i*r   If a very respectiue feare of y*o*ur displeasure, and a
doubt, that my L*o*rd whom I know owt of y*o*ur worthines to loue yow much,
would be so compassionate w*i*th yow, as to add his anger to y*o*urs, did not
so much increase my sicknes, as that I cannot stir I had taken the
boldnes, to haue donne the Office of this letter by wayting vpon yow
my self: To haue giuen yow truthe, and clearnes of this Matter
between y*o*ur Daughter and me; and to show to yow plainly the limits
of o*u*r fault, by w*hi*ch I know y*o*ur wisdome wyll proportion the punishm*en*t.
So long since, as her being at Yorkhouse, this had foundac*i*on: and so
much then of promise and Contract built vpon yt, as w*i*thowt violence
to Conscience might not be shaken. At her lyeng in town this last
parliam*en*t, I found meanes to see her twice or thrice: we both knew
the obligac*i*ons that lay vpon vs, and wee aduenturd equally, and about
three weeks before Christmas we married. And as at the doinge, there
were not vsd aboue fyue persons, of w*hi*ch I protest to yow by my saluation,
there was not one that ∧had∧ any dependence or relation to yow, so in all the
passage of it, did I forbeare to vse any such person, who by furtheringe
of yt might violate any trust or duty towards yow. The reasons, why
I did not foreacquaint yow with it, (to deale w*i*th the same plainnes that I
haue vsd) were these. I knew my p*re*sent estate lesse then fitt for her; I
knew, (yet I knew not why) that I stood not right in y*o*ur Opinion; I
knew that to haue giuen any intimac*i*on of yt had been to impossibilitate
the whole Matt*er*. And then hauing those ∧honest∧ purposes in o*u*r harts, and those
fetters in o*u*r Consciences, me thinks we should be pardoned, if o*u*r fault be but
this, that wee did not by fore-reuealinge of yt, consent to o*u*r hindrance
and torment. S*i*r, I acknowledge my fault to be so great, as I dare scarse
offer any other prayer to yow in myne own behalf, then this, to beleeue this
truthe, that I neyth*er* had dishonest end nor meanes. But for her,
whom I tender much more, then my fortunes, or lyfe (els I would I might
neyth*er* ioy in this lyfe, nor enioy the next) I humbly beg of yow, that she
may not, to her danger, feele the terror of y*o*ur sodaine anger. I know
this letter shall find yow full of passion: but I know no passion can
alter y*o*ur reason and wisdome; to w*hi*ch I aduenture to com*m*end these
perticulers; That yt is irremediably donne; That if yow incense
my L*o*rd, yow destroy her and me; That yt is ∧easye∧ to giue vs happines; And
that my Endevors and industrie, if it please yow to prosper them, may
soone make me somewhat worthyer of her. If any take the

[verso]

aduantage of your displeasure against me, and fill yow with ill
thoughts of me, my Comfort is that yow know that fayth and
thanks are due to them onely, that speak when theyr informa=
cions might do good: which now yt cannot work towards any party.
For my Excuse I can say nothing except I knew, what were
sayd to yow.   Sir, I haue truly told yow this Matter, and
I humbly beseeche yow, so to deale in yt, as the persuasions of
Nature, reason, wisdome, and Christianity shall informe yow;
And to accept the vowes, of one whom yow may now rayse or
scatter, which are, that as all my loue ys directed vnchange=
ably vpon her, so all my labors shall concur to her con=
tentment, and ∧to∧ show my humble Obedience to your selfe.

From my lodginge by the
Sauoy. 2º Februa: 1601

Yours in all Duty and
humblenes

J: Donne.

57, 58, 59, 60

John Donne (1572–1631)
Autograph letter signed, to Sir Thomas Egerton
The Fleet, February 12, 1601/2
Folger MS L.b.528

Autograph letter signed, to Sir George More
"from my Chamber," February 13, 1601/2
Folger MS L.b.529

Autograph letter signed, to Sir Thomas Egerton
February 13, 1601/2
Folger MS L.b.530

Autograph letter signed, to Sir Thomas Egerton
ca. February 14–22, 1601/2
Folger MS L.b.534

These letters are fully transcribed and annotated in *John Donne's Marriage Letters* (Folger Shakespeare Library, 2005), the companion volume to *Letterwriting in Renaissance England*.

POAST
WITH A
PACQUET
OF
LETTERS

Newly Imprinted.

For Loue

For Lif

The postal "system"

"HAVING SO CONVENIENT A MESSENGER," "having the opportunity of a bearer," "I have sent you by this bearer," "I received no letter from you by our carrier," "you may write by this messenger," "I have promised this messenger 2 shillings for bringing your letter," "I was willing to write unto you but had not so convenient a messenger as I would therefore I sent this letter by 2 footmen to Derby to be conveyed unto you," "my messenger failed in the delivery thereof. I know not better how to convey it." Phrases such as these are commonplace in early modern letters —and they betray how "mailing" a letter in England was no simple matter. Before the royal post began officially accommodating private letters in 1635, mailing a letter involved paying a carrier, bearer, servant, or messenger, or enjoining a friend or stranger headed in the desired direction, to carry the letter for you. Even once an established postal service became available to all, most people still relied on personal messengers or hired carriers to deliver letters and goods between households. But the likelihood of a letter arriving in a timely fashion was iffy at best, and the chances of it getting "miscarried" (lost, stolen, or misdelivered) were considerable. Given these complicated logistics, then, it is not surprising that many letters from this period devote the first sentence or two to describing the resourceful means for both sending and responding to letters.

Carriers, bearers, or messengers, as they were variously called, were the lifeline between families and friends, court and country. They were the source of both vexation and gratitude: a poetical miscellany includes William Hall's 1631 jest elegy, "Upon the death of Hobson the Carrier of Cambridge" (Hobson's death was the subject of two poems by Milton as well), while a 1581 letter complains, "I have sent you a letter by a carrier and fearing that either the sloth or negligence of my messenger may keep the letter too long from your hands and considering the matter therein concerning your self have thought good hereby to repeat it again" (Folger MSS V.a.322, p. 129; L.e.621). It was not unusual for bearers to carry not just the letter itself and any accompanying goods or money, but also for them to convey the actual message—indeed, letterwriters often entrusted the most sensitive information to the bearer instead of writing it down, adding a line to the letter such as, "the bearer will explain more at large." Like a secretary, a trusted bearer was essential for safely communicating the thoughts of his master or mistress to others. When a recipient was faced with an unfamiliar bearer, on the other hand, suspicion could be cast on the letters he was delivering: "I have received no letter by this Carrier, but my Master have received one brought by a stranger," writes one servant, while William Peterborough skeptically observes to the earl of Danby: "I have received your lordship's letter by a Gentleman whom I never saw before which creates in me a doubt whether this letter came from your lordship" (Folger MSS X.c.51 (9); F.c.3).

Account books provide details about payments to unnamed letter carriers, goods carriers, and messengers, indicating that some kinds of letters and goods were indeed carried by anonymous "professional" (but unregulated by the Crown) carriers. In 1637, John Taylor published the schedules of weekly carriers to London in *Carriers cosmographie. Or a briefe relation of the innes, ordinaries, hosteries, and other lodgings in, and neere London, where the Carriers, Waggons, Foote-posts and Higglers, doe usually come . . . whereby all sorts of people may finde direction how to receiue, or send, goods or letters.* While acknowledging that carriers "doe often change and shift from one Inne or lodging to another," he still believed that "this booke will give instructions where the Carriers doe lodge that may convey the said letter, which could not easily be done without it: for there are not many that by hart or memory can tell suddenly where and when every carrier is to be found." Such was the problem of Edward Walker, who writes in 1672 that "On Thursday in Expectacion of the Carriers beeing heere I sent to the Inne an Hogshed of white Wine and a Terine of Excellent Claret but it seemes hee came not till the last night . . ." (X.d.155 (5)).

Royal post was another matter altogether, although it suffered many of the same problems of unreliability. Since the successful operation of a centralized government depended on its ability to communicate quickly with all parts of its realm, a reliable and efficient postal system was of paramount political importance. This system was known as the "post," although the term referred to a number of its elements—the system of transporting letters itself, the person carrying the letter, the horse used for transporting letters, and the person at the inn or post-house, which itself was located in the post-town or post-stage.

The six main postal roads emanated out from London like uneven spokes on a wheel—the Dover or Kent Road led to the Continent; the North or Berwick Road led to Scotland, the Chester Road led to Dublin (via Holyhead), the Western Road to Plymouth, the Bristol Road to the southwest, and the Yarmouth Road to the east coast—and were dotted with stage stops every ten to twenty miles. At each stage, the packet was supposed to be subscribed with the name of the town, the day and the hour, and the name of the local postmaster, in addition to being entered into an official ledger. The postmaster of each town was required to have ready riders and fresh horses located at the post-house, and be prepared to dispatch a delivery of letters within fifteen minutes. They were to supply saddles and other "furniture" for the horses, leather bags lined with cotton for the letters, and horns to blow along the way, at least three times a mile. If a royal messenger were carrying the packet of letters himself (a "through post") rather than passing the packet onto a new rider, he would receive a fresh horse and be accompanied by a post-boy, or guide, who would bring the horses back. It was decreed by proclamation that post should travel seven miles an hour in summer and five miles an hour in winter, and riders were to pay for both the horse and the guide (STC 8144). At some point in Elizabeth's reign, the post began carrying private mail as well, but only if it did not interfere with the delivery of government letters. The local postmasters received meager salaries, but were also given the monopoly on hiring out horses to ordinary travelers when the horses were not needed to carry royal mail. In Elizabethan England, letters authorized to travel by official post were usually signed on the address leaf by the sender (generally a member of the Privy Council). The phrase "For her majesty's affairs" was written at the top, followed by a variation of the command, "Post haste for life," and occasionally a crude illustration of a gallows to indicate particular urgency to illiterate post-boys. Sir Ralph Sadler provides a plausible explanation for the "for life" moniker in a 1559 letter to Secretary of State Cecil: "when we wryte, we indorse our lettres for lyef, though the matier requyre not so much hast; and so must you do, or ells the post will make no spede at all" (*The state papers and letters of Sir Ralph Sadler*, ed. Arthur Clifford (Edinburgh, 1809), vol. 2, p. 123).

A number of postal milestones and innovations took place in the seventeenth century, many of them resulting from complaints emanating from all levels —the Privy Council, the postmasters themselves, merchants, and the public at large. Wagon wheels and inclement weather made the highways impassable. Wages were in serious arrears. Fresh horses were frequently unavailable. Postboys were lazy and irresponsible. Letters were arriving late, or not arriving at all. In an attempt to control the transmission of treasonous letters or dangerous intelligence, proclamations throughout the century declared, or re-declared, a state monopoly on the carriage of letters, and frequent attempts were made to monitor letters sent to, and coming from, overseas. Politics and religious wars led to Elizabeth's 1591 proclamation outlawing the use of the well-established Merchant Strangers' post, run by foreign merchants in England, for overseas letters. A close eye also was kept on the Merchant Adventurers' post, run by English merchants overseas, and the Thurn and Taxis postal system, based on the Continent. Surveillance of mail, which included opening and reading letters and then resealing them, was rife.

The most important change occurred in 1635, when Charles I issued a proclamation (item 65) officially permitting his subjects to use the royal post to convey their private mail. He appointed Thomas Witherings as the first Postmaster General, and stipulated that for journeys under eighty miles, a single letter would cost two pence to post, for journeys from 80–140 miles, four pence, and for journeys over 140 miles or to Scotland, eight pence. The decision to broaden the scope of the royal post was largely a financial one—it was seen as a way to make the service of conveying official government mail self-supporting.

For the rest of the century, the official post was plagued by frequent changes in leadership, the monopoly being claimed by numerous individuals because of the valuable perquisites. At various points, the system returned to limiting itself to letters pertaining to "his majesty's business," and under Oliver Cromwell, "the service of the Commonwealth." In the 1650s, competing services were established, and shut down. In 1657, Cromwell passed an act "for settling the Postage of England, Scotland and Ireland," which lowered the rates for hiring horses and permitted government officials to use the post without charge (what became known as "franking"). By this time, postmaster positions were being "farmed out" to individuals who paid increasingly expensive fixed rents. At the Restoration, Charles II passed another act "for erecting and establishing a Post Office" (1660), largely a reiteration of the provisions of the Commonwealth Act.

Postmarks were established in 1661 as a way to increase efficiency through accountability. Originally called Bishop marks after Henry Bishop, the Postmaster General, these early postmarks consisted of a circle divided into two semicircles, one with the abbreviated name of the month, the other with the day of the month (see item 72). Bishop also developed the "postage due" stamp, a rectangular box divided into two squares, indicating the payment required in either shillings or pence. The by-post system was also developed in the 1660s to connect towns that were situated between the trunk routes. This was seen as an improvement on the hub-and-spoke system that required letters to go first to London. The General Letter Office in London was affected by the plague of 1665, when all letters were doused in vinegar, and the great fire of 1666, which destroyed it.

In 1680, the merchant William Dockwra set up a penny post for London and Westminster, recognizing the fact that it was more difficult, time-consuming, and expensive to send a letter across town than it was to send it across the country since the royal post made no provisions for intra-city conveyance. His pamphlet *A Penny Well Bestowed, or a Brief Acount of the New Design contrived for the great Increase of Trade, and Ease of Correspondence, to the great Advantage of the Inhabitants of all sorts, by Conveying of Letters or Pacquets under a Pound Weight, to and from all parts within the Cities of London and Westminster; and the Out Parishes within the weekly Bills of Mortality, for One Penny* outlined the ambitious undertaking, which included district offices, regional sorting stations, and hundreds of receiving houses with broadsides reading "Penny post letters taken in here," where letters were collected every hour. Dockwra claimed not to be in conflict with the General Letter Office since the area he served was not serviced by the government. However, his private commercial undertaking was deemed an infringement on the government monopoly and was subsumed by the Duke of York in 1682. Renamed the London Penny Post, the service adopted, with very minor changes, Dockwra's distinctive "penny post paid" stamps indicating prepayment, as well as the heart-shaped time stamps marking the hour of the day and whether it was "morning" or "afternoon."

Despite this fine-tuning and its increasing comprehensiveness, the system of sending letters and packets by continous relay on horses along designated routes remained largely unchanged from the time of Brian Tuke's appointment by Henry VIII as Master of the Posts around 1516 until the late seventeenth century. The post was a troublesome fact of life that left its anxious marks on and in virtually every letter of the period.

61

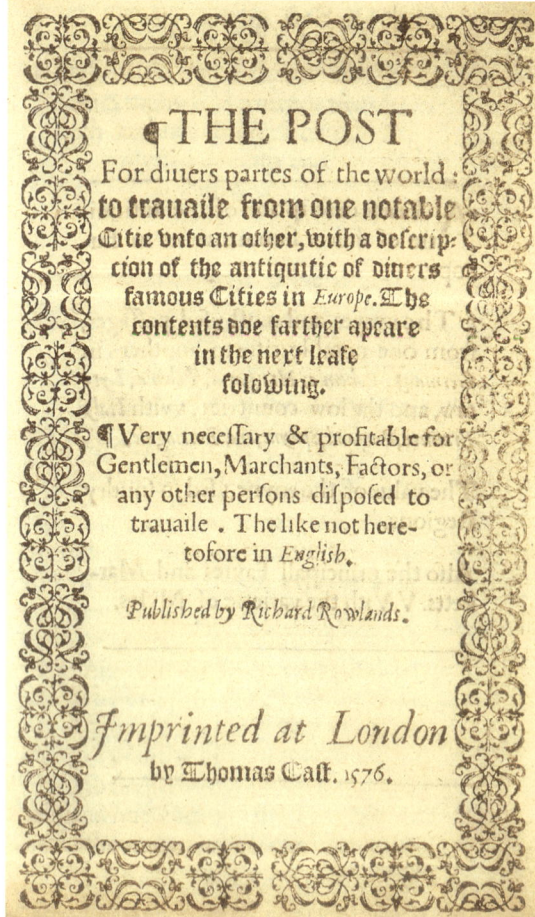

LETTERWRITING IN RENAISSANCE ENGLAND

61

Richard Rowlands [i.e., Richard Verstegan] (ca. 1550–1640)

The Post for diuers partes of the world: to trauaile from one notable Citie vnto an other, with a description of the antiquitie of diuers famous Cities in Europe . . . very necessary & profitable for Gentlemen, Marchants, Factors, or any other persons disposed to trauaile. The like not heretofore in English

London: Thomas East, 1576

Folger STC 21360

The Post for diuers partes of the world was the first English road book, intended for merchants and "all suche Gentlemen as are adicted to trauaile." In addition to supplying mileages between cities in England, between England and Continental cities, and between cities on the Continent, the book provides a 22-year almanac, a prayer for travelers, an explanation of the differences between Italian, German, French, Spanish, English, Hungarian, and Swiss miles (5 English miles equals 2 German miles), brief histories of the cities, an explanation of different coinages, and a list of principal fairs and markets.

[p. 52]   Certaine vsed wayes and passages in
England

From the cittie of London to Douer.

Darteforte	12
Grauesend	6
Rochester	5
Sittingborn	8
Caunterbury	12
Douer	12
The summe of myles.	56

———

62

John Ogilby (1600–1676)

Mr. Ogilby's pocket book of roads with the computed & measured distances and the distinction of market and post townes the third impression to which is added more roads and remarkable place omitted in the former allsoe a table for the ready, finding any road & the distance from London by William Morgan His Majesty's cosmographer

London: For the author, 1679

Folger O177a

While Rowlands' miles were based on the hazy measurement of 1,500 paces to the mile, Ogilby used the fixed distance of 1,760 yards per mile for his survey of the roads of England. Thus, Rowlands cites the distance between London and Dover as 56 miles, while Ogilby calculates the distance as 71 miles and 4 furlongs. This had major implications for post-riders, who paid by the mile. Ogilby's book also made it easy to distinguish between post-towns, cities, and market-towns by marking the former with asterisks, and the latter two with capital letters and italics. The book's narrow width made it suitable for carrying in one's pocket. In the following example (p. 5), the number in the first column signifies "the vulgar computation" while the number in the second column is the "measured distance by Miles and Furlongs."

62

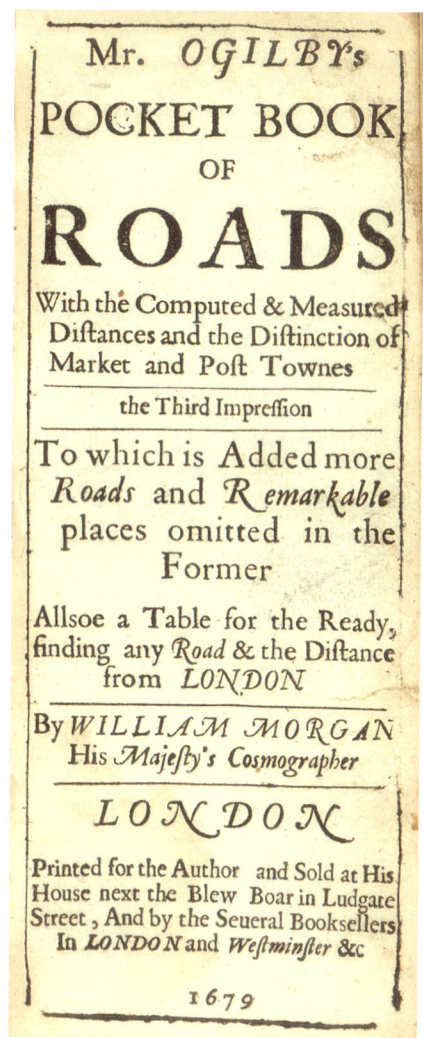

LONDON to Dover		
From London		
to halfe way house	2	2–7
Deptford	2	2–1
Shooters Hill	-	4–0
Wellen	5	2–1
Crayford	-	2–5
Dartford	3	2–0
Northfleet	4	5–2
Chalkstreet	-	3–2
Gads Hill	4	2–3
ROCHESTER	3	3–3
Chatham	1	1–3
Raynham	3	3–6
Newington Street	2	2–7
Key Street	1	1–1
Sittingborn	1	1–7
Bapchild	1	1–1
Greenstreet	1	1–5
Bocton Street	6	6–6
Harpledown	3	4–4
CANTERBURY	1	1–2
Bishopscourt bridg	3	3–2
Liddon	6	7–4
Ewel	1	1–4
Douer	2	2–6

63

Elizabeth I (1533–1603)

Articles set downe by the right worshipfull Thomas Randolph . . . to be kept by the Postes from London to the Northerne borders against Scotland

London, January 22, 1583/84

[London: B. Norton and J. Bill, ca. 1618]

Folger STC 8145a, bound in 7758.3, vol. 2, p. 228

Rapid and reliable communication between England and Scotland was a necessity in Elizabethan England. When these articles were published, the English succession was still in question; Mary, queen of Scots, was being held prisoner in England; and her son, James VI, was king of Scotland. Thomas Randolph, Master of the Posts from 1567 to 1590, set down the following articles in association with a proclamation published by the queen, in an attempt to standardize the postal system and address some of its weaknesses.

Articles set downe by the right worshipfull Thomas Randolph Esquier, Master and Comptroller generall of all her Maiesties Postes, and straightly by him commanded to be kept by the Postes from London, to the Notherne borders against Scotland, for the better obseruation, and due execution of such orders, as lately were appointed by the Lords of her Maiesties priuie Councill.

First, that euery Post for the seruice of the Packet for her Maiesties affaires, shall haue in his stable, or in a readinesse throughout the yeere, three good and sufficient post horses, with sadles and furniture fitte and belonging. Three good and strong leather bagges well lined with bayes or cotton, to carrie the Packet in. And three hornes to blowe by the way, as by their Lordships order is commanded. Whosoeuer shall faile hereof, at any time when they shall be surueyed, shall abide the punishment that the Master of the Postes shall lay vpon him.

2. That euery Post, so soone as the Packet directed for her Maiesties affaires shall be brought vnto him, shall foorth with or within one quarter of an houre after, with all speede and diligence carrie the same, or cause it to be carried to the next Post, according to the orders by their Lordships also set downe. The breach of this article shall also be punishable at the Master of the Postes pleasure.

3. That euery Post, either of his owne, or such as he shall keepe or appoint vnder him, shall haue always in readinesse, foure good and sufficient Post horses, and two hornes, to serue at all occasions for such as either by commission, or other wise for better expedition shall ride in Post. And if the number of horses exceede their owne furniture, then that they supplie their want, as by their Lordships is prouided for, and set downe.

4. That euery Post from henceforth keep two faire paper bookes, or one large and great one, aswel to register the names, dates, and number of horses, of such as either with commission, or without shall runne the Post, as also to enter the Packets, that for her Maiesties affaires shall passe and be caried by them. And the same shall signifie at the end of euery moneth, or within ten dayes after vnto the Master of the Postes. And so often as he shall vpon occasions, either generally or particularly call and send for the same.

5. That no Post shall hazard or send any Packets directed for her Maiesties affaires by any person whatsoeuer, but by an expresse seruant of his owne, and that in post, Upon paine of forfeiture of one quarters wages for the first offence, whereof the halfe to be giuen to the informer thereof whosoeuer, and the other halfe to bee at the disposing of the Master of the Postes. And for the second offence, expulsion out of his office, the same being deuly prooued against him.

6. That all Postes and guides ryding with any Currior, or Through Post, either with Commission, or without, shall bring the partie so riding vnto the house and dwelling place of the next standing Post, that is also to furnish him of fresh horses, or shall signifie the same vnto him (the partie being a personage or man of sort, that for his pleasure will make choice of his lodging.) And shall not suffer him so ryding, to passe the next ordinarie stage without the consent

and liking of the Post of the place. Upon paine of forfeiture of ten shillings to the Post offended, and a full restitution of so much as he should haue gained.

7. Also be it especially and duely obserued by all her Maiesties Postes, as they will answere to the contrary, That if any Inholder, Hackneymen, or other whatsoeuer, hauing horse to hyre, shall take vpon him contrarie to their Lordships orders to deliuer any horses with horne and guide, to any man running the Post, either with Commission or without, Without the knowledge and consent of the ordinarie Post of the place where the horses were deliuered (if any Postes there bee appointed.) The Post of the next stage, by whom he passeth, shall in this case stay and charge the officer with safe custodie of the guide or conductor, and shall not deliuer anie horses to the partie so ryding, till notice be giuen either to her Maiesties Secretarie, or the Master of the Postes.

8. That no Post or guide ride without his horne, and the same to blow as is prescribed by their Lordships: bee it either with the Packet, or with Through Post. Neither shall he refuse to carrie the male or other cariage of the partie ryding behinde him, so that the same exceed not the weight of fourtie pounds at the vtmost.

9. That no Postes seruant or boy ryding with the packet, shall deliuer any by letteres or priuate packets, before he haue first discharged himselfe of the packet for her Maiesties affaires by deliuering the same into the hands of the next sanding Post. Unto whom also he shall commit and deliuer all the by letters and priuate packets as well as the other, vpon paine of the forfeiture of ten shillings to the Post offended, and the displeasure of the master of the Postes.

10. That no Postes seruant or boy riding with the packet, and hauing by letters or priuate packets, or other kinde of carriage committed vnto them, shall aduenture to open or breake vp, or any other wayes directly or indirectly, shall fraudulently imbesill or conuey the same wilfully: but shall safely deliuer the same vnto the hands of the next Post as is abouesaid. And whatsoeuer he be that shall be found to be faultie herein, he shall lose his Masters seruice, and the Master shall vnderly such punishement as the Master of the Postes shall finde him worthie of.

11. Lastly, Because that the negligence of seruants and boyes hath alwayes bene the greatest cause of the former disorders, And that also to grow and fall out through the small care and want of gouernement in the Masters: These therefore for a warning in time to come, shall be to signifie vnto all the Postes in generall. That whose seruant or boy soeuer shall hereafter either directly or indirectly, breake, disobey, or be found faultie of any of these Articles aboue said. The penaltie and forfeiture thereof shall lye vpon the Master himselfe, without fauour or remission.

12. And hereunto I will all her Maiesties Postes to haue a speciall care and regard, as they will answere to the contrary. London, the xxii. of Ianuarie. 1583.

Tho. Randolph Comptroller of all her Maiesties Postes.

64
Privy Council
Warrant to Thomas Sackville, earl of Dorset
Whitehall, April 8, 1603
Folger MS X.d.30 (42)
Reproduced at 85%

"In this tyme of vrgent occasion," immediately after the death of Elizabeth I on March 24, 1603 and the accession of James VI/I, it became even more of an imperative to maximize the efficiency of the post between London and Berwick "for the often and speedy Conveyance of Pacquett*es* to and froe." To this end, Elizabeth's Privy Council directed the lord treasurer to pay 150 pounds to Thomas Myles, paymaster of the post, in order for him to ensure that each of the stages along the road had a fresh supply of horses, and that additional stages were established "in suche other places by the way where his M*ai*estie shall resolue to take his Journey." James I entered Berwick on April 6, 1603, and arrived at London on May 7, 1603.

[superscription]

To o*ur* very good L*ord* the Lord
Buchurst L*ord* highe Thr*easur*er
of Englande

[letter]   After o*ur* righte harty Com*m*endacions to yo*ur* good L*ord*   Whereas it is moste necessary in this tyme of vrgent occasion to vse the seruice of the Postmasters established betwene Berwick and London for the often and speedy Conveyance of Pacquett*es* to and froe for the speciall seruice of o*ur* Souueraigne Lorde the king*es* M*ai*estie that order be taken to assiste the saide Postmasters of the seuerall Stages w*ith* Convenyent supplies of freshe horses as there shall fall out occasion of necessity by the nexte adioyninge partes of the Countrey, And also for the better Conveyinge of his M*ai*esties Trayne from B*e*rwick hether to appointe newe Stages in suche other places by the way where his M*ai*estie shall resolue to take his Journey To dyrect and vndertake the w*hich* seruices, Choice is made of Thomas Milles Esquier Paymaster of all the Poste and Rowland White gent Postmaster of his M*ai*esties Courte to whom wee thincke it fitt that allowance be made of the Som*m*e of One hundred and ffyfty Pound*es* by way of Imprest, aswell for theire expence in the saide Journey as also to make any necessary disboursement*es* for the seruices aforesaide. These are therefore to pray and requyre yo*ur* L*ord* by vertue of the warrant and authority giuen vs by his M*ai*estie by his late l*ett*res of the 28th and 31th of Marche laste, to giue dyrection in all thinges necessary for his M*ai*esties seruice, to take order that the said Som*m*e of One hundred and ffifty pound*es* be paid out of his M*ai*esties Receipte of Thexchequer vnto the said Thomas Milles by way of Imprest for the seruices abouemenc*i*oned. And so wee wishe yo*ur* L: very hartely well to fare.   ffrom the king*es* Pallace of Whitehall the viij^th of Aprill 1603   yo*ur* good L*ords* very loving freind*es*

Jo: Cant	Tho. Egerton	T. Buchurst	E Oxenforde	Notingham
	Ro Sussex	Pembroke	E. Worcester	Rutland
Howard				
Ric: London				
Tho: Lawarre	Ro: Riche	T: Darce	Wyllyam Sandys	
Hen. Windsor	G Chandois	ffran Norreys		
W. Knollys	Ed: Wotton		Ro: Cecyll	
	J Popham			

After o[u]r right harty Comendac[i]ons to yo[u]r good L. Whereas it is moste necessary in this tyme of vrgent occasion to vse the s[er]uice of the Postmasters established betweene Berwick and London for the often and speedy Conveyance of Pacquetts to and froe for the speciall s[er]uice of o[u]r Soueraigne Lorde the Kinge Ma[jes]t[i]e that order be taken to assiste the saide Post: masters of the severall stages w[i]th Convenyent Supplie of fresshe Horsse as there shall fall out occasion of necessity by the neerest adioyninge p[ar]ties of the Countrey, Now also for the better Conveyinge of his Ma[jes]t[i]e Trayne from Berwick hether to appointe newe stages in suche other places by the way where his Ma[jes]t[i]e shall resolue to take his iourney to digest and vndertake the w[hi]ch s[er]uice, there is made of Thomas Miller Esquier [illegible] of all the Poste and Rowland White gent Postmaster of his Ma[jes]t[i]e Courte to whom wee thincke it fitt that allowance be made of the Some of One hundred and fifty Pounde by way of Imprest, as well for their expences in the saide iourney as also to make any necessary disbourstm[en]te for the s[er]uice aforesaide. These are therefore to pray and require yo[u]r L. by virtue of the warrant and authority giuen vs by his Ma[jes]t[i]e by his late l[ett]res of the 28th and 31th of Marche laste, to giue direction in all thinges necessary for his Ma[jes]t[i]e s[er]uice, to take order that the said Some of One hundred and fifty pounde be payed out of his Ma[jes]t[i]e receipte of Th[e]xchequer vnto the said Thomas Miller by way of Imprest for the s[er]uice aboue mentioned. And so wee wishe yo[u]r L. very hartely well to fare. From the Kinge Pallace of Whitehall the [illegible] of Aprill 1603

yo[u]r good L. very loving frinde

Jo: Cant[erbury]   Tho: Egerton C. L.   T. Buckhurst E. Oxenforde   Nottingham

    Ro: Suffolk   Pembroke   E. Worcester   Rutland

H. Howard
Ric: London

Tho: Lawarre   [illegible]   J. Hunn.   William Sandys

Jo: Ven Winchester   G. Chandois   Henry Norreys

W. Knollys   Ed. Wotton   Ro: Cecyll

Viscount Wallingford

Mr Skinner

make an order

TB

Lord Thr*easur*er

8 Aprill. 1603

The nobilitie & late priuie

Counsell

    for an Imprest of 150^{li}

    to Mr Tho*mas* Milles paym*ent*

    of the post*es*

65

Charles I (1600–1649)

By the King. A Proclamation for the setling of the Letter Office of England and Scotland

July 31, 1635

London: Robert Barker, 1635

Folger STC 9041

England did not have an official national postal service until Charles I established a continuously running post between London and cities in England, Scotland, Wales, and Ireland with this 1635 proclamation. It was thought that opening the post to personal mail would pay for the rising expense of conveying the king's official mail. Perhaps because people had relied on haphazard methods of conveyance for so long, the king was intentionally vague about the penalties for *not* using the new system.

> . . . And his Maiesties further will and pleasure is, that from the beginning of this seruice or imployment, no other Messenger or Messengers, Foot-Post or Foot-Posts, shall take vp, carry, receiue, or deliuer any Letter or Letters whatsoeuer, other then the Messengers appointed by the said Thomas Witherings to any such place or places as the said Thomas Witherings shall settle the conueyances, as aforesaid. Except common known Carryers, or a particular Messenger, to be sent of purpose with a Letter by any man for his owne occasions, or a Letter by a friend. And if any Post, Messenger, or Letter-Carryer whatsoeuer, shall offend contrary to this his Maiesties Proclamation; his Maiestie vpon complaint thereof made, will cause a seuere exemplary punishment to be inflicted vpon such delinquents. . . .

65

380

❧ By the King.

❧ A Proclamation for the setling of the Letter Office of England and Scotland.

Hereas to this time there hath beene no certaine or constant enter-
course betweene the Kingdomes of England and Scotland, His Maiesty
hath beene graciously pleased, to command His seruant Thomas
Witherings Esquire, His Maiesties Post-master of England for forraigne
parts, to setle a running Post, or two, to run night and day betweene
Edenburgh in Scotland, and the City of London; to goe thither, and come
backe againe in sixe dayes, and to take with them all such Letters as
shall be directed to any Post-towne, or any place neere any Post-towne
in the said Roade, which Letters to be left at the Post-house, or some other house, as the said
Thomas Witherings shall thinke conuenient: And By Posts to be placed at seuerall places out of
the said Roade, to run and bring in, and carry out of the said Roades the Letters from Lincolne,
Hull, and other places, as there shall be occasion, and answeres to be brought againe accordingly;
And to pay Post for the carrying and recarrying of the said Letters, Two pence the single
Letter, if vnder fourescore Miles; And betweene fourescore, and one hundred and fourty Miles,
Foure pence; If aboue a hundred and fourty Miles, then sixe pence; and vpon the borders of
Scotland, and in Scotland, Eight pence: If there be two three, foure, or fiue Letters in one packet,
or more, Then to pay according to the bignesse of the said Packet, after the rate as before; which
money for Post as before, is to be paid vpon the receiuing and deliuery of the said Letters here
in London.

The like rule His Maiesty is pleased to order the said Thomas Witherings to obserue to
Westchester, Holyhead, and from thence to Ireland, according to a prouision made by the Lord De-
putie and Councill there; and to take Post betwixt the City of London and Holyhead, as before to
the Northward; and to goe thither, and bring answeres backe to the City of London, from all
the places in that Roade in sixe dayes, which is constantly hereafter to be obserued, and to settle
By-posts in the said Roade, as there shall be occasion, for the benefit of all His Maiesties louing
Subiects.

His Maiesty is pleased further to command the said Thomas Witherings, to obserue the
like rule from the City of London to Plymouth; and to prouide sufficient messengers to run night
and day to Plymouth, and to returne within sixe dayes to the City of London, and for carriage of the

381

said Letters to Plymouth, Exeter, and other places in that Roade, His Maiestie doth Order the said
Thomas Witherings to take the like Post that now is paid as neere as possibly he can.

And further, His Maiestie doth Command and Order the said Thomas Witherings, so soone as
possibly may be, to settle the like conueyance for Letters from Oxon, Bristoll, and other places on
that Roade, for the benefit of all His Subiects, And the like the said Thomas Witherings is to obserue with all conuenient speed to Colchester, and so to Norwich, and diuers other places in that
Roade.

The three first conueyances from London to Edenburgh, from London to Westchester and Holyhead in
Wales, and from London to Plymouth and Exeter, are to begin the first weeke after Michaelmas next.

Now for the better enabling the said Thomas Witherings to goe forward with this seruice, and for
the aduancement of all His Maiesties Subiects in their Trade and correspondence; His Maiestie
doth hereby Command and Order all His Post-Masters vpon all the Roades of England, To
haue ready in their Stables one or two Horses, according as the said Thomas Witherings shall haue
occasion to vse them, to carry such Messengers with their Portmantles, as shall be imployed in
the said seruice, to such Stage or Place as his present occasions shall direct him to: If the said
Messenger shall haue occasion but for one Horse, then to leaue him at the place where he shall take
fresh Horse, paying for him Two pence halfe peny for euery Mile, if two Horses, then to take a
Guide and pay Fiue pence a Mile.

And that the said Post-Masters may be prouided for this seruice, His Maiestie doth hereby Order and Command, that such Horses as shall be prouided for the said seruice, shall not vpon that
day the Messenger shall be expected, let, or send forth the said Horses so prouided, vpon any other
occasion whatsoeuer.

And His Maiesties further will and pleasure is, that from the beginning of this seruice or im-
ployment, no other Messenger or Messengers, Foot-post or Foot-posts, shall take vp, carry,
receiue, or deliuer any Letter or Letters whatsoeuer, other then the Messengers appointed by
the said Thomas Witherings to any such place or places as the said Thomas Witherings shall settle the
conueyances, as aforesaid. Except common knowne Carryers, or a particular Messenger, to be sent
of purpose with a Letter by any man for his owne occasions, or a Letter by a friend. And if any
Post, Messenger, or Letter-Carryer whatsoeuer, shall offend contrary to this His Maiesties
Proclamation; His Maiestie vpon complaint thereof made, will cause a seuere exemplary punishment to be inflicted vpon such delinquents.

And His Maiestie doth hereby strictly require and Command all His louing Subiects whatsoeuer, duly to obserue and performe His Royall pleasure herein declared, as they will answere the
contrary at their perils.

And lastly, His Maiestie doth hereby charge and command all Iustices of Peace, Maiors, She-
riffes, Bailiffes, Constables, Headboroughs, and all other His Officers and Ministers whatsoeuer, to be aiding and assisting to the said Thomas Witherings, in the due accomplishment of this His
Maiesties will and pleasure.

Giuen at Our Court at Bagshot, the last day of Iuly, in the eleuenth yeere of Our Reigne. 1635.

God saue the King.

¶ Imprinted at London by Robert Barker, Printer to the Kings most Excellent
Maiestie: And by the Assignes of Iohn Bill. 1635.

66
Nicholas Breton (1545?–1626?)
A Poste with a packet of mad Letters. Newly imprinted.
London: For John Marriot, 1634
Folger STC 3693 (with the title page to part 2, reproduced below, from a later (1685?) edition)

Breton's title page depicts two men on post-horses, one blowing his post-horn and carrying the requisite leather post-bag. Through-posts (posts who carried packets to the final destination) were accompanied between post-stages by guides, who would ride with them to the next post-town in order to bring back the horses used during that stage. Post-horns were blown at regular intervals throughout the journey. Breton's letter to the reader, below, sets the stage for the ensuing fictional letters, which were allegedly dropped by a careless post.

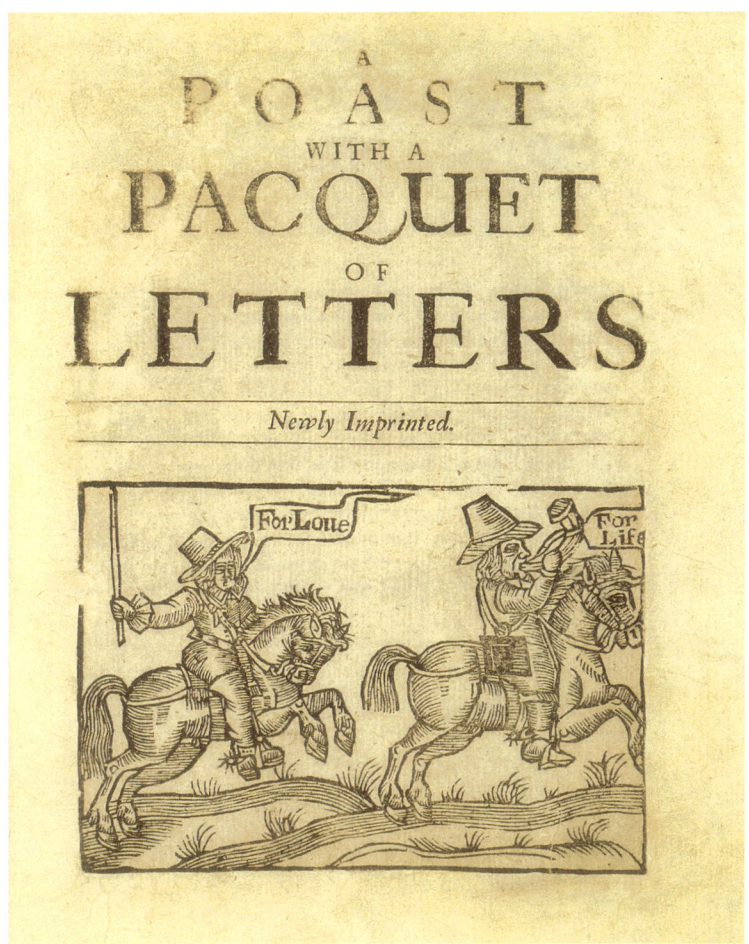

TO THE READER.

Gentle if you be, be you so, gentle Reader; you shall understand, that I know not when, there came a Poste, *I know not whence, was going I know not whither, and carried I know not what: But in his way, I know not how, it was his hap with lack of heed, to let fall a Packet of Idle Papers, the superscription whereof being only to him that finds it, being my fortune to light on it, seeing no greater style in the direction, fell to opening of the inclosure, in which I found divers Letters written, to whom, or from whom I could not learne. Now for the contents of the circumstances, when you have read them, iudge of them; and as you like them, regard them: And for my selfe, hearing you liked well of this first Part, I have adventured a second, which here I present you with, both in one: but fearing to be too tedious in this Letter, lest you like the worse of those which follow, I rest as I have reason,*

Yours, *N.B.*

———

67

Anthony Nixon

A Straunge Foot-Post, with a packet-full of strange petitions. After a long vacation for a good terme

London: E[dward] A[llde], 1613

Folger STC 18591

The title page to this fictional series of petitions depicts a foot-post with a walking stick and post-bag. After a packet of letters arrived by post-horse, foot-posts, or by-posts, would then distribute the contents of the packet to individual recipients in outlying areas.

68
George I (1660–1727)
Unopened letters to the duc de Bourbon and the duc d'Orléans
ca. January–May 1724
From the collection of Arthur L. Schwarz, Scarsdale, NY

Letters were often used to fulfil important political and diplomatic functions. When an ambassador or envoy was sent from one sovereign to another, for example, his credentials were established by the letters that he carried between the two. In October 1723, the English king George I sent Horace Walpole as envoy extraordinary to the court of King Louis XV of France. Louis was then only thirteen years old, and the government of the country rested in the hands of his protectors, the duc de Bourbon and the duc d'Orléans. In May 1724, the resident ambassador, Sir Luke Schaub, was recalled to England, and it appears likely that these letters were designed to confirm Walpole in his place. Although similar letters were delivered to the king and the duchesse d'Orléans, it seems that Walpole did not hand over these two letters, and so they remain intact and unopened, providing us with an extremely rare and fascinating example of what letters looked like as they were being delivered. In particular, they reveal just how small sealed letters were: these are of standard quarto paper size, folded three times.

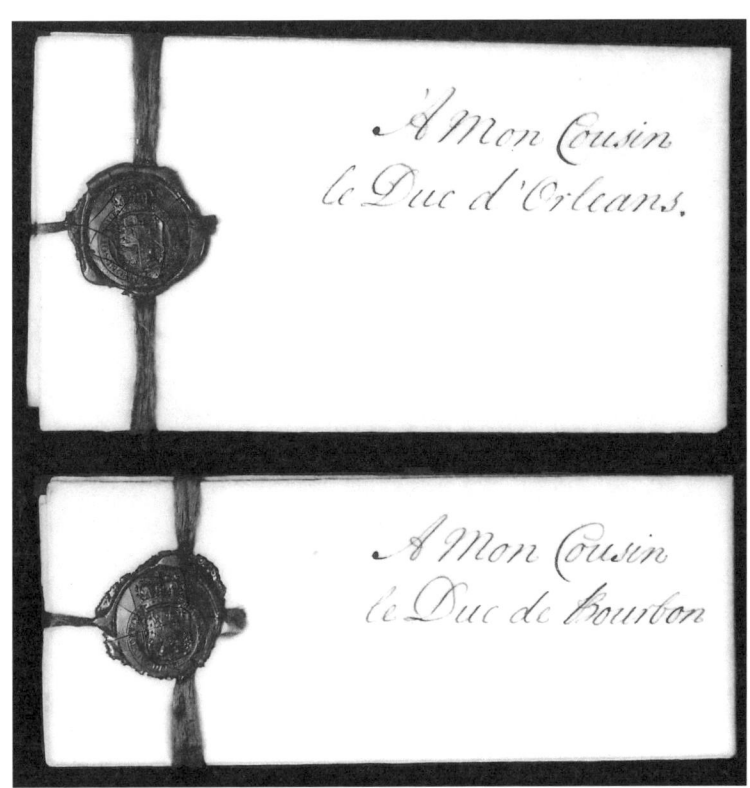

69

N. H.

The compleat tradesman: or, the exact dealers daily companion. Instructing him throughly in all things absolutely necessary to be known by all those who would thrive in the world; and in the whole art and mystery of trade and traffick; and will be of constant use for all merchants, whole-sale-men, shop-keepers, retailers, young tradesmen, countrey-chapmen, industrious yeomen, traders in petty villages; and all farmers, and others that go to countrey fairs and markets; and for all men whatsoever, that be of any trade, or have any considerable dealings in the world

London: John Dunton, 1684 (2nd edition with "large Additions")

Folger 154-806q

The author of this book intended it to be a pocket companion for the use of London merchants and tradesmen. His chapter on the post office extols the great improvements in the efficiency of the mail system, which now has to handle a "prodigiously great" number of letters compared to the quantity of mail "in our Ancestors days." This was due to the fact that even "the meanest People have generally learnt to write." He further cites the astounding statistic that "in five days, an Answer of a Letter may be had from a place 300 miles distant from the Writer."

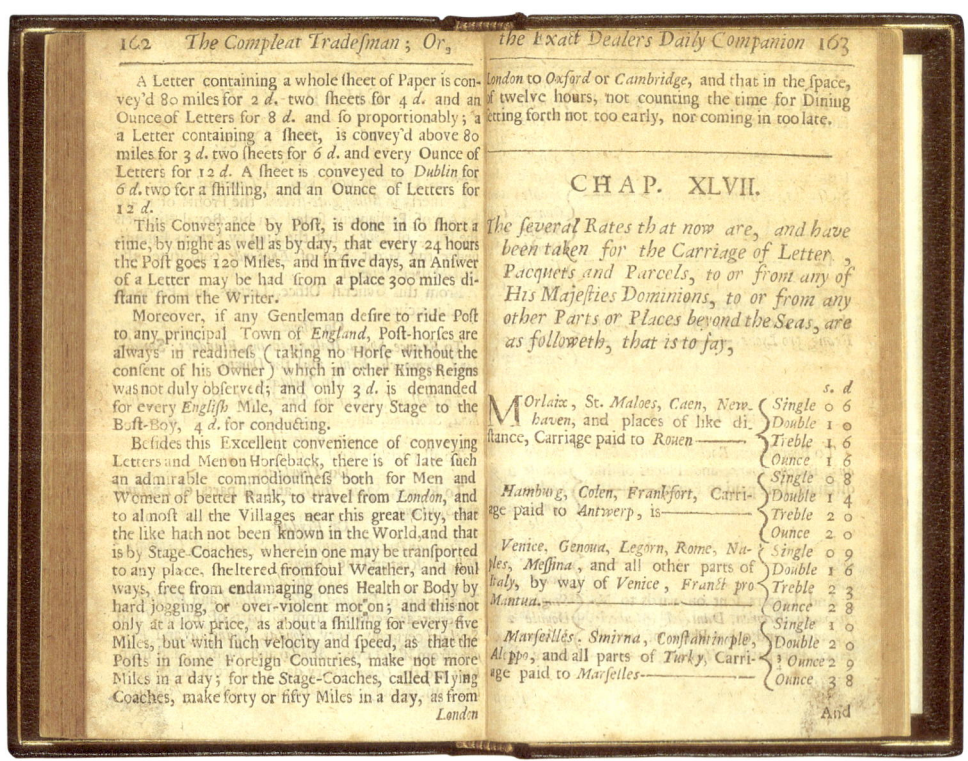

[p. 161]
CHAP. XLVI.
Of the Post-Office

This Office is now kept in *Lumbard-street*, formerly in *Bishopsgate-street*; the Profits of it are by Act of Parliament setled on his Royal Highness the Duke of *York*; but the King by Letters Patents, under the Great Seal of *England*, constitutes the Post-Master-General.

From this General Office, Letters and Pacquets are dispatched,

On *Mondays*,

To *France, Spain, Italy, Germany, Flanders, Swedeland, Denmark, Kent*, and the *Downs*.

On *Tuesdays*,

To *Holland, Germany, Swedeland, Denmark, Ireland, Scotland*, and all parts of *England* and *Wales*.

On *Wednesdays*,

To all parts of *Kent* and the *Downs*.

On *Thursdays*,

To *France, Spain, Italy*, and all parts of *England* and *Scotland*.

On *Frydays*.

To *Flanders, Germany, Italy, Swedeland, Denmark, Holland, Kent* and the *Downs*,

On *Saturdays*,

To all parts of *England, Wales, Scotland* and *Ireland*.

Letters are returned from all parts of *England* and *Scotland* certainly every *Monday, Wednesday* and *Fryday*; from *Wales*, every *Monday* and *Fryday*; and from *Kent* and the *Downs* every day; but from other parts more uncertainly, in regard of the Sea.

[p. 162] A Letter containing a whole sheet of Paper is convey'd 80 miles for 2 d. two sheets for 4 d. and an Ounce of Letters for 8 d. and so proportionably; a Letter containing a sheet, is convey'd above 80 miles for 3 d. two sheets for 6 d. and every Ounce of Letters for 12 d. A sheet is conveyed to *Dublin* for 6 d. two for a shilling, and an Ounce of Letters for 12 d.

This Conveyance by Post, is done in so short a time, by night as well as by day, that every 24 hours the Post goes 120 Miles, and in five days, an Answer of a Letter may be had from a place 300 miles distant from the Writer.

Moreover, if any Gentleman desire to ride Post to any principal Town of *England*, Post-horses are always in readiness (taking no Horse without the consent of his Owner) which in other Kings Reigns was not duly observed; and only 3 d. is demanded for every *English* Mile, and for every Stage to the Post-Boy, 4 d. for conducting. . .

[pp. 165–66] The said Office is managed by a Deputy, and other Officers, to the Number of seventy seven persons, who give their actual Attendance respectively, in the dispatch of the Business.

Upon this Grand Office depends one hundred eighty two Deputy-Post-Masters in *England* and *Scotland*; most of which keep Regular Offices in their Stages, and Sub-Post-Masters in their Branches; and also in *Ireland*, another General Office for that Kingdom, which is kept in *Dublin*, consisting of Eighteen like Officers, and Forty five Deputy-Post-Maseters.

The present Post-Master-General keeps constantly, for the Transport of the said Letters and Pacquets;

{*France*, two Pacquet-Boats.

Between *England* {*Flanders*, two Pacquet-Boats.

and — {*Holland*, three Pacquet-Boats.

{*Ireland*, three Pacquet-Boats.

And at *Deal*, two Pacquet-Boats for the *Downs*.

All which Officers, Post-masters, Pacquet-Boats, are maintained at his own proper charge.

And as the Master-piece of all those good regulations, established by the present Post-master-General, for the better Government of the said Office, he hath annexed and appropriated the Market Towns of *England*, so well to their respective Post-Stages, that there is no considerable Market-Town, but hath an easie and certain Conveyance for the Letters thereof, to and from the said Grand Office, in the due course of the Males every Post.

Though the Number of Letters missive in *England*, were not at all considerable in our Ancestors days, yet it is now so prodigiously great (since the meanest People have generally learnt to write) that the Office is Farmed for above 40. rather 50000 *l.* a Year.

70

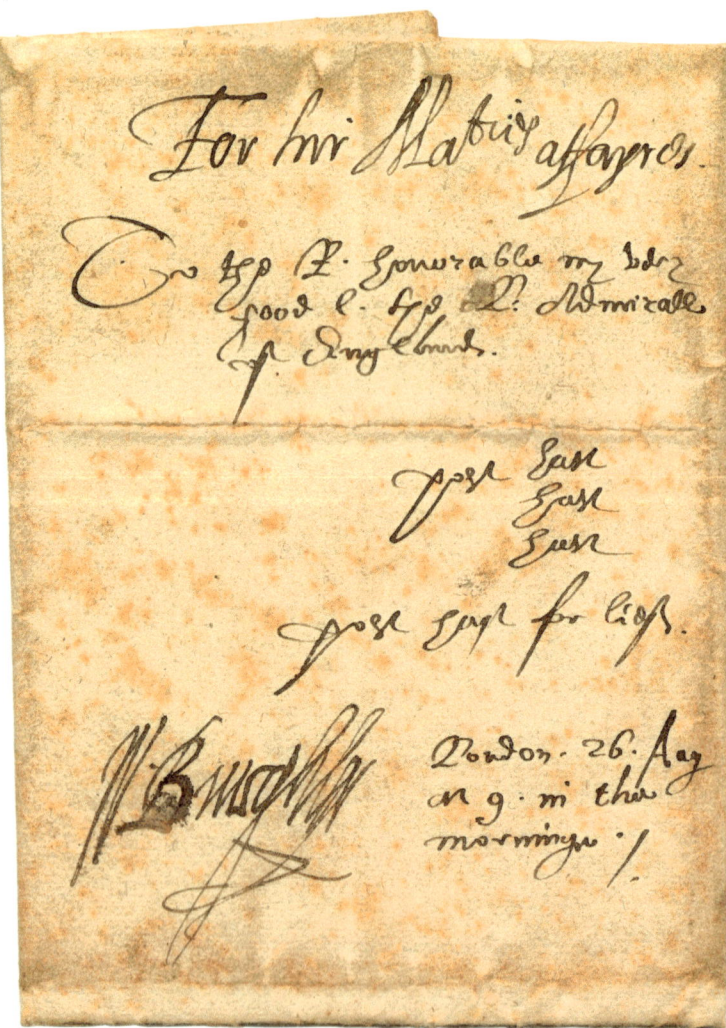
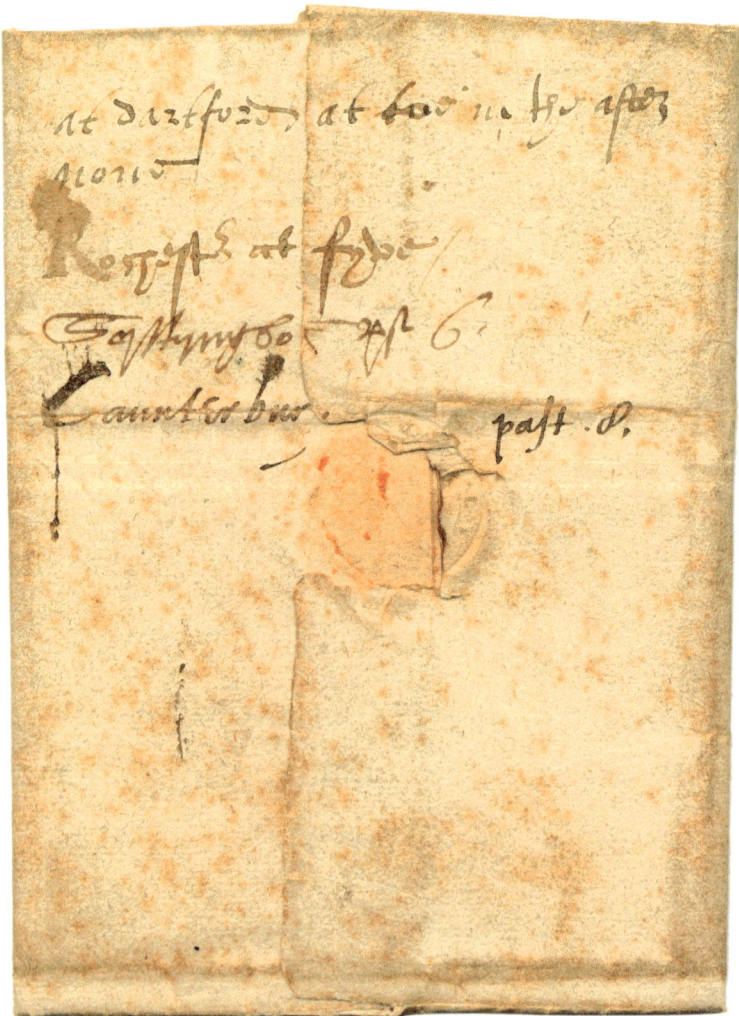

70
William Cecil, baron Burghley (1520–1598)
Letter signed, with autograph postscript, to Charles Howard, 2nd lord Howard of
Effingham (later 1st earl of Nottingham)
The Strand, August 26, 1588
Folger MS X.d.494
Reproduced at 100%

"Post hast hast hast post hast for lief" is the urgent command on this letter from
Lord Burghley to the Lord Admiral of England, who was on board the flagship
"Ark Royal," sailing against the retreating Spanish Armada. Dated August 26, 1588,
it concerns the supply of munitions to two English ships battling a Spanish ship
near New Haven. Like many letters from the period, this one was written by a personal secretary, with Burghley signing it and adding a postscript in his own handwriting. The letter endured an 80 mile journey between London and Dover. Local
postmasters have recorded the time of day or night when the letter passed through
their post houses: London at 9am, Dartford at 2pm, Rochester at 5pm, Sittingbourne
past 6pm, and Canterbury past 8pm (the last three entries can only be read when
the letter is completely folded). In his reply (located at the National Archives in
England), the Lord Admiral writes that he received it "about 5 of the clock in the
morning," for a total travel time of 20 hours, or 4 miles per hour.

[superscription] For hir M*ai*esties affayres

To the R*ight* honorable my very
        good l*or*d the l*or*d Admirall
        of England.

            post   hast
                      hast
                      hast
            post hast for lief.

W Burghley

[postmasters' notes] London. 26. Aug
at 9. in the
morninge./.
at dartford at tue in the after
none
Roches*t*er at fyve
Syttyngbor*n* p*as*t 6.
Caunterbury past .8.

[letter] After my most hartie Commendac*i*ons to yo*ur* good l*or*d
having this verie morning receiued the inclosed le*tt*re to yo*ur* l*or*dship
from my l*or*d of Sussex, and by his D*i*rection required to open the
same, to thend I might by mine acquaint yo*ur* l*or*dship w*i*th the
contents theareof, I haue been bold soe to doe, and to

send yt inclosed in this to your lordship by post, remitting to your lordship
to doe that which you shall thinke fitt to be done vppon
consideracion of that which is conteined thearein according to
the importance theareof. And so in hast I must hartely
bid your B. farewell.   ffrom my house in the
Strand this xxvj[th] of August 1588.

                                        Your good & assured loving frend.

                              W Burghley

[postscript in   I thynk your Lordship may spare
Burghley's hand]   to William fenner some more succor
                        for recovery of this shipp.
                        my Lord of Sussex hath delyverd
                        to the Ayd. Culverin shott & l. sacre shott iiij[20]
                        minion shott iiij[20] barrells of powder iiiij
                                    and to the Charles
                        fawcon shott iiij[20]/
                        barrells of powder ij

[endorsement]   Lord Threasorer
                        26 Aug. 88
                        with an enclosed lettre from
                        captain fener touchinge the
                        spanishe ship in Newhaven

────────

71
James Shiers
Autograph letter signed, to Sir Thomas Wentworth
February 10, 1662/63
Folger MS X.d.428 (158)
Reproduced at 95%

On the address leaf of this letter reporting the negative outcome of a King's Bench
case in London, John Shiers includes a note that the Ferrybridge postmaster should
forward the letter to West Bretton, home of the Wentworth family. The notation
"post paid 3 d" in another hand indicates that the sender had paid three pence, the
going rate for conveying a single sheet letter above eighty miles. West Bretton,
Yorkshire, was roughly twenty-five miles from Ferrybridge, which, in turn, was 185
miles from London.

        To the Right Worrshipfull Sir Thomas
        Wentworth knight at
                    Bretton, these
                        hast.

        To bee left with the Postmaster of -
        fferribridge to be speedily sent

        post paid. 3 [d]   Yorkeshire

To the Right Hono.ble Sr Thomas
Wentworth Knt. at
Bretton, these
hast.

To be left wth ye Postmr of —
Ferribridge to bee speedily sent
post pd. 3 d. Yorkshire

To the Right honorabell John Howard
Esq at his house in Beanes
yard in Westminster

72
Nicholas Parker
Autograph letter signed, to John Ferrers
February 27, 1663/64
Folger MS L.e.723
Reproduced at 90%

The postmark on this letter concerning rentals and tithes is February 29, two days
after Nicholas Parker dated it "February 27 1663." Because of the leap year day postmark, we know that the letter was actually posted in 1664, not 1663. Parker was
following the common practice in early modern England of observing Lady Day
(March 25) as the beginning of the new year.

———

73
Humphrey Higer
Accounts, ca. 1650
Folger MS L.e.345

This bill indicates that despite the increasing availability of a standardized national
post, individuals still relied on bearers as well. Highes, who was most likely keeping
the books for John Ferrers of Walton-on-Trent, Derbyshire, records that three letters
were sent by the post for one shilling (perhaps more, the page is damaged), and on
another occasion, a double letter by the post for six pence. He also paid three pence
to have a letter brought from Burton, and gave six pence to "Jorge a fule" to bring a
letter to him. He replenished some of his letterwriting supplies as well, purchasing
six pounds of Calais sand, a fine white sand used for blotting ink, two quires of cap
paper, and one quire of white paper. The manuscript is damaged, rendering some
of the text illegible.

humphrey
higers
bill
Jannuary *the* first

ffor 3 letters to *the* post by antony	0 - 1 - [obliterated]
pead to Callingwood for goeing	
4 times to burton w*i*th rabbits	0 - 1 - 0
ffor bringing a letter from burton	0 - 0 - 3
ffor a greate knife	0 - 1 - 0
giuen 3 musissenners	0 - 0 - 9
giuen *the* man for *the* bullit moules	0 - 0 - 6
giuen to Jorge a fule for bring a letter	0 - 0 - 6
ffor 3 gros tobackco pips at 3 shi*llings*	
2 pence a gros	0 - 9 - 6
ffor his peanes	0 - 1 - 0
ffor goeing to liesfield one time	0 - 0 - 6
ffor 8 bottells of seakk and twenty of	
white wine and a bottle of viniger	2 - 5 - 0

ffor 2 quier of cap paper and one of white	0 - 1 - 0
ffor tebs peaines	0 - 0 - 6
ffor a pound of Tobackco	0 - 2 - 0
ffor humphrey wetton goeing to formark	0 - 1 - 0
giuen to Anne kinke	0 - 1 - 0
giuen to John goodman by my mistres order and [?] man	0 - 3 - 6
to a peake musiscenner	0 - 0 - [obliterated]
ffor 6 pound of calli sand	0 - [obliterated]
ffor a dusson and a halfe of broumes	0 - 1 - 4
for a dubble letter to the post	0 - 0 - 6
ffor alane. siue to dres. meale	0 - 0 - 10
peal for bringing lettres from burton	0 - 0 - 2

———

74
Thomas Trevelyon (b. ca.1548)
"Carry-tale"
Miscellany, 1608
Folger MS V.b.232

The foot-post in this illustration wears a pouch of letters around his waist, holds a letter superscribed "To his frinde liar" in his hand, and carries a large post-bag with the inscription: "Newes from all parttes is in my sacke With lies and tales it Loades my backe." Trevelyon's image emphasizes the power of letters to disseminate information, whether it be false or true. The scriptural proverbs below it condemn "tale-bearers" for spreading lies and secrets.

A Poole
to Whitechurch
to Hunsterton
Bridgmore
156
157
Checkley
Bettley

Bunbury
169
the Cleys
168

enter Cheshire
Ashtree 155

Woret Owre
154
vulgo
Onneley
enter Shropshire

to Drayton 153
to Drayton
Apeyate

152

Sideway hall

151

to Drayton
150

Newcastle

STAFFORD SH

to Whitechurch

to Bulls Green
166
167
Stoke
Hall

Hurleston
165
to Tranmore Green

to Beam Heath
Burford Green
164
Acton

to
163
Whitechurch

Nampwich
162

to Betley & Sandbach
161

to Aulme
160
Stapley
Hotebock Hall

Bar Bridge
Mill
Watts Veld Pavement

Houses
Catveley Hall
to Orpram

Weaver Flu

to the Holt
Glass House
Rowton
to Whitechurch 180

Nampwich
& Stableford
Cart Road

Bough
to Odf 181

Chistert als Chr let

Gibbit
179
Bro Heath
178

Cotton Heath
3 Stone Bridge
177

to Sta bleford
Hocke n

to Chester
176

the Red Cap
175
Tutton Hall

Cotton
174
Utkint

Idenshen Hall

Ash Tree
to Utkinton
173

To perley

172

SHIRE

CHESHIRE

Lost and found

THE FACT THAT THERE WERE POSTAL SYSTEMS IN EXISTENCE did not guarantee a letter's safe delivery. Even from the anecdotal evidence contained in other letters that *did* arrive, it is obvious that a good many letters went missing *en route*, either lost, stolen or misdirected. While we don't know what percentage of letters never reached their destinations, the amount of ink devoted to instructions and caveats for the delivery of letters—the logistics of getting things from point A to point B—suggests it was high, and a source of unending concern to letterwriters. The frequent failure of the post had one positive side effect, however: it allowed writers to present their work as if it had been accidentally chanced on at the road-side. This was useful in the conveying of news—a typical publication in 1657 by the untraceable "O.P." bills itself as *A true copie of a letter sent from a friend in Paris, to his friend in London, with one inclosed, casually found neer the Louvre in Paris* (London, 1657). And the conceit worked particularly well in literature, prompting the appearance of the "packet of letters" supposedly discovered at the side of the road, which soon became a popular fictional genre.

Given the often haphazard postal systems, and the sometimes delicate nature of correspondence, letterwriters in the Renaissance had to come up with novel ways of protecting their letters—and themselves. Perhaps the most successful ways are obvious— dangerous information was not entrusted to letters but was given verbally to the bearers of letters. If a message needed to be sent on paper, then the writer would often instruct the recipient to burn the letter. Yet other messages were committed to "enclosures," loose pieces of paper inside the letter that could be promptly destroyed while the outside letter was kept. Letters could be sewn into clothing, or, as in the famous case of Mary, queen of Scots, placed in watertight containers in casks of ale.

The problem also provoked some more devious solutions, the stuff of children's detective stories—such as ink that became visible only when the letter was exposed to sunlight, or candlelight, or water, or even orange juice. Or one of the myriad ciphers, especially popular for conveying politically or militarily sensitive information, that exercised the minds of some of the period's greatest thinkers. Recipes for invisible ink, ciphers, and other ways to achieve secrecy, commonly appeared in popular "books of secrets." Johann Jacob Wecker's *18 Books of the Secrets of Art & Nature* (London, 1660), for example, contained instructions for "Letters not to be read but in the night," "The way to read Letters that are concealed upon the Paper," "How to make up Letters, that they cannot be privately opened," and "How a Letter is to be opened secretly" (pp. 270–71).

75
Thomas Crompton (ca. 1589–1645)
Autograph letter signed, to Lady Mary (Vanlore) Powell
Weston, November 28, 1630
Folger MS X.c.51 (21)

This letter was intended to inform Lady Powell of various financial dealings undertaken on her behalf by her steward Thomas Crompton, but Crompton was forced
to spend the first half of the letter defending himself against Lady Powell's charge
that he had not written. In fact, according to Crompton, he had written four times
previously, but clearly none of the letters had reached its destination. Crompton's
painstaking account of his correspondence testifies to the multiple ways letters
might be sent: the first is enclosed in a letter to his master, and taken by the carrier;
the second is carried by Mr. Powell, presumably a member of the family; the third,
taken by Mr. Powell's servant, itself enclosed a letter to his master; and the fourth
was taken by the carrier. With this fifth letter, Crompton gives a detailed description of its intended recipient, giving her name, her husband's name and rank, and
a specific address—evidently with success, since this letter reached Lady Powell.
Despite his assurances, it must be said that the 20% per cent delivery success rate of
Crompton's five letters seems suspiciously low.

[superscription]
To the right wor*ship*f*u*ll and
my much honor*e*d good Lady
the L*ady* Powell wife to S*ir*
Edward Powell k*nigh*t and
barronett and one of
his Ma*i*esties Mast*er*s of
requests dwellinge at
Westminster next
to the scoolehowse.
dd this I
pray.

[letter]
Good Maddam,
I haue rec*eived* yo*u*r last lett*er* w*hi*ch doeth reporte of my
neclect in not wrightinge to yo*u*r La*dy*shi*p* / I will
asshure ~~your~~ yo*u*r La*dy*shi*p* *that* this is the fiffte lett*er* I
haue wrote vnto yow, *the* first I sent by *the* Carrier
Burrowes, the next I sent by M*r* Powell. The next
after *tha*t I sent by his man sam w*hi*ch was a lett*er*
to my M*aste*r and one inclosed to yo*u*r La*dy*shi*p* and *the* first
lett*er* I sent to yo*u*r La*dy*shi*p* was inclosed in my M*aste*r his
lett*er*./ and *the* last I sent but this, was by the
Carrier. / and soe is this, beinge *the* fifft; And
I protest I haue sent euery weeke sithence I
came hether; if not by *the* Carrier, it by those
w*hi*ch I knowe haue deliu*er*ed them, and if it were to
wright every day one; I would not misse, if it
did please God:)
I haue sould sithence I cum hether aboute forty

Busshells of wheate, sum at 8^s:6^d: a bus*h*ell and sum at 8^s:
and at 7^s: six pence: and fiue hundred bushels of
Barly at 5^s: a bus*h*ell and sum six score bushels of Beanes
at 4^s: and 3^s: - 8^d and 4^s-6^d, a bus*h*ell. /
I haue hempe seede enough to sowe *that* pleck w*h*ich
was sowed *the* last yere. /
I will talke w*ith* Newman before I cum, and bringe
word aboute his ∧^{sonn}∧. I thinke hee hath noe great
skill: Nan remem*b*ers her dutie, and promises to
bee carefull. / and please God I will bee at
fullham the Sat*t*er day befor Christide or nere
there abouts. I haue a note of yo*ur* La*dys*hips sheepe
wh*i*ch I tooke when I was at Pengethly./ and of yo*ur*
woole beinge fowre score and two stone w*h*ich sum ors
all w*h*ich I will make playne vnto yow when I cum. /
Thus w*ith* my dutie to my M*aster* and my la*dy*
Vanloore, and yo*ur* La*dysh*ip and my loue to my
Aunte, my Falentine, M*ist*ris Jane, Joane, and to all
the rest of my fellows. prayinge for yo*ur* la*dys*hips
health I rest. / yo*ur* poore servantte till death:

Tho: Crumpton

[vertical, in left
hand margin]

from Weston *the*
28⁰: No*vember* 1630:

———

76
Richard Bagot (d. 1597)
Draft of letter to William Cecil, baron Burghley
Blithfield, February 27, 1595/96
Folger MS L.a.84

This short draft of a letter provides a revealing glimpse into the unofficial but
always vigilant systems of surveillance practised by the Elizabethan government. In
February 1596, a carrier found two letters on the road to Chester, about two miles
from Nantwich. He took them to an innkeeper in Stone—possibly the regular stag-
ing post for the mail in that town—who opened them and then, alarmed at their
contents, handed them over to the local dignitary Richard Bagot, who himself sent
them to the heart of government, in the person of Lord Treasurer Burghley. These
letters, sent from London and destined for two men named Haughton, talk crypti-
cally of a change coming soon; Bagot thinks that one may be written from a brother of a man executed for conspiring to murder the queen in a Catholic plot. Copies
of the two letters survive as Folger MS L.a.542.

Right honorable my verie good lord I send you herein two
letters found by a carrio*ur* in the highe way to Chester, two myles
on this side the towne of Nantwich, w*h*ich he brought w*ith* him to
Stone to one Tho*mas* Rathbon, Inkep*er* ther at the signe of the crowne
who breakinge them vp, & pervsinge the content*es* sent them

to me, And for *that* ther is matter in the one manifestinge ~~the~~
the trayterous myndes of vnloyall subiect*es*, envyinge the
quiet estate of o*ur* countrie, with desire of alteracion as may
appeare, Thother not importinge so much, yet for *that* I
greatlie suspecte him to be the brother of one executed with
Babington might cause him to beare a Revenginge mynd
w*h*ich I hope by yo*ur* l*ordshi*ps good meanes wilbe p*re*vented, And
so w*ith* all humble dutie co*mm*it you to the mercie of the Allmightie
Blithfild the xxvij[th] of ffebruarie. 1595.

———

77

John Ogilby (1600–1676)

Britannia Depicta Or Ogilby Improv'd; Being a Correct Coppy of M[r]. Ogilby's Actual
Survey of all the Direct & Principal Cross Roads in England and Wales

London: for Thomas Bowles, 1720

Folger DA615 O3 Cage

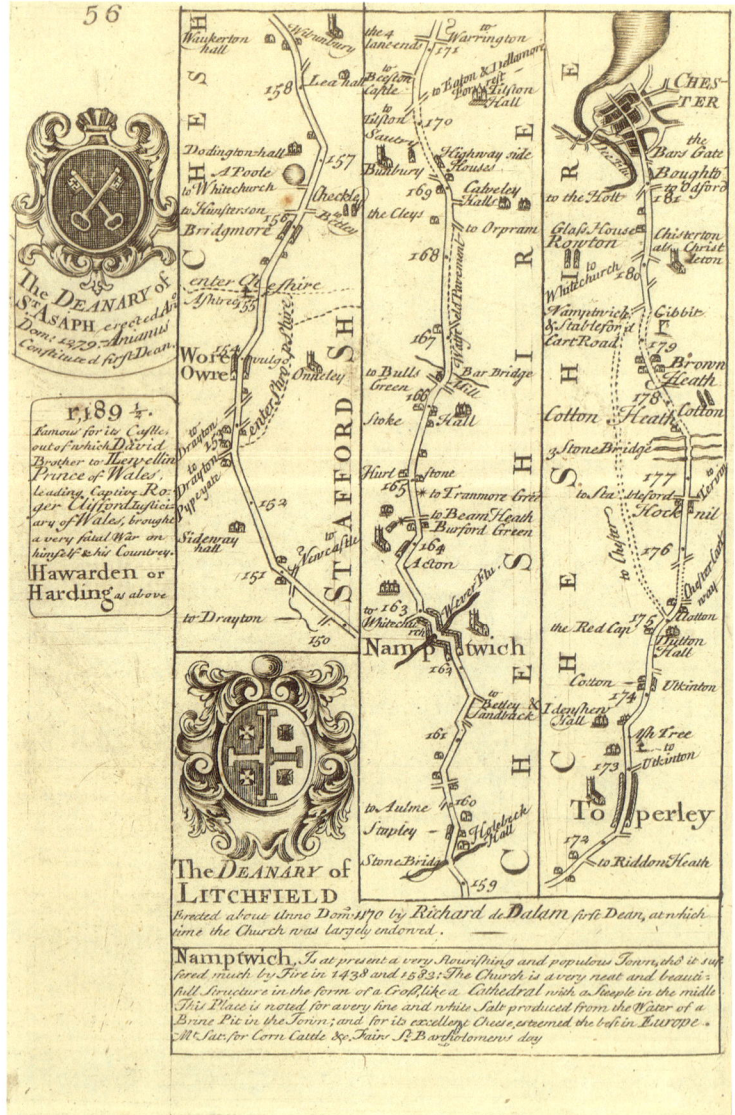

This popular edition of John Ogilby's *Britannia* contains maps of the major postal routes in England and Wales, and allows us to place Richard Bagot's story in geographical context. Page 56 shows the "highe way to Chester," and the middle of its three columns shows Nantwich ("Namptwich") some nineteen miles away from Chester. Stone is about twenty miles from Nantwich, and thus about twenty-two miles away from where the carrier found the letters.

————

78

Thomas Blount (1618–1679)

The academy of eloquence: containing a compleat English rhetorique, exemplified; common places and formula's digested into an easie and methodical way to speak and write fluently, according to the mode of the present times: with letters both amorous and morall, upon emergent occasions

London: H[enry] L[loyd] for Anne Moseley, 1663 (3rd edition, with additions)

Folger B3323

Collections of form letters reveal that the loss of letters was an everyday occurrence. Blount's manual, for example, contains among its "Letters both amorous and morall, Upon emergent occasions," one letter entitled "A second Salutation, upon the miscarriage of a former letter." The sender explains to the recipient that he had "Address'd my salutes before," but he understands that his letter "miscarried," that is, failed to reach its destination. He sends another letter not only to rectify this, but also to correct the impression the recipient might have, "that I was as silent as their miscarriage makes me seem." Note also how the letters come to personify their writer: "If they stammer in the delivery [of their message], they best express my self."

[p. 154]

A second Salutation, upon the miscarriage of a former Letter.

SIR,

I Address'd my salutes before, but here they miscarried. The labour to repeat them is not burthensome; yet lest their loss might bring you into suspition, that I was as silent as their miscarriage makes me seem, I adde these to try better fortune; in which, if more happy, they know their errand, to present me and my loves to your devotion. If they stammer in the delivery, they best express my self, who (surcharg'd by your deserts) must conceive more obligation, smother more affection, than I can utter. You can mend both by the clearness of a candid interpretation, till both are able to be more articulate and plain; None can better expound gratitude, than he who most merits it. Sir, I forget not the delights of your ingenious conversations, those sweet (but too short) moments of my contents. I remember your ready favors, your reall endearments, I remember all, and for all am thankfull. Will you have more? More than this you cannot, I am (what I am),

Sir,

Very much yours,

D.W.

79

Thomas Nash (1567–1601)

Strange Newes, of the intercepting certaine Letters, and a Conuoy of Verses . . .

London: Iohn Danter, 1593

Folger STC 18377b.2

The possibilities of the phenomenon of the intercepted letter—and better, the intercepted packet of letters—were not lost on writers of fiction. In 1592, as part of his longstanding print battle with the Cambridge scholar Gabriel Harvey, the satirist Thomas Nash published what purported to be a collection of letters and verses, which had been intercepted "as they were going *Priuilie* to victuall the Low Countries," one of his many lavatorial puns. The Folger possesses the only known surviving copy of this 1593 edition of *Strange Newes*.

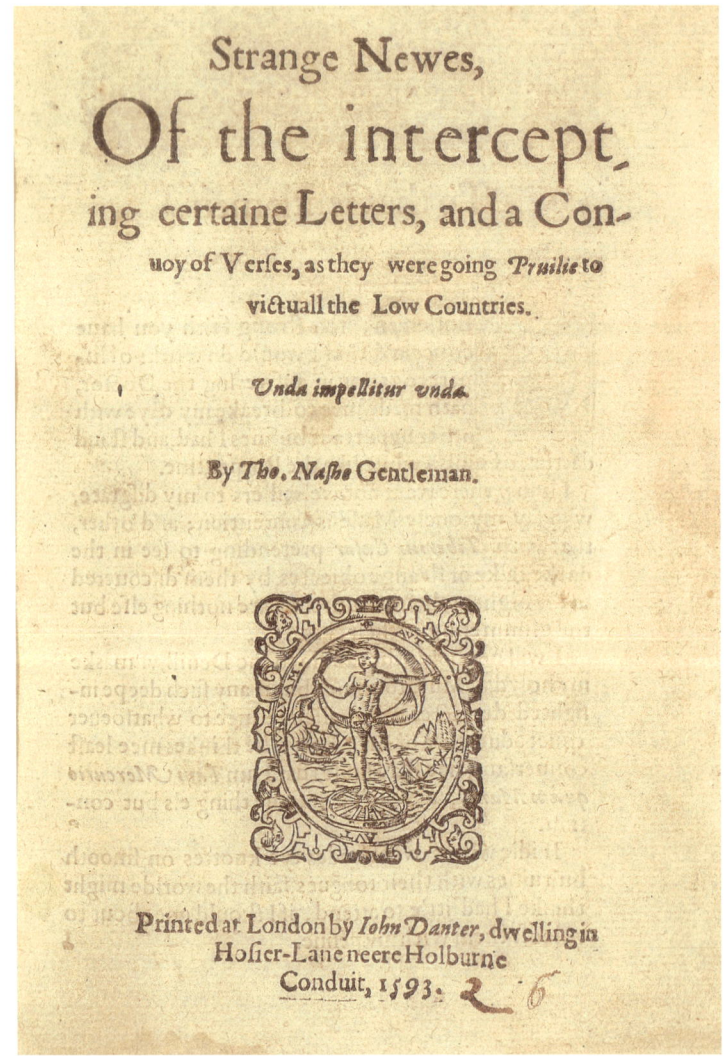

80

Thomas Ogle (d. 1671)

A letter of dangerous consequence, from Sergeant Major Ogle, to Sir Nicholas Crisp
at Oxford. As it was intercepted by Colonell Goodwin of the Parliaments forces.
Together with the examination of the messenger, in the coller of whose doublet the
said letter was found

London: For Edw[ard] Husbands, 1642 [i.e., 1643]

Folger O187

In times of political and military unrest, letters were especially vulnerable to inter-
ception, despite the lengths to which their bearers would go to hide them. The
English Civil War spawned a wave of intercepted letters which were then promptly
delivered to printers and gleefully published. The title page of this pamphlet, dated
February 27, 1642/3, tells some of its story. With the authority of the clerk Henry
Elsying, it proclaims that it was "Ordered by the Commons in Parliament, That this
Letter and Examination be forthwith printed and published."

[p. 8]

The Examination of *Henry Commins*, Servant to
Master *Daniel Colwell*, one of the searchers of the
Custome-house London, taken before Colonell *Good-*
win and Colonell *Bulstrode*, the 16. of February,
1642.

He saith, that his Master went from his house in
Bartholomew-lane London, to Oxon, upon Friday
last, with Sir *Nicholas Crisps* his Lady, and that Captain
Ogle, dwelling over against Pallace-yard conduit Westminster, sent by him a Letter to Sir *Nicholas Crisp* to
Oxon: Which Letter the said Captain did, together
with his Maids help sow up in the Coller of the Doublet
of this Examinant, giving him a great charge to deliver
the Letter carefully, and not to confesse from whom he
had it: And there coming one to speak with Captain
Ogle, whiles he was sowing in the Letter, he suddenly
called this Examinant into his Closet, that he might not
be discovered.

And this inclosed Note, the Examinant saith, was sent
from Sir *Nicholas Crisp* his Servant, unto his Master.

Henry Comens.

81

The Kings cabinet opened: or, certain packets of secret letters & papers, written
with the Kings own hand, and taken in his cabinet at Nasby-Field, June 14. 1645.
By victorious Sr. Thomas Fairfax; wherein many mysteries of state, tending to the
justification of that cause, for which Sir Thomas Fairfax joyned battell that
memorable day are clearly laid open; together, with some annotations thereupon.
Published by speciall order of the Parliament
London: For Robert Bostock, 1645
Folger C2358.2

King Charles himself fell victim to the genre when in 1645 Robert Bostock published a series of letters that were purportedly removed from the king's personal
cabinet or closet. The prefatory epistle to the Reader explained the value of having
the King's own letters made public.

It were a great sin against the mercies of God, to conceale those evidences of
truth, which bee so graciously (and almost miraculously) by surprizall of
these Papers, hath put into our hands; nor doe we smother this light under a
Bushell, but freely hold it out to our seduced brethren, (for so in the spirit of
meeknesse labouring to reclaim them, we still speak) that they may see their
errors, and return into the right way: For those that wilfully deviate, and
make it their profession to oppose the truth, we think it below us, to revile
them with opprobrious language, remembering the Apostle St. *Jude*, and that
example which he gives us in his Epistle. They may see here in his privat
Leters what affection the King beares to his people, what language and titles
he bestowes upon his great Councell; which we return not again, but consider with sorrow, that it comes from a Prince seduced out of his proper sphear;
one that has left that seat in which he ought, and hath bound himselfe to sit,
to sit (as the Psalmist speakes) in the *Chair of the scornfull*; & to the ruine
(almost) of three Kingdoms, hath *walked in the counsels of the ungodly*; and
though in our tenents we annex no infallibility to the seat of a King in
Parliament, as the *Romanists* do to the Papall Chaire, (since all men are subject to errour) yet we dare boldly say, that no *English* King did ever from that
place, speak destruction to his people, but safety and honour; nor any that
abhorred that Seat and Councell, but did the contrary. Therefore, Reader, to
come now to the present businesse of these Letters; thou art either a friend or
enemy to our cause: If thou art well affected to that Cause of Liberty &
Religion, which the two Parliaments of *England* and *Scotland* now maintain
against a combination of all the Papists in *Europe* almost, especially the
bloody Tygers of *Ireland*, and some of the Prelaticall an Court Faction in
England: thou wilt be abundantly satisfied with these Letters here printed,
and take notice therefrom, how the Court has been *Caiolde*, (that's the new
authentick word now amongst our Cabalisticall adversaries) by the Papists,
and we the more beleeving sort of Protestants, by the Court. If thou art an
Enemy to Parliaments and Reformation, and made willfull in thy enmity
beyond the help of miracles, or such revelations as these are, then tis to be
expected, that thou wilt either deny these papers to have been written by the
Kings own hand, or else that we make just constructions and inferences out of
them: Or lastly, thou wilt deny, though they be the Kings own, and beare such
a sense as we understand them in, yet that they are blameable, or unjustifiable

against such rebels as we are. As to the first, know that the Parliament was never yet guilty of such forgery, the King yet in all the Letters of his, which have been hitherto intercepted, never objected any such thing, and we dare appeale to his own conscience now, knowing that he cannot disavow either his own hand writing, or the matters themselves here written. All the Ciphers, Letters, all circumstances of rime, and fact, and the very hand by which they are signed (so generally known and now exposed to the view of all) will averre for us, that no such forgery could be profitable.

———

82
Thomas Lupton
A Thousand Notable things, of sundry sortes, Wherof some are wonderfull, some straunge, some pleasant, diuers necessary, a great sort profitable and many very precious
London: Iohn Charlewood, for Hughe Spooner, [1579]
Folger STC 16955

This copy of recipes, with the ownership mark of one John Dean, is annotated throughout in the margins with handwritten notes. A recipe for invisible ink is partially obscured by a large ink blot, while another page contains a large drop of red sealing wax.

[p. 150]
Salt Armoniacke stampte, and myxt with water, doth make whyte Letters nothing differing from the cullour of Payer [Paper]. But if you holde the same Paper to the fyre, the Letters wyll waxe blacke. *Mizaldus.*

[p. 166]
If you put the powder of Allom in water, whatsoeuer you wryte therwith, the wryting or Letters wyl not appeare: vnlesse you put ye same paper in water, and then you shall reade it perfectly. *Bapt. porta.*

[pp. 214–15]
Wryte what you wyl, on fayre whyte paper, with the iuyce of a redde Onion, well myxed and tempered with the whyte of an Egge, which being drie: wyll appeare as though it were onely playne paper, without any wryting. But if you holde it against the fyre, you maye then easilye reade it, or perceyue the letters.

[p. 232]
To put a Shedule, or lytle wryting into an Egge, lay an Egge certaine dayes in strong vynegar, vntyl it be soft, and wryte your name or what you lyst in a lytle peece of paper, and folde the paper as harde together as you can: then with a Raser cut the sayd Egge in the toppe fynely, and aduisedly: through the which, put the little paper into the Egge cyrcumspectly, and then put the Egge into cold water, and immediately the shell wyl be hard as it was before. A proper secrete.

83
Francis Bacon (1561–1626)
De Dignitate & Augmentis Scientiarum Libros IX
London: John Haviland, 1623
Folger STC 1108

Francis Bacon's definition of the perfect cipher was the one that is never perceived to be a cipher, and so is never subjected to deciphering. While working on an embassy in France, he developed a cipher that fit the bill: the writer should have two alphabets "one of true letters, the other of non-significants." He should "infold in them two letters at once; one carrying the secret, the other such a letter as the writer would have been likely to send, but that does not contain anything dangerous." This way the letter would not appear to be a cipher, and the bearer would not be questioned about it.

The infolding writing, he wrote, "shall contain at least five times as many letters as the writing infolded; no other condition or restriction whatever is required. The way to do it is this: First let all the letters of the alphabet be resolved into transpositions of two letters only. For the transposition of two letters through five places will yield thirty-two differences; much more twenty-four, which is the number of letters in our alphabet." This is the biliteral alphabet (top of p. 279), into which the "interior epistle" must be rendered. Taking as his example the Latin word "fvge" (flee) Bacon renders the four letters F V G E into a sequence of twenty a's and b's: Aababbaabbaabbaaabaa.

Then comes the tricky part. "Have by you at the same time another alphabet in two *forms*; I mean one in which each of the letters of the common alphabet, both capital and small, is exhibited in two different forms – any forms that you find convenient." The two forms Bacon has here (on p. 280) are two different *handwritten* forms of each letter: each capital and each small letter. In some cases the differences are obvious: the capital 'E' for example. But most are more subtly differentiated: the final loop on the second version of a lowercase d, for example, or the final loop on the second version of a lowercase h. "Then take your interior epistle, reduced to the biliteral shape, and adapt to it letter by letter your exterior epistle in the biform character; and then write it out."

Bacon gives as his example exterior (i.e. cover) epistle the phrase "*Manec te volo donec venero*": "I want you to stay until I come" (the opposite, of course, to "flee"). It is in the way that it is handwritten that the first twenty characters of this message come to give us aababbaabbaabbaaabaa, which can then be rendered back using the biliteral alphabet as FVGE. So: you'll note that Bacon chooses the "a" version of capital M rather than the "b" version; the "a" version of small "a" but the "b" version of small "n". What is crucial here is that the content of the message is utterly irrelevant: Bacon could have written any phrase of twenty or more characters in any language using the Roman alphabet: it is in the careful *handwriting* of each letter that the message is encrypted. Various parts of these strategies are by no means unique or original to Bacon, but his original contribution lies in his deployment of handwriting.

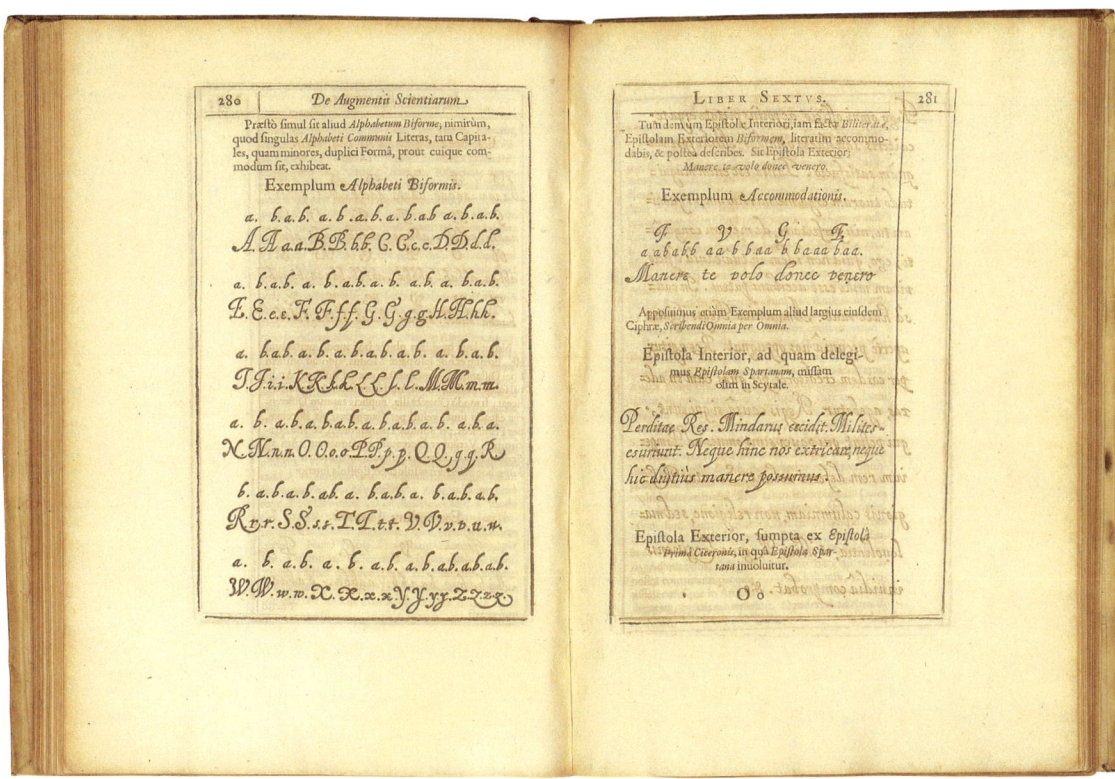

84

George Digby, earl of Bristol (1612–1677)

Letter signed, written on king's behalf to Prince Rupert or Maurice

Oxford, April 27, 1645

Folger MS Add 1285

Reproduced at 98%

This letter, lacking both an address and a seal, was written during the Civil War on behalf of king Charles I, then trapped at Oxford. The writer, George Digby, earl of Bristol, writes to an unidentified party, either Prince Rupert or Prince Maurice, advising that as a result of Oliver Cromwell's recent incursions, Rupert needs to march on Oxford in order to prevent the city from being besieged. Owing to its acute political sensitivity, the letter has been written partially in cipher—or rather a combination of ciphers. Several major players are denoted by numbers: King Charles is 241, Prince Rupert 354, the Marquis of Hertford 223, and so on. Also given numbers are key terms such as "counsel" (130), "haue" (211) and "horse" (214). Some common words are given codes consisting of a letter and a number, for example "and" (A1), "be" (A5), "but" (B1), "can" (B2), and so on. Other words are translated, letter by letter, into a numerical code. Each letter has four numbers by which it can be denoted—from "e" (1–4) to "t" (77–80). Some words are made up by a combination of different ciphers—so "hinder" at the end of the seventh line is given by 38.C5.6.1.66, 38=h, C5=in, 6=d, 1=e and 66=r, hence "hinder." Any number over 80 is a blank—the decipherer has underlined these to remind himself to ignore them.

The decipherer decoded the letter successfully, in the process exposing one error in the original coding. The cipherer, no doubt rushing to get the letter ready, slipped by one number in coding the letter "m," so the letter now gives the order "to larch immediately." The deciphered version is transcribed below, mistakes included.

May it please *your* Highnesse

       In my last by Steevens I gave *your* Hign*ess* an account
of Cromwells incursion into our quarters with 3000. horse
and dragoones of his successe in the base delivery vp of Blecking=
ton howse, and in Routinge some of our horse, since that hee
hath beaten vpp other of our quarters. I believe his first
designe was to goe Joyne with Massye, but these successes
will make them stay in these parts, hopinge to hinder
the Kings march to P. Rupert and by the reputation of
it to draw an armye quicklye out of London to distresse vs
heere. the truth of it is it is imposs
ible in the King to march till the
y be remoued which how to doe but by your d
rawing your army this way I knowe not
the Kinge hath sent orders in al
l gorings horse and what foote can be
consented by the M: of Hartfords counsell upon
due consideration of the west
to larch immediately hithe
r if those horse here they would suf
fise to doe the worke but it must bee
expected that ere they can come hither
the Rebels will haue in our quarters a goo
d body of foote and then if wee not f

[fol. 1ᵛ] oote al shee enough to deal
e with them those horse will be exposed to the
same hazards and inconveniences that the horse so now have
here are besides that the contrey is
so eaten up that if wee have not a
force that can support itselfe or put
it to an issue quickly it
will bee impossible in those horse when y co
m to subsist it is therefore proposed unto
your highn*ess* whether vpon this occasio it be not
necessary for P: Rupert to march hi
ther as strong as P: Rupert can and to
frame our body of an army he
rabouts with out which not only
the Kings coniunction with you will be
impossible but he will be in danger of being
beseidged here and then P: Rupert will be
forced to march hither to relee
ue him upon worse tear
mes then now to preuent all this
the truth is that the distresse of che
ster is an vnhappy obiection; but since *your*
highn*ess* sayes you can not cleeue to pla

[fol. 2ʳ] ce without the trayne and that it is not
possible for the King to bring

May it please y'r Highnesse

In my Last by Steevens I gave y'r High: an account
of Cromwells incursion into our quarters with 3000. horse
and dragoones of his successe in the bare delivery vp of Blechin-
=ton howse and in Routinge some of our horse, since that hee
hath beaten vp other of our quarters. I beleeve his first
designe was to ioyne with Massye, but their successe
will make them stay in these parts, hopinge   to h m d r r
n1. 38. e5. 6. 1. 66.
the Kings m a r c h to P. Rupert
n3. 241. 58. 26. 15. 64. 13. 40. n1. 554. and by the reputation of
it to draw an armye quicklye out of London to distresse vs
heere.   the t r u t h of that is that is i m P o s s 58.
n3. 80. 64. 74. 79. 40. k1. f2. f1. f2. f1. 32. 25. P 37. 46. 57. 58.
i b l e   m the king to m a r c h t i l l the
30. 23. 28. 4. e5. n3. 241. n1. 26. 16. 66. 12. 40. 80. 30. 27. 28. n3.
y b e r e m o u e d which how to doe but by your
67. 24. 66. 1. 25. 45. 76. 2. 6. k6. 39. 46. 55. n1. c2. 01. a5. 425. 6.
r a w i n g your army this w a y   I know not
65. 16. 54. e5. 19. 425. 906. n4. 56. 17. 70. 89. 31. 244. k1. 71. 81.
the Kinge hath.   s e n t o r d e r s m a l
58. 1. 48. 80. 83. 44. 64. 6. 1. 65. 58. e5. 16. 27.
l   g o r m g s horse and what f o o t e can be
27. 87. 20. 46. 66. e5. 19. 57. 214. a1. k1. 8. 45. 47. 80. 4. 12. a4.
c o n s e n t e d by the M'r of Hartford s counsell up on
12. k2. 58. 2. 48. 79. 4. 5. a5. n3. 223. 59. 89. 130. 75. 35. k2. 84.
d u e c o n s i d e r a t i on of the w e s t
6. 76. 1. 11. k2. 57. 30. 6. 1. 64. 15. 80. 32. k2. k1. n3. 55. 4. 58. 79.
to m a r c h i m m e d i a t e l y hithe
n1. 27. 16. 65. 12. 39. 30. 24. 26. 1. 6. 31. 14. 26. 2. 28. 67. 39. 33. n.
r w i t h horse with another t they s u f t
66. 86. 4 horse. 214. n3. n3. 64. 64. 4. n3. 67. would. 57. 77. 8.
f i s i t to doe that w o r k e
10. 33. 58. 1. n1. c2. n3. 53. 44. 65. 42. 4. 88. but it must bee
expected that   they can come hither
15. n3. 68. 62. 13. 45. 25. 3. 83. 39. 31. n3. 64.
the Rebels will haue in our quarters   a g o o
n3. 357. 59. 89. 03. 211. e5. 45. 75. 65. 85. 339. 59. 89. 16. 18. 46. 49.
b o d y of f o o te and then it will not b
6. 85. 21. 44. 5. 67. k1. 8. 45. 47. 80. 3. 21. n3. 50. 90. e4. 02. k1. 78. 9.
                                                    o o
                                                44. 47.

84

foo 4 e a l sh e n o u g h t o d r a l
44.47.79.4.88.16.27. m3.3.50.44.74.18.38. n1.6.1.15.

& with th e m + h o s e horse
2. p5. n3. 24. 78. 38. 47. 58. 1. 82. 214. will bee exposed to th

that the horse so now ha
same hazards and inconveniences. n2. n3. 214. 02. n3. e1.

there are be s i d e s that the c o n t r y is
04.66.1. a2. a4.58.30.6.4.2.58. n2. n3.12. k2.80.65.68. th

so e a t e n u p not a
m2.4.14.80.2.49.87.77.37. that if wee have. n1.80.81.15

force that ca n s u p p o r t it s e l f e of put
186. n2. 02. 57. 76. 36. 34. 44. 66. 80. f2. 57. 4. 27. 9. 2. n4. k5.

fit to a n fiss u e q u i c k l y
f2. n1. 16. 49. 89. f1. 58. 76. 1. 82. 62. 75. 32. 13. 43. 28. 68. it

in t h o s e horse when y e o
will bee impossible. c5. 80. 38. 44. 58. 4. 214. 04. n3. 70. 12. 45.

m to s u b s i s t
25. 85. n1. 59. 76. 22. 58. f1. 79. 89. it is therefore proposed in

it be not
your high whether upon this occasion f2. a4. n1. 80. 81

necessary for P. Rupert to m a r c h hi
50. 3. 11. 1. 57. 58. 16. 64. 69. c5. 354. n1. 24. 16. 65. 11. 40. 84. 38.

the r a s s t r o n g a s P. Rupert's an and
n3. 66. 10. 57. 87. 58. 80. 04. 44. 50. 19. 90. 15. 58. 354. 62. a1. n

t r a m e o u r b o d y off an army he
8. 65. 15. 25. 2. 3340. 74. 64. 84. 21. 47. 7. 70. k1. 17. 49. 106. 64.

r a b o u t s with o u t which not son l y
65. 16. 23. 46. 76. 80. 60. p5. 46. 77. 79. 70. n1. 80. 82. k2. 28. 6

the kings c o n u n c t i o n with yo u will be
n3. 241. 57. 87. 17. k2. 30. 77. 50. 13. 78. k2. p5. 69. 47. 75. 03. n4.

i m p o s s i b l e but he will be in danger of be ing
33. 26. 96. 46. 57. 60. 31. 21. 28. 1. b1. 04. 03. n4. e5. 154. k1. n4. e5.

be s i d g e d here and th e n P. Rupert will be
19. 81. n4. 58. 1. 31. 6. 18. 2. 5. e3. 3. a1. n3. 49. 354. 03. n4. 186

forced to m a r c h hi there to r e l i e
6. 86. n1. 26. 17. 66. 12. 39. 89. 40. 33. n3. 65. n1. 66. 4. 29. 1.

u e him u p one wor s e t i a t
77. 3. 88. 40. 30. 24. 84. 74. 35. k2. 56. 47. 66. 57. 2. 82. 8. 2. 16. 6.

m e s the n now to pre u e n t a ll thi
24. 1. 58. n3. 48. n3. n1. 35. 65. 3. 76. 1. 50. 80. 83. 16. 28. 27. n

the d i s t r e s s e of the
the truth is that. n3. 88. 7. f1. 79. 65. 1. 57. 60. 4. k1. 11. 39. 4.

s t r
58. 80. 1. 66. 86. 90. is an vnhappy obiection; but since y

ny can not be l e u e to p l a
high sayes you. b2. n1. 66. 1. 27. 14. 77. 2. n1. 35. 28. 15

13. 3.

c e without the t r a y n e and that it is not
13. 3. 25. k3. n3. 82. 80. 66. 16. 69. 49. 2. 21. n2. 2. 71. k1. 79.

p o s s i b l e for the king to b ring
89. 35. 46. 59. 58. 30. 21. 28. 4. 84. c5. n3. 241. n1. 22. 64. c5. 19.

thet r a y n e to P: Rupert that o i e e t i on e
n3. 80. c5. 15. c5. 1. n1. 354. n2. 45. 23. 33. 3. 12. 79. 30. k2. 12.

t a s t s by the Lawe off n e c e s s i t
15. 57. 2. 58. 25. n3. 28. 16. 55. 3. k1. 50. 3. 12. 4. 57. 60. 30.

70. 82. 90. This is all I have to say by his Ma: Comand
submittinge all to yr Highn: Judgment. I rest

Your Highnesse most faithfull
humble servant

George Delove

traine to P: Rupert that obiection c
eases by the lawe of necessity
y. This is all I have to say by his Ma*iestie*s Co*mm*and
submittinge all to *yo*ur Highn*ess* Judgment. I rest

Oxford
Aprill 27th   Your Highness most faithfull
1645   humble servaunt

George Digbye

*Lo*rd Digby to P Rupert
Aprill 27 1645 Oxford
Cromwells incursions into their
Quarters with 3000 horse & Dragoons
hath taken Bletchington howse. his
success may make him alter his designe
to joyne with Massey, & stay in these
p*ar*ts to hinder the K. from marching
to P.R. the K. desires PR to march
with his Army to Oxford

———

85
John Cotgrave (fl. 1655)
Wits interpreter, the English Parnassus. Or, A sure guide to those admirable accom-
plishments that compleat our English gentry, in the most acceptable qualifications of
discourse, or writing.
London: N. Brooke, 1655
Folger C6370

John Cotgrave's *Wits Interpreter, The English Parnassus* is typical of the kind of miscellany volume that became popular in the mid-seventeenth century. It advertised
itself as "A sure Guide to those Admirable Accomplishments that compleat our
English *Gentry*, in the most acceptable Qualifications of *Discourse*, or *Writing*,"
accomplishments that would vouchsafe the reader access to "those pleasing
Witchcrafts of *Eloquence* and *Love*." Appended to the usual suspects of "New Songs,
Fanciers, Epigrames, Drollery, Letters, &c." was a surefire way of keeping love letters
secret: "Cardinal Richelieu's Key to his manner of writing Letters by Cyphers,"
which was "counted so rare a secret, and of such dangerous consequence if ill
imploy'd, that it was death in his army to have it or to make any use of it." Cotgrave
also supplies recipes "To make white Characters appear upon black paper," "That a
Letter may not be read unless it be dissolv'd in water," and one "That a letter may
not be seen by Star-light or Candlelight," as well as some replacement ciphers fea-
turing odd characters.

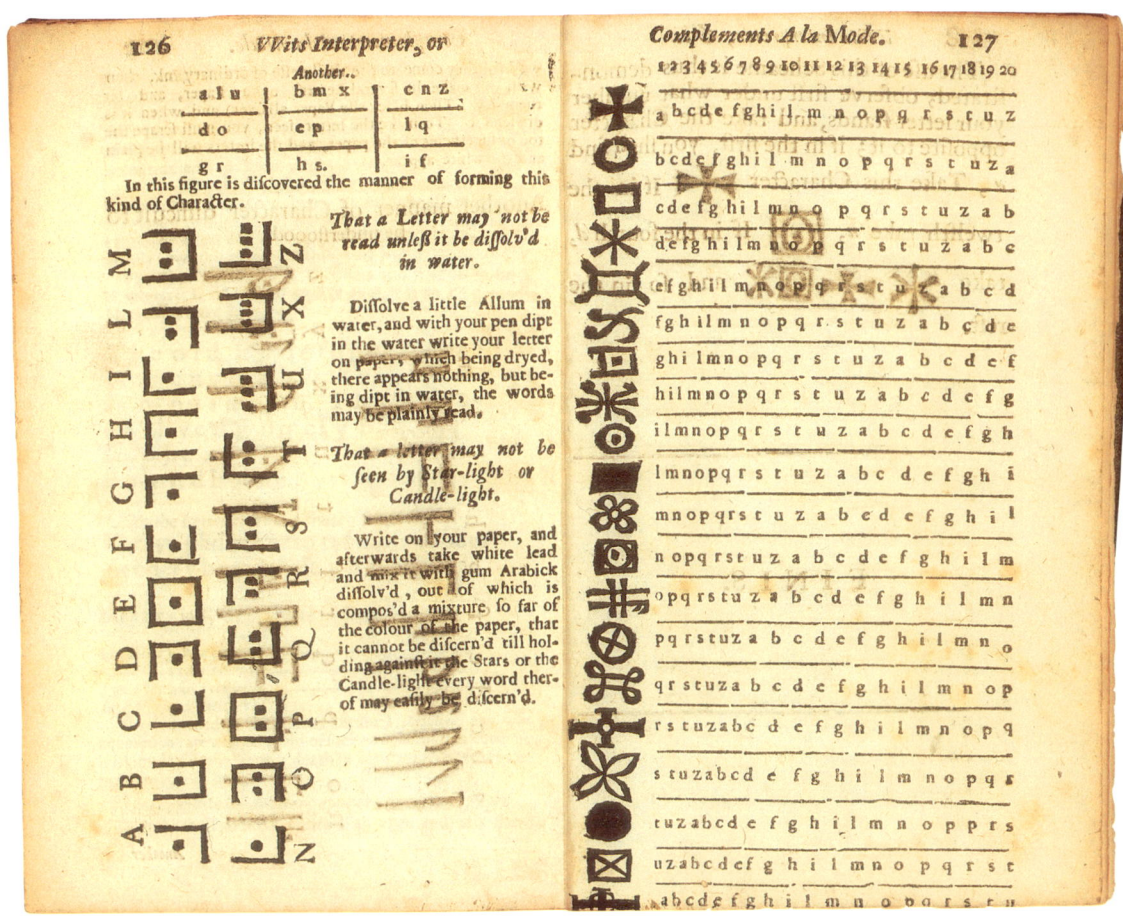

86
Isabel Kinardesley
Letter signed, to Walter Bagot
Loxley, July 27, 1609
Folger MS L.a.593
Reproduced at 90%

This emotional letter was written at a time when Isabel Kinardesley was, against her own will, separated from her husband and under physical threat from an unspecified "she" who, she claims, had planned "to haue thruste me downe the stayers & to haue broken my necke." Kinardesley begs Bagot "not to fayle" to represent her at the assizes—but just as importantly, not to "lett this my letter be seene" nor reveal "that any of this shoulde come from me, but by word of mouth to you," otherwise the messenger (the person carrying the letter) will be blamed. She claims that she is being held prisoner in her chamber, denied access to friends, and that "it is almost vnpossible for me to gett one to wryte for me." Once again, in the midst of this dramatic story, we see the central importance of the mechanics of letter-writing in the period: how Kinardesley needs someone to write for her, someone to deliver the letter, and for all involved to deny that such a letter ever existed.

To the wo.r Walter Bagot
Esq.r deliver these
at blithfeilde

Good Sr hauing dispenced somme parte of my mynde vnto you
at your last being at Loxley I had thoughte to haue sayrde
those thinges vnto you that now I ame force'd to weyte
vpon that instant beinge then put in daunger of my lyffe
for that shee had thoughte to haue thruste me downe the
stayers & to haue broken my necke had not you haue byne
so neere, which I stond daly in daunger of.

These are for gods cause and as euer you loued god or
any good christian to stand my good frende so muche as to
speake for me vnto my husband at the sisses, and that then you
my husband and Mr Richarde will apoynte somme tyme to make
amendes of this businesses heere at Loxley with earnest expeditiõ
For If greate spuches may preevayle the treuthe shall alwayes
be as it is now, drowned in the osion of oblivion and the certinty
of thinges neuer comme to lyghte, that my husband and I
mayse either live as man & wiffe ought to doe or ells that he woûl
showe any lawfull and Just cause why I should not (As
I thanke god he cannot) but that I may liue with him as
man and wyffe oughte to liue to gether, But to liue this vngodly
lyffe contrairy to al mankynde besides it is a greate greiffe to me
and a greatre daunger to our soules, beinge that we make
our promysses before the most almyghtye god to ths contrary
and for to liue this vngodly lyffe it is the greatst greiffe to
my soule But god he knowes ther is no defaulte in me.
If that my Husband will not, that then I may departe in
quietnesse hauing so resonnable aportion as I had when
I was at Dupster which was to my greefe to repeen both
that & this you partly knowing what a good dowrey
hee had with me bothe in Landes and goudes.

490

Lett me intreat you not to foyle me at the Sisses because of
my wretched estate, I beseeche you as I haue made my
selfe boulds to trubell you so I proye you that you
willnot lett this my letter be seene nor that any of this
shoulds come from me, but by word of mouth to you
at your being at Loxley for feere of further blame of
the meisenger For as I ame kepte as a poore prisnon heere
inmy chaumber and connot goe abraude so lickewisse
is expelled all people out of my presence that it is almost
vnpossible for me to gett one to wryte for me but that god
of his great goodnes dothe rayse frendes for them that put
theyr trust in him, or so much as once let me speke with
any: but they strayght doe mak great matters of suspitie
vpon it being with out cause atall and as god shall me
saue this is treew: thus in hast I leaue you to the tuition
of almyghty god Loxley this present xxvij th day of July 1609

                    your louing frende

                        Isabell Kinardesley

To the wor*shipfull* Walter Bagot
Esq*uire* deliver these
at blithfeilde

Thus

Good S*ir* hauing dispenced some parte of my mynde vnto you
at your last being at Loxley I had thoughte to haue sayed
those thinges vnto you that now I ame forc'd to wryte
vpon that instant beinge then put in daunger of my lyffe
for that shee had thoughte to haue thruste me downe the
stayers & to haue broken my necke had not you haue byne
so neere, which I stand daly in daunger of.
        These are for godes cause and as euer you loued god or
any good Christian to stand my good frende so muche as to
speake for me vnto my husband at the sisses, and that then you
my husband and Mr Ridiarde will apoynte some tyme to make
amende of this businesses heere at Loxley with ernest expeditio*n*
For If great speeches may prevayle the truthe shall always
be as it is now, drowned in the oscion of oblivion and the certenty
of thinges neuer come to hyghte, That my husband and I
maye ether live as man & wiffe ought to doe or ells that he wolde
showe any lawfull and Just cause why I shoulde not, (As
I thanke god he cannot) but that I may liue with him as
man and wyffe oughte to liue together, But to liue this vngodly
lyffe contrary to al mankynded besides it is a greate greeffe to me
and a greatere daunger to our soules, beinge that we made
our promysses before the most almyghtye god to the contrary
and for to live this vngodly lyffe it is the gretest greeffe to
my sowle But god he knowes ther is no defaulte in me.
If that my Husband will not, that then I may departe in
quietnesse hauing so resonnable a portion as I had when
I was at Vtuxeter which was to my greefe to repeete both
that & this you partly knowing what a good dowrey
hee had with me bothe in Landes and Gooudes.

Lett me intreate you not to fayle me at the sisses because of
my wretched estate, I beseeche you as I haue made my
selfe bould to trubell you so I praye you that you will not
lett this my letter be seene nor that any of this
shoulde come from me, but by word of mouth to you
at your being at Loxley for feere of further blame of
the meisenger, For as I ame kepte as a poore prisnor heere
in my chaumber and cannot goe abraude so lickewisse
is expelled all people out of my presence & that it is almost
vnpossible for me to gett one to wryte for me but that god
of his great goodness dothe rayse frendes for them that put
theyr trust in him, or so much as once let me speeke with
anye but they straght doe mak great matters of susspitio*n*
vpon it being with out cause atall and as god shall me

saue this is trew thus in hast I leaue you to the tuition
of Almyghty god   Loxley this present xxvijth day of July 1609

your louing frende

Isabell Kinardesley

———

87
Elizabeth Knyvett
Autograph letter signed, to Roger Townshend
Ashwellthorpe, December 11, 1626
Folger MS L.d.386
Reproduced at 100%

Elizabeth Kynvett, writing with family news to her nephew Roger Townshend, demonstrates the simultaneous pleasures and dangers of letterwriting: by writing she unburdens herself, but by setting down her thoughts on paper she runs the risk of being read by others. "I pray lett this be burnt, to tell no tales," she orders Townshend, before admitting "Yet is it som ease to my Hart; to vtter my Greife." Many letters survive with the instruction to "burn this letter"—often in a post-script, as in Folger MS L.d.628, a letter to Townshend from Henry Woodhouse which contains as an afterthought the command "I pray burne this letter. . . ." Of course, that they survive to this day betrays the fact that, for whatever reason, the recipients could not bring themselves to destroy their correspondence.

[superscription]   To my Honored & Beloued Ne=
                    phew Sir Roger Townshend
                    at Rainham giue these

[letter]   Honored Sir//
        To heare of your good health & safe Returne, I do much Reioyce: My Daugh*ter*
Receiued a Testimony of y*our* Loue, for w*hich* she thinkes her selfe highly Honored by you.
And if she could but find out such another Messenger *tha*t might haue *the* same acceptance
from you, she would haue Auns*wered* your Lett*er*s. If I should not be to Troublesom: I would
make you Partaker of my Occurrences here. I haue oftentimes tould my Cos*en* Sidley
since he would not lett his Kinseman Marry before he cam of Age; *tha*t he should not be
2 Daies Elder, before I would haue them Marrried: so he did Consent therto for a
great while; saing t͡he 5th of February was his Birth Day. And now he will not lett
them Marry vntill Easter; it is Deferred som 7 weekes because of his Grandm*other*s Re=
ligeon. And I had rather they had Married in Lent: to avoid Superstition & also for
Privacy sake: For neyther is my Sones House, nor his Estate fitt to make it a Publike
meeting. Indeed this protracting is a great vexation to me. I do not speak this to
alter, any of your Resolutions; for if you be reddy to pay; I am reddy to Receiue
with many thankes, for houlding so long.
I am suar M^r. Mason told you whatt a Suit I made to y*o*u for *the* Nomin*ation* of a Bayleif: so I
thank him, he Sollicited my Suit to *the* Next High Sher*iff* Ther was no hurt in this. After my
Son Groos Cam Down, ther was one made Suit to my Son Kny*vett* for his Lett*er* when I
heard it, I tould him it was to late; for I had already written for a Friend of mine. (Now I

must tell you; I first asked my Son, if he had any Mind to itt, before I would write for my Frind. He Aunswer. No, he Cared not who had it). Notwithstanding did whatt I could; I tould I took it very vnkindly, nay for a great wrong; *that* he would so oppose me. Yet did he send away his Man with great violence; I having no opportunity to wright against him. I made full account I had lost it. But God *that* Guideth all thinges, to his owne Glory; Guided my Son Groos; who Auns*wered that* I had first spoken for it, & therefore he desired my Son Kny*vett* to excuse him. Now when I had gotten *the* history, I yielded it to him. This is my good Son, whom you haue praised so Highly. I pray lett this be burnt, to tell no tales. Yet is it som ease to my Hart; to vtter my Greife. I must be gone, wherfore since I cannot be at Hemsby; The next is to Lon*don* to M^r. Buckitts. when my Daugh*ter* is Married. M^r. Mason wrott me word of M^r. Noah his Counsaile must cost me 40^s But I would faine Know if he do Prophecy good vnto vs. You think, you shall sitt quiett now, for a wife; I protest, I cannot hould my Toung; Oh *that* I might liue to see you happely Married, then should I Desiar to go to Heaven, to carry *the* first Newes. Good Sir Pardon my Tædiousnes, And Now with my best Reme*m*brance of my vnfeigned Loue to you I Rest now & Euer

Your most Louing & poor Aunt

Elizabeth Knyuett

From Ashwelth

This -11- of Decemb*er* // 1626 -

87

To my Honored & Beloued Nephew Sir Roger Townshend
at Rainham giue these

Honored Sir//

To heare of your good health & safe Returne, I do much Reioyce: My Daugh[ter]
Received a Testimony of y[ou]r Loue, for w[hi]ch she thinkes her selfe highly Honored by you—
And if she could but find out such another Messenger y[a]t might haue y[e] same acceptance
from you, she would haue sun[t] your Lett. If I should not be to Troublesom; I would
make you Partaker of my Occurrencies here. I haue oftentimes tould my Cos: Bidleys—
since he would not lett his Kinseman Marry before he cam of age; y[a]t he should not be
3 Daies Elder, before I would haue them Married; so he did Consent therto for a
great while; saing y[e] 5[th] of February was his Birth Day. And now he will not lett
them Marry untill Easter; it is Deferred som—7—weekes, because of his Grandm[other]s Re-
ligeon. And I had rather they had Married in Lent; to auoid Superstition & also for
Priuacy sake. For neyther is my Sones House, nor his Estate fitt. to make it a Publike
meeting: Indeed this protracting is a great vexation to me. I do not speak this to—
alter any of your Resolutions; for if you be reddy to pay; I am reddy to Receiue
w[i]th many thankes, for houlding so long. —

I am suar M[r]. Mason tould you what a Suit I made to y[ou] for y[e] Nomin[ation] of a Bayleif: So I
thank him, he Sollicited my Suit to y[e] Next High Sher[iff]. Ther was no hurt in this. After my
Son Groos Cam Down, ther was one made Suit to my Son Kny. for his Lett. when I
heard it, I tould him it was to late; for I had already written for a Friend of mine. (Now I
must tell you; I first asked my Son, if he had any Mind to itt, before I would write for my Friend)
He Aunswea. No, he cared not who had it). Notw[i]thstanding did what I could; I tould I took it
very unkindly, nay for a great wrong; y[a]t he would so oppose me. yet did he send away his Man
w[i]th great violence: I hauing no opportunity to wright against him. I made full account I had
lost it. But God y[a]t Guidets all thinges, to his own Glory; Guided my Son Groos; who sun[t]
y[a]t I had first spoken for it, & therfore he desired my Son Kny. to excuse him. Now when I
had gotten y[e] victory, I yeilded it to him. This is my good Son, whom you haue praised so
Highly. I pray lett this be burnt, to tell no tales. yet is it som ease to my hart; to uter my
Greife. I must be gone. wherfore since I cannot be at Hemsby; The next is to Lon. to
M[r]. Bucketts. when my Daugh. is Married. M[r]. Mason wrott me word of M[r]. Noah
his Counsaile must cost me—40[s]. But I would faine know if he do Prophecy good unto us—
you think, you shall sitt quiet now, for a wife; I protest, I cannot hould my Toung; O y[a]t I
might Liue to see you happely Married, then should I Desiar to go to Heauen, to carry y[e]
First Newes. Good Sir Pardon my Tediousnes, And Now w[i]th my best Remebrance of
my Unfeigned Loue to you I Rest now & Euer

Your most Louing & poor Aunt

From Ashwells.
this—11—of Decemb. // 1626—

Elizabeth Knyuett

James I's secret letters: a case study

Robert Carr was twenty-three years old—"straight-limbed, well-favored, strong-shouldered, and smooth-faced, with some sort of cunning and show of modesty"—when he came to King James's attention in 1607 by falling off a horse during a court joust and breaking his leg. The king involved himself personally with Carr's recuperation, and before long Carr had won his affections: James, it was said, "leaneth on his arm, pinches his cheek, smoothes his ruffled garment, and, when he looketh at Carr, directeth discourse to divers others" (Henry Harington, ed., *Nugae Antiquae* (London, 1804), 390-97). Over the next few years, James showered Carr with honors—making him a knight, a Gentleman of his Bedchamber, a viscount, a Knight of the Garter, a Privy Councillor, Lord Chamberlain, and ultimately earl of Somerset. When Carr fell in love with a married woman, Frances Howard, the countess of Essex, James smoothed the path to Frances's divorce and footed the bill for the elaborate wedding celebrations. But he was less amenable to Carr's friend Sir Thomas Overbury, who had a great influence over the favorite; James offered Overbury several postings overseas, and when he politely refused them, imprisoned Overbury in the Tower in April 1613, where he died later that year.

In September 1615, it was revealed that Overbury had been the victim of poison. An investigation revealed a complex plot involving an apothecary's boy, the Lieutenant of the Tower, The Lieutenant and the Deputy Keeper of the Tower, a woman named Mrs. Turner, and through her, the countess of Somerset. It seems that the Countess, disliking Overbury's hold on her husband, and well aware of his personal antipathy to her, had decided to get rid of him by poison. The earl and countess of Somerset were arrested. The countess confessed her part in the murder, but claimed that her husband was not involved. But James wanted the earl to confess—so that Somerset, an emotional man liable to violent outbursts, would not say anything compromising to the king in front of a packed court. As the May 1616 arraignment approached, James made increasingly frantic attempts to persuade Somerset to talk. Since Somerset was now being held in the Tower of London, in the custody of Sir George More, Lieutenant of the Tower, the King was forced to resort to a series of confidential messengers and secret letters. Four letters survive, two of them bearing James's personal seal (Folger MSS L.b.652, L.b.655).

First, James sent a personal messenger to Somerset in the Tower "with suche directions unto him, as if thaire be a sponke of grace lefte in him, I hoape thaye shall worke á goode effecte." He asked the new Lieutenant of the Tower, Sir George More, to allow him into Somerset's presence "in suche secreatie none liuing maye knowe of it & that after his speaking with him in priuate he maye be returned bakke againe as secreatlie" (Folger MS L.b.652).

When the first mission failed, James wrote to engage More's services to persuade Somerset to do "that, quhiche is both most honorable for me & his owin best." More was to assure him, in James's name, that if Somerset confessed his guilt to the commissioners before the trial, James would not only perform what he had promised through his previous messenger, but would "enlarge it." More should remind Somerset that last winter he had confessed to the prosecutor, Sir Edward Coke that "his cause was so euill lykelie, as he knew no iurie coulde quyte [acquit] him;" that it was feared that the Countess would plead only "weaklie for his innocencie;"

that the commissioners have "some secreate assu[ra]nce, that in the ende she will confesse of him"—all the while keeping James's involvement secret. To More, James noted that he did not mean that Somerset should confess if he were innocent, "but ye knowe how euill lykelie that is" (Folger MS L.b.653).

Even with the "enlarged" promises, More's attempts failed, prompting a third letter from the King. In this letter, we perhaps get nearest to understanding what James feared from Somerset: "[G]od knowis it is only á trikke of his ydle braine, hoaping thairby to shifte his tryall, but it is easie to be seene, that he wolde threattin me, with laying an asperion upon me of being in some sorte accessorie to his cryme." Now, James orders, Somerset should write or send a message to James "concerning this poysoning"— but it must not be a private letter since "I can not heare á priuate message from him without laying an aspersion upon my selfe of being an accessorie to his cryme." Once again we see the double-edged nature of the personal letter. James asks More to "urge him by reason, that I refuse him no fauoure quhiche I can graunte him without taking upon me the suspition of being guiltie of that cryme quhairof he is accused" (Folger MS L.b.654).

As the date for the arraignment grew nearer, Somerset's behaviour became more bizarre until, in a "strainge fitte," he refused point blank to attend his own trial. James insisted that unless he was "ather apparantlie seike or distractid of his wittes" the trial was not to be delayed; if he was, then the trial would be adjourned for a few days, in which time "if his sikenesse or madnesse be counterfitted it will manifestlie appeare" (Folger MS L.b.655).

The Somersets were tried separately in May 1616, both found guilty, and sentenced to death. While Somerset was being tried on May 25, James was at Greenwich, "so extreme sad and discontented, as he did retire himself from all company, and did forbear both dinner and supper until he had heard what answer the Earl had made"(Edward Sherburn to Dudley Carleton, May 31, 1616, National Archives, Kew, SP14/87/40). Anthony Weldon later alleged that James had spent the entire day in "restless motion," "sending to every boat he saw landing at the bridge, cursing all that came without tidings." To Weldon this was evidence that "all was not right, and there had been some grounds for his fears of Somerset's boldness" (Walter Scott, ed., *Secret History of the Court of James the First* (Edinburgh, 1811), vol.1, pp. 411–12, 424). James still feared that Somerset might be prone to an outburst in court. "It seemed something was feared should in passion have broken from him," wrote Edward Sherburn, "but when his Majesty had heard that nothing had escaped him more than what he was forced to answer to the business then in hand, his Majesty's countenance soon changed, and he hath ever since continued in a good disposition." Whatever secrets Somerset knew about James, he had not spilled them, and he escaped with his life: the Somersets were held in the Tower until January 1622, after which they were permitted to reside at fixed places and ultimately granted formal pardons. Somerset never regained James's affection and died in relative obscurity in July 1645.

88
James I (1566–1625)
Autograph letter signed, to Sir George More, with seal
May 9, 1616
Folger MS L.b.652

[letter]

Goode sir george as the onlie confidence I hadde in your honestie made me
without the knowledge of any, putte you in that place of truste quhiche
ye nou posesse, so muste I nou use youre truste & secreatie ~~for~~ ^in^ a thing
greatlie concerning my honoure & seruice, ye knowe Somersettis daye
of tryall is at hande & ye knowe also quhat faire meanis I haue
usid to moue him by confessing the trewthe to honoure god & me
& leaue some place for my mercie to worke upon, I haue nou at last
sent the bearare heerof, an honeste gentleman & quho once follo ^wid^
him, with suche directions unto him, as if thaire be a sponke of grace
lefte in him, I hoape thaye shall worke á goode effecte, my onlie de
syre is, that ye wolde make his conuoye unto him in suche secreatie
none liuing maye knowe of it & that after his speaking with him
in priuate he maye be returned bakke againe as secreatlie, so repo=
sing my selfe upon youre faithfull & secreate handling of this busienesse,
I bidde you hairtelie fairwell.

James R.

[endorsement]

9th of May. about
one of the clock in
the afternoone _____ 1616.

[later endorsement]

Letter from King James the first
his own hand Writing, to
Sir George More, Lieutaneant of the Tower

————

89
James I (1566–1625)
Autograph letter signed, to Sir George More
May 13, 1616
Folger MS L.b.653
Reproduced at 98%

Goode sir george althogh I feare that the laste message I sent
to youre infortunate prisoner shall not take the effecte that
I wishe it shoulde, yett I can not leaue of to use all meanes
possible to ~~mak~~ moue him to doe that, quhiche is both most
honorable for me & his owin best. ye shall thairfore
giue him assurance in my name, that if he will yett before
his tryall confesse cleerelie unto the comissionars his guil=
tienesse of this fact, I will not onlie performe quhat I pro=
meised by my last messinger, both towardis him & his

Goode Sir george althogh J feare, that the laste message J sent

to youre infortunate prisoner, shall not take the effecte that

J wishe it shoulde, yett J can not leaue of to use all meanes

possible to ~~will~~ moue him to doe that quhiche is both most

honorable for me & his owin best. ye shall thairfore

giue him assurance in my name, that if he will yett before

his tryall confesse cleerelie unto the comissionars his guil-

tinesse of this fatt, J will not onlie performe quhat J pro-

meased by my last messinger, both towardis him & his

wyfe, but J will enlarge it, according to the phrase of the

ciuill lawer, quod gratiæ sunt amplianda, J meane not that

he shall confesse if he be innocent, but yett nowe howe

euill lyke lie that is & of youre selfe ye maye discusse

with him, quhat shoulde meane his confidence now to endure

a tryall, quhen as he rembers that this last wenter he confes-

sid to the cheefe iustice that his cause was so euill lyke lie, as

he knew no iurie coulde quyte him, assure him that J protes-te

upon my honour, my ende in this is, for his & his wyffes goode, & will
doe well lyke ueryes, of youre selfe to caste out unto him, that ye feare
his wyfe shall pleade weaklie for his innocencie & that ye fynde,
the comissioners haue, ye know not how, some secreate assurance,
that in the ende sho will confesse of him, but this muste be layed
as from youre selfe, & thairfore ye muste not lette him knowe
that I haue written unto you, but onlie that I sent you priuatelie
to deliuer him this message, lett none liuing knowe of this & if it
take goode effecte, moue him to sende in haiste for the comissioners
to giue thaime satisfaction, but if he remaine obstinate, I desyre
not that ye shoulde trouble me with an ansoure, for it is to no
ende & no newis is bettir then euill newis, & so fair well &
god blesse youre labours.

James R

wyfe, but I will enlarge it, acording to the phrase of the
ciuill lawe, quod gratiæ sunt ampliandæ, I meane not that
he shall confesse if he be innocent, but ye knowe how
euill lykelie that is & of youre selfe ye maye dispute
with him, quhat shoulde meane his confidence nou to endure
á tryall, quhen as he rem[em]bers that this last winter he confes
sid to the cheefe iustice that his cause was so euill lykelie, as
he knew no iurie coulde quyte him, assure him that I protes$_\wedge$te$_\wedge$

[verso]

upon my honour, my ende in this is for his and his wyefes goode. ye will
doe well lyke wayes, of your selfe to caste out unto him, that ye feare
his wyfe shall pleade weaklie for his innocencie & that ye fynde
the comissioners haue, ye know not how, some secreate assurance,
that in the ende she will confesse of him, but this muste onlie be
as from your selfe, & thairfore ye muste not lette him knowe
that I haue written unto you, but onlie that I sent you priuate worde
to deliuer him this message, lett none liuing knowe of this, & if it
take goode effecte, moue him to sende in haiste for the comissioners
to giue thaime satisfaction, but if he remaine obstinate, I desyre
not that ye shoulde trouble me with an ansoure, for it is to no
ende & no newis is bettir then euill newis, & so fair well &
god blesse youre labours.

James R.

[endorsement]   13th of May 1616.

———

90
James I (1566–1625)
Autograph letter signed, to Sir George More
May 1616
Folger MS L.b.654

Goode sir george I ame extreamelie sorie that youre unfortunate
prisoner turnis all the greate caire I haue of him, not onlie against
him selfe, but against me also, as farre as he can, I can not blame
you, that ye can not coniecture quhat this maye be, for, god knowis
it is only á trikke of his ydle braine, hoaping thairby to shifte
his tryall, but it is easie to be seene, that he wolde threattin me,
with laying an asperion upon me of being in some sorte acces=
sorie to his cryme, I can doe no more, (since god so abstractes his
grace from him,) then repeate the substance of that letre quhich
the lorde haye sent you yester night, quhiche is this, if he
wolde writte or sende me any message concerning this poy$_\wedge$soning$_\wedge$
it needis not be priuate, if it be of any other bussienesse, that
quhiche I can not nou with honoure ressaue priuatlie, I maye
doe it after his tryall & serue the turne as well, for ex$_\wedge$cepte$_\wedge$

ather his tryall, or confession præcede, I can not heare á
priuate message from him without laying an aspersion upon
my selfe of being an accessorie to his cryme, & I praye
you to urge him by reason, that I refuse him no fauoure ∧~~quhiche~~ quhiche I can graunte him∧ with∧out∧
taking upon me the suspition of being guiltie of that cryme

[left margin, vertical]

quhairof he is accused & so fairwell.

James R.

———

91
James I (1566–1625)
Autograph letter signed, to Sir George More, with seal
May 1616
Folger MS L.b.655

[superscription]

To o*ur* trustie and well
beloued *Sir* george more
knight o*ur* lewetenent of
o*ur* tower of London

[letter]

Goode sir george, for ansoure to youre straunge newis, I ame
first to tell you, that I expecte the lorde haye & sir robert
carr haue bene with you before this tyme, quhiche if thaye
haue not yett bene, doe ye sende for thaime in haiste that
thaye maye first heare him, before ye saye any thing unto him,
& quhen that is done, if he shall still refuse to goe, ye muste
doe youre office, excepte he be ather apparantlie seike or distrac=
tid of his wittes, in any of quhiche cacis ye maye aquainte the
chancellaire with it, that he maye adiorne the daye till
mondaye nexte, betwene & quhiche tyme, if his sikenesse
or madnesse be counterfitted it will manifestlie appeare, in
the meanetyme I doubte not but ye haue acquainted the chancellair
with this strainge fitte of his & if upon these occasions
ye ~~brig~~ bring him á litle laiter then the houre appointed, the
chancellaire maye in the meanetyme protracte the tyme the
best he maye, quhom I praye ~~your~~ you to acquainte lykeways
with this my ansoure as well as with the accident, if he haue saide
any thing of moment to the lorde haye I expecte to heare of it
with all speede, if otherways, lette me not be trublit with it

[left margin, vertical]

till the tryall be past. fairwell. James R.

92
Coversheet to James I letters
with L.b.652–655

Sir George More evidently valued these four handwritten letters from James I,
placing them in a special envelope in which they have survived to this day.
According to a label on the envelope by his descendants, Sir George More "in his
Lifetime made mutch accoump of these lettors beinge euery word of Kinge James
his owne wryghtinge."

These 4 lettors weare all of Kinge James his
Owne hand wryghtinge, Sent to Sir George
More, Liftennant of *the* Tower, (beinge putt in
to that place by his owne apoyntment without
*th*e Priuitie of any Mann) Concerninge my
Lorde of Sommersett, whoe beinge in
the Tower, and ∧heringe∧ that he should come to
his arrayngnement begann to speak Bigg
woordes Tuchinge on *the* Kinges reputatio*n*
and Honnour,   The Kinge Therfore
desird as mutch as he Cowld to make
him Confes The poysoninge of Sir Thomas
Ouerberry, and so not to Come to his A[rray]
ngnement but to Cast him Selue on his
Mercye / But beinge a Courtiour and Beaten
to those Courses, woold not. // ffully Imagi=
ninge that the ∧kinge∧ Durst not; or woold not
bringe him to his Tryall. The Gentlema*n*
the Kinge sent in one of *the* Letters to my
Lord wase Waltor James soomtime my Lordes
Secretarye. But *the* Kinge althoughe he weare
the wissest to woorke his Owne endes that euer
wase before him, it all that Could not woorke on Somersett

[left margin,
vertical, lineation
not maintained]
But that he euer stoode on his innocency, and woold neuer
 be brought to Confes that he had any hand with his wyfe
in *th*e poysoninge of Ouerberye, knewe not of it, nor Consented vnto itt,
And I haue often tawlked with m^r James his Chyfe servant aboute it, whoe
euer wase of Opinion *tha*t my Lord wase Cleere and his Ladye only
Guyltie. for one time m*istr*is Tournor tolde him, that littell did my Lord
knowe what she had aduentured for his Ladye: but *the* Trewth ∧is∧ Kinge
James wase wearye of him: Buckingham had supplyed his place:

[endorsement]   4 Letters of kinge James his owne wryghtinge

Sir George Mores my father in Lawes Legacie. whoe in his Lifetime made
mutch accoump of these lettors beinge euery word of Kinge James his owne
wryghtinge. James *the* first:

OVIDIVS NASO

OVIDS
HEROICALL
Epistles.
Englished by W. S.

Veniam pro laude
peto ————

—— nunc mitibus
Mutaræ quæro Tristia

Second Edytion

The afterlife of letters

READING A PERSONALLY-ADDRESSED LETTER may seem to us the most
private of activities. But once again we need to un-think our instinctive reactions
to letters to understand how they operated in early modern England. As we have
already seen, there was a good likelihood that a secretary might be involved in the
penning, and possibly even the composition of, supposedly "private" letters. Those
letters would be transported by a third party, the bearer, who might be entrusted
with a verbal message to complement the letter. And the letter, once received, might
well be read by people other than its named recipient. There is ample evidence that
letters were read aloud, lent to friends and family, and even circulated more widely.

The Cavendish-Talbot collection at the Folger yields a variety of circulating
letters. When James VI of Scotland came to the English throne in March 1603,
Gilbert Talbot, 7th earl of Shrewsbury, wrote from Whitehall Palace to his friend Sir
John Harpur in Derbyshire to let his friends in Derbyshire and Staffordshire know
that he might well be entertaining the new king at his estate at Worksop (indeed,
(the king spent the night of April 20 at Worksop, en route from Edinburgh to
London). He asked for their company, with the jocular stipulation that they bring
extra fat capons, hens, or partridges. The earl clearly wrote with the intention that
his letter would be circulated; the Folger's copy (Folger MS X.d.428 (116)) is in the
hand of one John Curzon, who adds a postscript stating that he had received the letter
from his cousin Harpur so that his friends could consider it. In the same collection
of letters, Gilbert's father, George, 6th earl of Shrewsbury, writes to his wife Elizabeth
(Bess of Hardwick) that he enjoyed her letters so much that he sent them to Gilbert,
and mentions in other letters to her that he is enclosing letters that he has already
read (X.d.428 (89, 93, 97)). In most cases, the original sender would assume that his
letter would be passed around, unless he specified otherwise.

The reading of a letter was an integral part of the letter's transaction. Bearers
were sometimes ordered to watch for the recipient's reaction, and quite frequently
surviving letters contain accounts of responses to letters. Sometimes these are fleeting
impressions—"I delivered your letter to Justice Warburton who smyled before he
opened it & said he did imagyne what was the cause . . ." (Folger MS L.e.579).
Sometimes, however, the reports are more complex: "the letter which I brought
hither seemed a surprise & trouble to the receiver, who red it presently by mee, so I
observed it to be a long & puzleing letter: immediatly he told his Lady, who came
in, & mee the import of it . . ." (Folger MS Add 902).

Dutch genre painters were the first to include letters in scenes of everyday life.
In the mid-seventeenth century, artists such as Gerard van ter Borch, Jan Steen, and
Johannes Vermeer began depicting the wide range of emotions that could be evoked
by the receipt and reading of a letter, ranging from wistfulness to pleasure, anxiety,

and despair. Letterwriters and readers were shown alone in their closets, as well as in taverns or in the presence of servants, secretaries, or messengers. These epistolary scenes portray letters as ubiquitous, powerful, and often intense documents, capable of transforming the lives of their recipients in a myriad of ways.

John Donne writes to Sir Henry Goodyer that his letters "are permanent, for in them I may speake to you in your chamber a yeare hence before I know not whom, and not heare my selfe" (*Poems*, 1635, p. 292). Donne's observation speaks to the afterlife of letters—the realization that once a letter leaves his hands, he no longer has control over the trajectory of its words. His letter remains a living testimonial that could be read and reread, not just by the recipient at the moment of its receipt, but a year from thence, by anyone. As we have seen earlier, even a request to have a letter burned did not ensure its "impermanence" (item 87). It is difficult to know what percentage of letters were saved by their owners, and likewise, what percentage of these saved letters have survived, but items 103–106 indicate that letters were preserved for a variety of reasons. And household manuals such as Thomas Lupton's *A thousand notable things of sundrie sorts* (London, 1579), with its recipes for preventing mice from eating letters and for treating paper so it won't burn, suggest that preservation was taken seriously, both for record-keeping purposes and sentimental reasons.

What happened to a letter after it was read? The recipient, or his clerk or secretary, would often fold the letter and write on the top of the outer leaf an endorsement consisting of the date, and/or the name of the sender, and/or a brief summary of the letter. The letter would then be filed in a bundle, alongside copies or drafts of relevant outgoing correspondence, with the endorsements easily visible for quick recall and retrieval. Contemporary *trompe l'oeil* paintings show letters folded back into their original form and tucked haphazardly in wall-mounted letter racks, but it is unknown if this was an artistic device or an actual method of keeping letters. Some business letters and receipts have holes in the upper left corner, indicating that they may have been strung together and hung from a wall, as they are depicted in Dutch paintings of lawyers' offices.

Letters could take on a talismanic quality, serving as a substitute for the absent sender. Queen Elizabeth famously preserved Leicester's last letter in a box by her bed, and endorsed it, "Leicester's last letter." Likewise, Sir Walter Bagot endorsed a packet of his son's letters, "Lewes his last *letters*" (item 19) and Mary Hatton and Randolph Helsby both endorsed each other's courtship letters with each other's names and the date (item 50). The last entries in John Martin's unfinished letterbook consist of copies of his wife's first and last letters to him (item 103).

Personal letterbooks took many forms. They could contain copies of letters actually sent and received by the compiler, as well as letters collected by him or her—including copies of historical, scurrilous, or anonymously-written letters that circulated widely (and may have been, in fact, intended for "scribal publication"), letters taken from printed books, advice letters from parents, letters preserved for legal and financial reasons, or letters simply worthy of imitation. Lydia Dugard kept a letterbook in which she transcribed all of her letters to her cousin Samuel. On at least one occasion, however, the imminent departure of a messenger prevented her from having time to make a copy, leading her to ask: "pray cousin will you doe so much as send me this letter again tis call'd for, and so I cant have time to transcribe it. I know it is not worth it but Im loath to break an old custome. dont forget to send it" (X.d.477 (22)).

A considerable number of the manuscript volumes that survive from the sixteenth and seventeenth centuries are collections of what might loosely be termed "state papers" —documents pertaining to the political, parliamentary, governmental, diplomatic, court and military issues of the day, many of them naturally in letter form. It seems that individuals were drawn to the idea of having in their possession a set of such documents, partly out of historical interest, and partly as a repository of information and models for future documents. From the English Civil War onwards, these manuscript collections started to appear in printed form—perhaps because of the radical changes in the country's government, printers and booksellers felt what had previously been state secrets, *arcana imperii*, were now fit materials for popular consumption. Alongside such general collections as the *Cabala*, *Scrinia Ceciliana*, and *The Compleat Ambassador* were letter books publishing the correspondence of individuals such as Francis Bacon, John Donne, and Tobie Matthew.

All too often surviving early modern letters tell only half their story. Letters were often, literally and figuratively, covers for other documents or objects, and frequently we only have a tantalizing mention in the letters of what they once enclosed or covered. Some of these enclosures were quite prosaic—receipts and bills. But sometimes a letter would contain other letters, perhaps letters to be distributed within a household or a small community, or letters to be read and then sealed and sent on. This sharing of letters, usually lost to history, is revealed in a letter dated May 26, 1600, from "Thro: kinfell" in Smithfield to John Ferrers, at "the Lady Puckerings house in Warwicke." Kinfell reveals that "at my Comming from home in the heate of all my busines I forgotte to send you the letter you lent me, which I haue now heere returned you with." He also prays Ferrers "also to be warie of distrebuteng to many Copies of that reformed poetrie you had of m^r Combes," testifying again to the copying and sharing of papers, and hinting at possible dangers (Folger MS L.e.664).

Even a cursory trawl through the Folger's manuscript collection reveals that letters could "enclose"—or their bearers could carry—virtually anything: six pairs of gloves (Folger MS X.c.51 (10)); some peaches, nectarines, and grapes (Folger MS Add 805 (1)); even "a fatt oxe (I hope)" (Folger MS X.c.51 (26)). Oxford student William Bagot, in a letter to his father Sir Walter Bagot, writes, "I haue sent you by this barer a pen knife the best that I coulde get being a smale remembrerance of my duti" (Folger MS L.a.176). Once again they suggest that the culture of letterwriting was wide-ranging in its practical implications—the basis for a whole set of social transactions that extended far beyond the written page.

93

Woman receiving a letter in her chamber, ca. 1690
Oil on oak panel (46 x 238 cm)
From the collection of George Way, Staten Island

The slyly-smiling woman standing in her bedchamber appears to refuse a letter from a bearer as two maidservants observe with undisguised curiosity. The scene is reminiscent of Dutch genre paintings of women reading and writing letters in intimate settings, with the familiar props of a curtained bed and a table accessorized with a mirror, a tortoise-shell comb, a round silver box, a silver candlestick, and a silver ewer and basin.

————

94

Man reading a letter, ca. late 17th century
Oil on oak panel (24.2 x 18.23 cm)
From the collection of George Way, Staten Island

In a spare interior, a well-dressed man with a gray beard sits in a red leather-backed chair at a simple wooden table covered in green cloth, concentrating on the contents of a letter. The letter rests on a writing box; next to the writing box are an inkwell, pen, and penknife, suggesting that he intended to reply to the letter. His walking stick leans against the wall; above it are a bookshelf and a circular object hanging from the wall.

————

95

Woman reading a letter, ca. 17th century
Oil on oak panel (223 x 19 cm)
From the collection of George Way, Staten Island

While reading a letter, an old woman casts a concerned glance in the direction of the man sitting opposite her, who is smoking a pipe and holding a glass of wine. In this typical Dutch tavern scene, a clay pipe rests on the table between them and a wooden tobacco-jar and clay pipe rest on a barrel in the foreground.

————

96

Katharine (Cromwell) Whitstones Jones (b. 1597?)
Autograph letter signed, to her cousin Mrs. Wind of Bargen
Ely, February 16, 1648/49
Folger MS X.c.53
reproduced at 100%

Two weeks after Charles I's execution, Oliver Cromwell's sister Katherine Whetstone Jones, writing to her cousin Mrs. Wind, declared that she would have sacrificed her own life to save the life of the king, a dangerous opinion to air in the Cromwell circle. Despite her openness in the confines of the letter, Whetstone Jones does her best to limit the effects of her letter: "I cowld & would saye more but I am afraid you will lett my letter bee seene by some *that* I desirs showld not see it, for my noble cousin your hu[s]band if hee peruse it I am content & desire it, hee can but laugh at the foolish, at best, weake expressions of a poore woman...."

[superscription]

ffor my honoured cousin
Mrs Wind, at hir house
in Bargen these

[letter]

Elye this 16th off ffebruarye 1648

Sweet cousin,

I acknowledg my selfe extreamlye oblieged to
you for your kinde letter, & had sattisfyed your
Noble ffather & husband's w*i*th your owne desires
w*i*th the newes of these parts out there needes
not my penn to declare wh*a*t is soe in the mouths
& eares of all men, allass deare cousin, I am
very darke & knowe not wh*a*t to Judge of sutch
high things they are farr aboue my capase
tye, I confess I was verye much troubled at
*tha*t strooke, wh*i*ch tooke the head of this poore King
dome from vs, & trulye had I bin able to haue
purchased his life, I am confident I couwld wth
all willingness haue layed downe mine, but
Gods word hath silenced mee for till I was
sett downe by yt I did nothing but murmur
neither indeed cowld I containe my selfe soe *tha*t I haue
now gotten, a name heere wh*i*ch I neuer had in Bargen, they
saye I am a royallist, the Lord make mee what hee
will haue mee to bee, soe shall I submitt to his
will in all things, & lett vs striue to posses our selues
w*i*th patience as well in the publique, as our more pri=
uate affayres, because will wee, or nill wee, the
counsell of the Lord shall stand, Oh how happye are
they *tha*t can saye from a singell true heart, the Lords will &
wayes are best, I wish & praye I maye attaine to it,
trulye cousin, you haue not a freind or seruant
*tha*t showld or would more faithfullye serue you then
my selfe, but soe longe as I am in the countrye, I can not
possible performe your commands, I hope eyre longe
to goe to London to see & speake w*i*th my brother, whoe I haue not seene a sight
since my comming ouer, & then I shall bee your humble seruant to my power, as
for the newes about Captaine Pye, I much reioyce I confess at any good that

shall befall him, but I beleiue hee allowes the good, or bad counsell of some, whoe
intended to worke mee discontent, I beseetch God forgiue them, but I am affraid
God will in the end lett them feele what now peraduenture they littell dreame of, I leaue
to the Lord & there owne contiencyes, & it may bee in time, hee will find the wronge hee

[verso]

hath had & done in listninge affter soe vnworthy people, for my
part they shall find I will not runn affter him as they peraduenture
Imagen, yet if I had binn with child as some of them, spake, I might haue bin inforsed to it,
I suffered more in Bargen, then euer I did in any place in my life,
but I am now gotten by prouidence vnder the wings of a deare and
tender mother, wheare as In either feele nor see the greatness
of the world soe I liue not in any want, saue what pleaseth the
Lord to deny mee, tis not Just a husband, for if it were, happelye
I might haue my desires, but were I worthy of the best man
of this Kingdome, & might haue him if I would, I deale trulye
with you & all the frends I haue in the world showld neuer
alter my determination, & yet I haue a brother tenders mee as
dearlye as a brother can doe, & I knowe will not deny mee any
thing, vppon good & Iust grounds I cowld & would saye more but
I am afraid you will lett my letter bee seene by some that I desire
showld not see it, for my noble cousin your hu[s]band if hee perused
I am content & desire it, hee can but laugh at the foolish, at
best, weake expressions of a poore woman, yet his true freind
& seruant, deare cousin I much reioyce to heare of the health
of your wholle ffamelye, the Lord in mercye continue it, I see
you are carefull to increase the world still, the Lord make you
a Joyfull mother, to the comfort of you & yours, I cowld wish I
were neare you to serue you in your need, to my power, bee
pleased to present my due respects to Sir Robert Wind, &
my worthy cousin your husband with your selfe, kiss littell Bette
from mee, my loue to all yours, assuring you I am,

Deare cousin

Your faithfull freind
& humble seruant
Ka Whitstones

praye cousin bee pleased to present
my respects to all that wish well
toe mee, Lauena presents her due
respects to you & all yours, shee is
eyre longe to goe from mee, my chilldren)
haue & doe finde a louing & carfull Vnkell I prayse God

[endorsement]

K Whitstone
1648
Feb 16

Lynches the 12th of ffebruary 1648

Sweet Cousin

acknowledg my self exceeding obliged to
you for your kindnesse that satisfyeth mee
... my ffather & ... your owne ...
... in the newes of ... parts but there needs
not my paine to ... you of ... in the younge
... of ... all as deepe cosins ... am
very loake ... not to trouble you wth such
sleight things they are far aboue my goods
... I confess twas ... much much ... at
... to wake the ... of this ... you ...
... confident I could to
... downe geuing ...
... all ... my fort ... I was
... wch is ...

to goe to London to see & speake wth my brother, whch I haue not ffroue as yet
since my comeing ouer & this shall bee your humble servant to my power as
for the nuers about Castynge Dyer, my cheife ioyes I confess at any good that
shall befall him, but I beliue hee followes the good or bad counsell of for, who
is mindes to worke mee discontent, soe helpe God forgiue them, but I am affrayd
God will in the end lett them feele what now peraduenture, they little dreame of leaue
to the Lord & there owne consciences, & it may bee in time hee will find the wrode his

he Whitstone
Feb 1648
16

... they shall ... listning to ... the ... [illegible handwritten text] ...

Dear Cusin

Your faithfull frend
& humble servant
R L

... Elnis, is write by ...
olive crommwells ... letter

97
Lydia Dugard (1650–1675)
Autograph letter signed, to Samuel Dugard
March 22, 1668
Folger MS X.d.477 (13)

Lydia Dugard's letter to her cousin Samuel Dugard has an ultimate motive beyond
enquiring about his poor health. Originally enclosed inside it was another letter
written by Lydia to one Mr. Jekyll, which she wants Samuel to read. If he thinks it
unsuitable to be passed on to Jekyll, Lydia asks that Samuel make her apologies to
Jekyll for not writing. If he thinks it suitable, however, Lydia asks that he will seal it
with his own seal, his "seal of approval" making it clear that he has read and
approved the letter.

Dear Cousin,

I was not a little troubled when I heard of the continuance of your
cough, fearing it would grew worse. but how I am cheered sinc you
told me the good news of its decrease, and put me in hopes it
will take a finall farwell: now I shall hope to be in health too,
for it was vain for me to think I could long be so when I
was tortured with tears you would be cough'd into a consumtion.
Cousin (however you may think or hope), I cant be well if y[ou]
are not. and if I have health at any time I could willingly [   ]
it if it would contribute to yours. but methinks my late reso[lve]
of being lese free in the expresion of my afection is soon forgotten
and broke. I hope you will not conclude from the breach of this
others are no better kept. You see I can't keep my heart lockt
and it wil not be hid from him that has it. nor will I endeavor
it should for the future but resolve against resolutions impossible
[to be] kept. Cousin this inclosed was half writ the last week; but
Carls playing the good husband came so soon I had not time
to finish it. it is unsealed that you may peruse it, and I refer
it to you whether to deliver it or not. if it have not your
approbation withhold it and excuse me to Mr Jekyll for not
writing. all are well here and salute you. Dear Cousin

March 22. 1668

your truly faithfull

youl seal Mr Jekylles letter
if you give it him

Lydia DuGard.

98

Cabala, mysteries of state, in letters of the great ministers of K. James and K. Charles. Wherein much of the publique manage of affaires is related. Faithfully collected by a noble hand

London: M.M., G. Bedell, and T. Collins, 1654 (i.e., 1653)

Folger C183 c. 1

This collection of nearly 200 letters dating from 1617 to 1625 was read by its original reader with pen in hand. Most of the letters are annotated and underlined, with the occasional query (i.e., "quaere if some amours were not between *the* Queen of fra*nce* and *the* Duke wh*ich* *the* King of Fra*nce* did vent") (p. 298). The letter shown here illustrates two layers of reactions to letters: the original sender of the letter reports the vacancy of the deanery of York to the duke of Buckingham, since the former dean of York was "struck dead suddenly, by a Letter, which one Dr. Scot procured from his Majestie, to be his Coadjutour," and the reader of this copy, who writes in the margin next to this passage: "struck dead with a letter from the King."

The Lord Keeper to the Duke. 99

3. If your Grace ſhall make him your ſervant with this favour ſo nobly condition'd, he hopes your Grace may proceed on with his Patent thus forward, without any ſtay for any other Corrival, which notwithſtanding he humbly refers.

4. But deſires, if his preſentment be accepted, he may have leave by me to render his thanks unto your Grace perſonally ſometime to morrow.

And ſo I leave your Grace for this time in Gods protection. And reſt

Yours, &c.

The Lord Keeper to the Duke. 24. December, 1624.

My moſt Gratious Lord,

I Moſt humbly beſeech your Grace for Gods ſake, and his Churches, to conſider of this motion, which I do make unto your Grace, concerning the Deanerie of *York* now vacant, the Dean being ſtruck dead ſuddenly, by a Letter, which one Dr. *Scot* procured from his Majeſtie, to be his Coadjutour.

It is not for any man in particular; but againſt Doctor *Scot*, that he may not by the importunity of any one upon your Grace be promoted to this place, being the ſixth, or ſeventh place of preferment Eccleſiaſtical within this Kingdom, but that your Grace would be pleaſed to remove Doctor *White*, or Doctor *Hall*, or whom your Grace ſhall pleaſe, unto this great Deanery, and beſtow the leſſer Deanerie (far above his merit) upon him.

For theſe Reaſons.

1. I know that he hath ſold away all his Livings which he hath had in this Church, and hath at this day never an one.

2. I am credibly informed, he oweth 5000 l. at the leaſt. A vaſt ſumme for a poor Scholar, and too much to be got up in a poor Church. And moſt of this money in York.

3. I know he is a great Gameſter, and of no fitting converſation for a Church-man; but of very mean parts, either of Learning, or government.

4. I am certified at this time, that he is a man often overſeen in drink; but this I do not know.

O 2 If

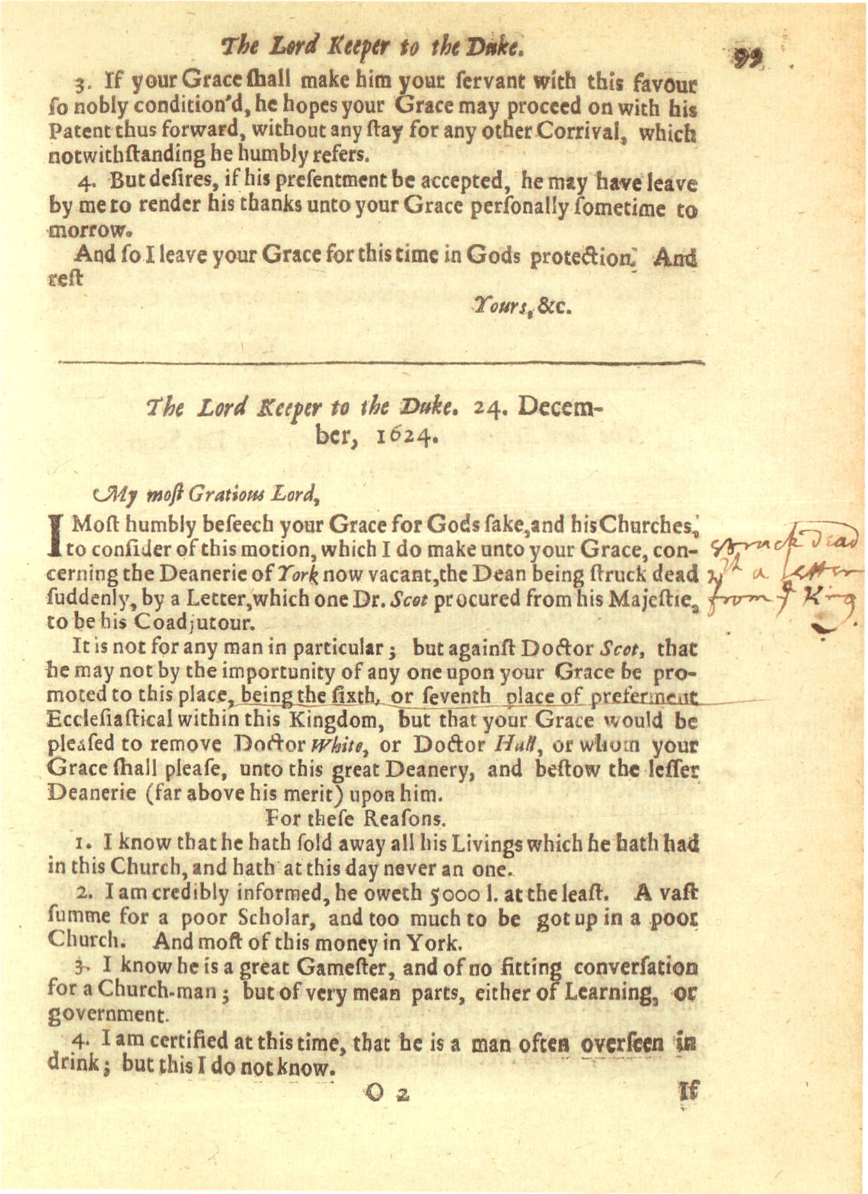

99

Ovid's heroicall epistles. Englished by W[ye] S[altonstall]
London: I. D[awson] for Michael Sparke Junior, 1639
Folger STC 18946

The engraved title page from the 1637 edition of *Ovid's heroicall epistles* has been added to some copies of the 1639 edition, including the Folger copy. The middle panels depict a lady and a knight (holding an inflamed heart) enthusiastically reading love letters received from each other.

100

William Shakespeare (1564–1616)
M. William Shak-speare: his true chronicle historie of the life and death of King Lear and his three daughters
London: printed [by Nicholas Okes] for Nathaniel Butter, 1608

One of the most moving moments in *King Lear* relies entirely on an appreciation of the culture of letterwriting. Cordelia hears of the sad fates of her father and Kent, and the cruel behavior of her sisters, in a letter brought to her by a gentleman. Her passionate response to the news is never seen on stage, but instead reported to Kent by the gentleman. What he is reporting, therefore, is Cordelia's reading of a letter—an event that the audience must have recognized as one filled with emotional possibility.

Kent. Did your letters pierce the queene to any demonstration of griefe.

Gent. I say she tooke them, read them in my presence,

And now and then an ample teare trild downe

Her delicate cheeke, it seemed she was a queene ouer her passion,

Who most rebell-like, sought to be King ore her.

Kent. O then it moued her.

Gent. Not to a rage, patience and sorow streme,

Who should expresse her goodliest you haue seene,

Sun shine and raine at once, her smiles and teares,

Were like a better way those happie smilets,

That playd on her ripe lip seeme not to know,

What guests were in her eyes which parted thence,

As pearles from diamonds dropt in briefe,

Sorow would be a raritie most beloued,

If all could so become it.

Kent. Made she no verball question.

Gent. Faith once or twice she heau'd the name of father,

Pantingly forth as if it prest her heart,

Cried sisters, sisters, shame of Ladies sisters:

Kent, father, sisters, what ith storme ith night,

Let pitie not be beleeft there she shooke,

The holy water from her heauenly eyes,

And clamour moystened her, then away she started,

To deale with griefe alone.

———

101, 102

Scrinia Ceciliana: mysteries of state & government: in letters of the late famous Lord Burghley, and other grand ministers of state: in the reigns of Queen Elizabeth, and King James. Being a further additional supplement of the Cabala. As also many remarkable passages faithfully revised, and no where else published. With two exact tables; the one of the letters, the other of things most observable
London: For G. Bedel and T. Collins, 1663
Folger S2109

Francis Bacon (1561–1626)
"Sundrie letters, conteyning matter of elegancie, worth, & moment, at seuerall times, & upon seuerall occasions, written to the excellent Maiestie of King James, & diuers other persons of honor & eminencie by Sir Francis Bacon deceased: aswell before he was his Maiesties Sollicitor: as in the after passages of his life, dignities & fortune wherein are inserted 3. Letters of K. James his owne: & some of others."
ca. 1630
Folger MS V.b.132

The overlap between manuscript and print cultures can be seen quite strikingly with these two volumes. In 1663, *Scrinia Ceciliana* appeared, which made public "Mysteries of State and Government: in Letters of the late Famous Lord Burghley, And other Grand Ministers of State: In the Reigns of Queen Elizabeth, and King

James." A ca. 1630 manuscript letterbook at the Folger, replete with a decorated title page and an index "of all the seuerall [i.e., 110] Letters conteyned in this Booke," suggests the influence of the practice of keeping manuscript letterbooks on the development of the genre of the printed "letterbook." Both volumes contain, among other similar entries, a series of letters sent out by Sir Francis Bacon along with presentation copies of his 1605 work *The Advancement of Learning*, to the Lord Treasurer Buckhurst, the Lord Chancellor Ellesmere, and the earl of Northampton (whom Bacon hoped would present the book to King James). The final letter asks the Cambridge preacher Dr. Thomas Playfere if he would consider translating the book into Latin; when Dr. Playfere died, Bacon undertook the work himself.

———

103
John Martin
Letterbook, 1652–1663, 1668, 1659–1663
Folger MS V.a.454

Typical of many letterbooks from the period, John Martin's book contained business and personal letters as well as a series of speeches and proceedings of the House of Lords. Both incoming and outgoing letters are transcribed, including letters to and from his mother, his brothers, his cousin, his uncle, his mother-in-law, and most touchingly, his wife Anne. Two of the last entries in the unfinished volume are devoted to her memory, serving as a reminder of their enduring love for each other. After the last letter from his wife, he inscribes a Latin passage from the Book of Job, which, translated into English reads: The Lord gave, and the Lord hath taken away; blessed be the name of the Lord.

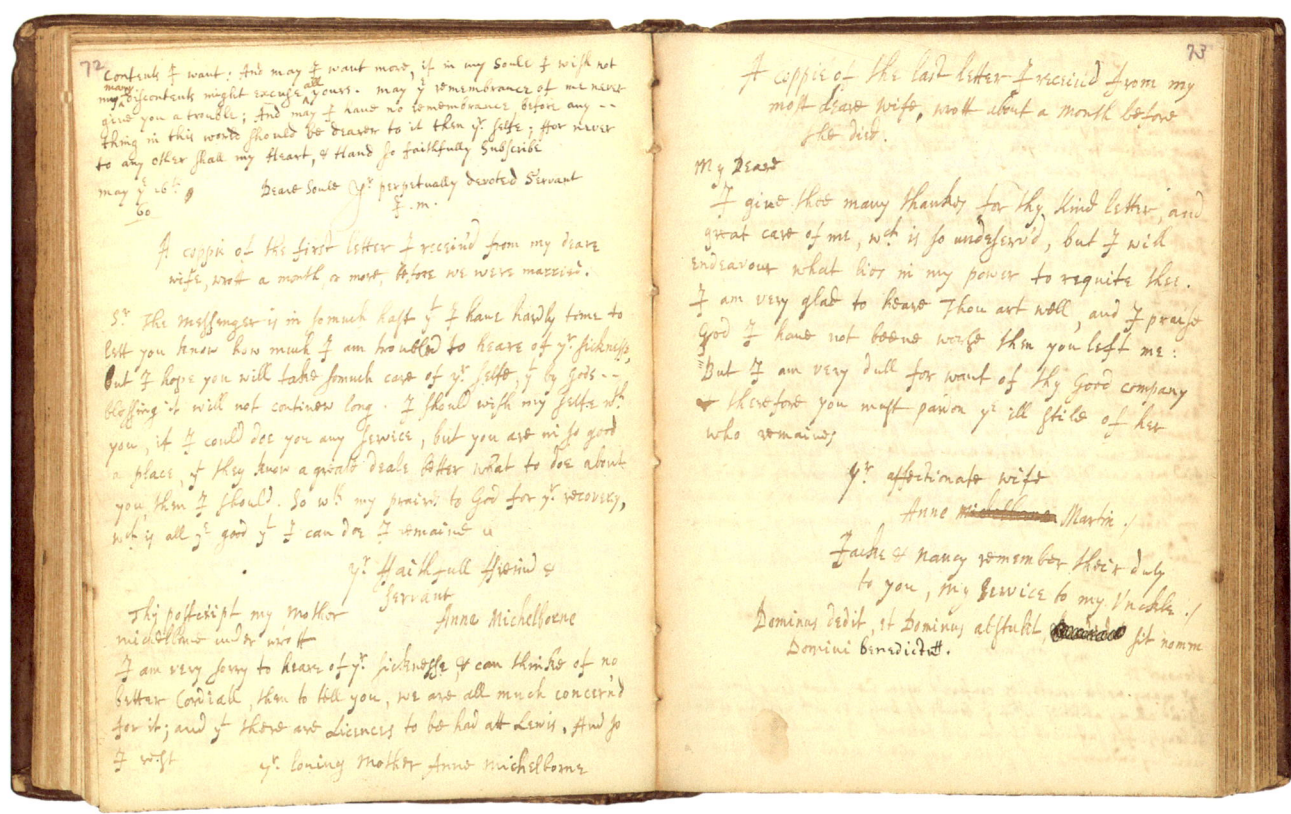

A coppie of the first letter I receiu'd from my deare
wife, wrott a month, or more, before we were married.

Sir. The messenger is in so much hast *tha*t I haue hardly time to
lett you know how much I am troubled to heare of *you*r sicknesse,
but I hope you will take somuch care of *you*r selfe, *tha*t by Gods
blessing it will not continew long. I should wish my selfe *wi*th
you, if I could doe you any service, but you are in so good
a place, *tha*t they know a greate deale better what to doe about
you, then I should. So *wi*th my praiers to God for *you*r recovery,
*whi*ch is all *the* good *tha*t I can doe I remaine
                              *you*r ffaithfull ffreind &
                                   servant
                                        Anne Michelborne
This postscript my Mother
Michelmore under wrott

I am very sorry to heare of *you*r sicknesse, & can thinke of no
better Cordiall, then to tell you, we are all much concern'd
for it; and *tha*t there are Licences to be had att Lewis, And so
I rest
                              *you*r louing Mother Anne Michelborne

A coppie of the last letter I receiu'd from my
most deare wife, wrott about a Month before
she died.

My Deare
I giue thee many thankes for thy kind letter, and
great care of me, *whi*ch is so undeserv'd, but I will
endeavour what lies in my power to requite thee.
I am very glad to heare thou art well, and I praise
God I haue not beene worse then you left me:
But I am very dull for want of thy Good company
Y therefore you must pardon *th*e ill stile of her
who remaines
                    Y*ou*r afffectionate wife
                              Anne ~~Michelborne~~ Martin ./

                    Jacke & Nancy remember their duty
                    to you, my Service to my Vnckle ./

          Dominus dedit, et Dominus abstulet, sit nomen
                    Domini benedictat.

104
Sir Francis Fane (d. ca. 1681)
Miscellany, compiled ca. 1655/56
Folger MS V.a.180

This book of aphorisms, anecdotes, and verse (about Holland, Germany, France, Italy, and England), was compiled by Sir Francis for his son Henry to entertain and enrich him while traveling on the Continent. It opens with a series of ten advice letters written for their sons by Henry's parents, grandparents, and great-grandparents between 1570 and 1656. In the initial letter, Sir Francis explains: "Your age now calling vpon me to send you abroad in to the world, where (by God's blessing) and your owne industry) you may advantage your internall and externall parts, better then in your fathers house; I thought good to make you Master of this litle Manuall," which includes "what fell from my worthy Progenitors penns, vpon the like occasion." Sir Francis included a copy of the letter below, which was written to him by his own mother, Mary (Mildmay) Fane, countess of Westmoreland.

[fols. 13ᵛ–14ʳ]

To my deare sonne Sir Francis Fane
Kni*gh*t of *the* Bath at Westmorland house
in Great St Bartholmews
London

Deare Boy
God hath made it *the* parents duty to take
care over their chilldren & *the* childrens
duty to expresse their thanks & loue by
liueing in their subiection & obedience,
and if you pe*r*form but yo*u*r part as
faithfully as I will (with Gods helpe
perform mine; wee shall help to
make each other extraordinarily
happy, w*h*ich is Gods blessing annexed
therevnto from *the* providence & vertues
of those from whom you are come,
You haue receiued honor and
maintenance, learne *the* rules of
vertue & practice nothing but
what is honest & noble, that you may
be an honour to that family that hath
honoured you, Now you come first into
the world be silent & observing, shew
not what is in you, till you haue putt
there by industry, that w*h*ich is worth
shewing, and when you obserue others
play *the* Bee, select for yo*u*r vse and
imitac*i*on onely the best, I never knew
any young man *that* was over open, that
was ever wise, but I haue knowne
some wise men that would talke

much, if you could doe but as well
as I can wish, and I were able to do
for you, as my heart desires; you
should be great both in vertue & estate,
but if you doe the best you can in the
first, I will doe *the* best I can in the
latter, and soe I hope you shall be
competently provided of both, which with
Gods blessing is as much as more to
his grace by my heartyest prayers
I dayly commend you, & desire you soe
to doe your selfe, & soe I rest

              Your affectionate loueing mother
                Mary Westmorland

Apthorpe *the* 25th
of January
1628.

———

105
Ben Jonson (1573?–1637)
Copy of a letter to an unknown woman, ca. mid-1605
Letterbook, ca. 1614
Folger MS V.a.321

This copy of a letter to the countess of Bedford (most likely) is one of a series of ten consecutive letters from Ben Jonson and George Chapman relating to their imprisonment for referring to James I and his Scottish entourage in the play "Eastward Ho!" The letterbook, written in two distinct hands, contains 140 letters originally written between 1582 and ca. 1614, and includes letters written by Elizabeth I, Francis Bacon, Robert Cecil, and John Dowland in addition to countless unidentified writers. It is thought that the letterbook was compiled by Peter Ferryman, who was acquainted with many of the letterwriters included in the volume.

Excellentest of Ladies./
And most honor'd of the Graces, Muses, and mcc; if it be not a sinne
to prophane your free hand with prison polluted Paper, I wolde intreate
some little of youre Ayde, to the defence of my Innocence, which is as cleare
as this leafe was (before I staind it) of any thinge halfe=worthye
this violent infliction; I am commytted, and with mee, a worthy Friend,
one Mr Chapman, a man, I can not say how knowne to your Ladishipp, but
I am sure knowne to mee to honor you; And our offence a Play, so
mistaken, so misconstrued, so misapplied, as I do wonder whether their
Ignorance, or Impudence be most, who are our aduersaries. / It is now
not disputable, for we stand on vneuenbases, and our cause so vnequal=
ly carried, as we are without examyninge, without hearinge, or with
out any proofe, but malicious Rumor, horried, to bondage and fetters;
The cause we vnderstand to be the Kinges indignation, for which we

are hartelye sorie, and the more, by how much the less we haue deseru'd
it. / What our sute is, the worthy employde soliciter, and equall
Adorer of youre vertues, can best enforme you. / .

Ben: Ihonson./.

————

106
Sir Humphrey Ferrers (son of Sir John Ferrers)
Copies of four letters to and from him, ca. October 1631
Folger MS L.e.677 (1–4)

This series of four letters exemplifies one kind of record-keeping—simply making
copies of letters and their responses and identifying them at the head with their
position in the series. In this instance, Ferrers has labeled the letters, copied onto
four sheets of paper with identical watermarks, as "my first letter," "the answeare,"
"my reply," and "his rejoinder." The letters concern an adultery case against one Mr.
Manley in the High Commission court in London, for which Ferrers needed the
unidentified correspondent to examine witnesses. Ferrers was in Dunstall, Staffordshire, at the time, and hoped not to have "to take an vnnecessarie Journey to
London." The case was of utmost concern to him, however, since "the world hath
an eye of thes proceeding*es* wherin my creditt (vpon vndertaking*es*) lies at stake,"
and "my honor lies at stake herein & I must defend it *with* the best guard I can."

————

107, 108, 109
Examples of endorsements
Lady Katherine (Lenthall) Hamilton Paisley (d. 1696)
Autograph letter signed, to her cousin, Col. Robert Warcupp
[November 1681]
Folger MS X.d. 375 (14)
Reproduced at 90%

Sir Richard Browne (1605-1683)
Autograph letter signed, to Robert Long
Paris, December 14, 1649 (New Style)
Folger MS Add 897 (1)
Reproduced at 100%

Lady Anne (Bacon) Townshend (1573-1622)
Autograph letter signed, to Sir Roger Townshend
[n.d.]
Folger MS L.d.594

Endorsements allowed the recipients of letters to be reminded of their contents
without having to unfold and reread them. The endorsement on the first example,
"Lady Pasley ab*out* S*ir* Johns ffunerall," provides the name of the individual whose
fate can already be deduced by the presence of a black seal.

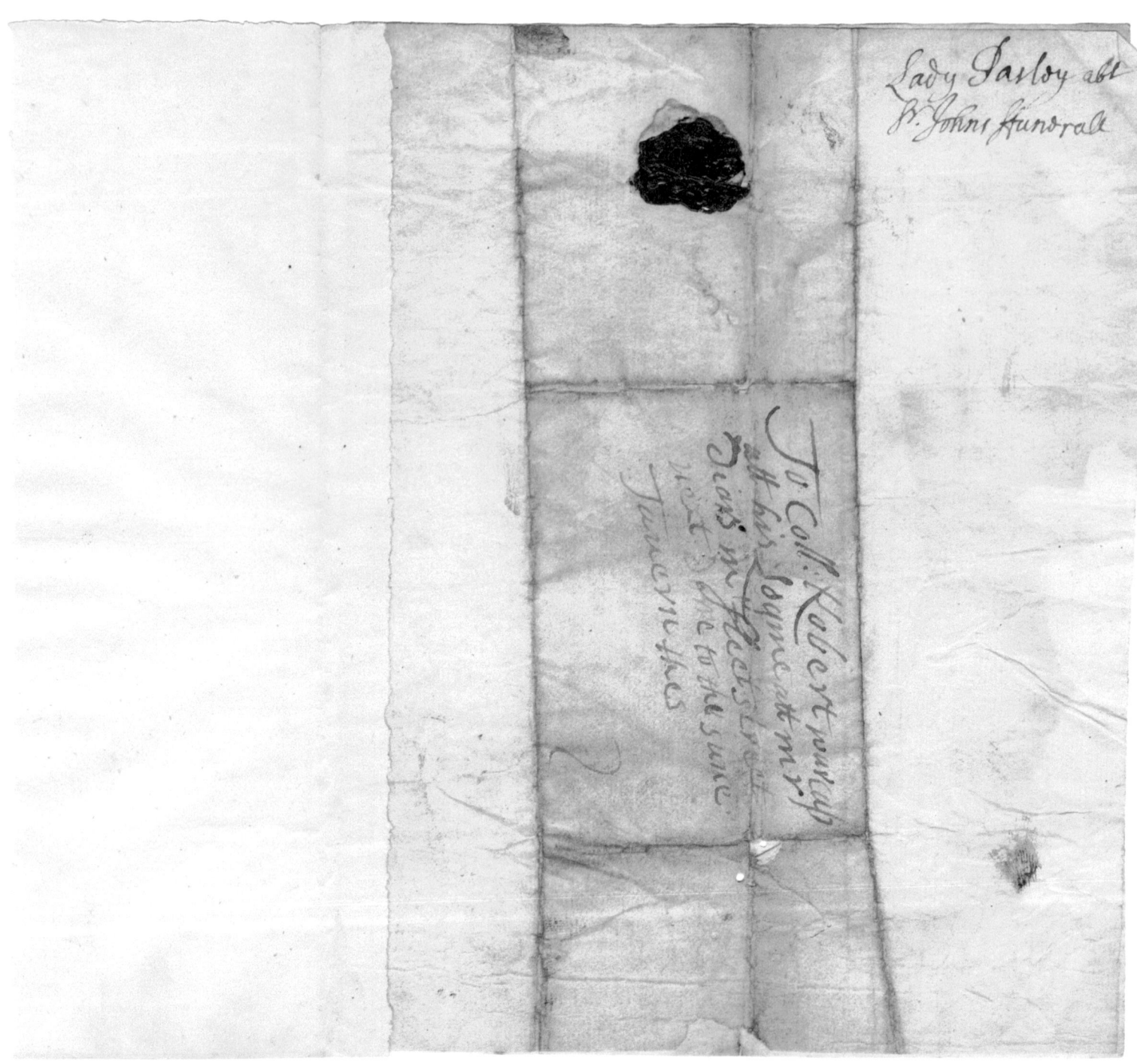

The second example,

> Sir Richard Browne of
> the 14th of december new
> stile
> Receyued the 11th old stile

exemplifies the complications associated with dating letters sent to or from the Continent, since England used the Julian, or "old style" calendar, which lagged ten days behind the Gregorian, or "new style" calendar, which had been adopted by most Continental countries in 1582. This letter appears to have been received three days before it was even sent, but by adding ten days to the "received" date, we see that it in fact took a week for the letter to arrive in London from Paris (in 1649).

Sir Roger Townshend patiently endorses a long letter from his mother (superscribed "To hir very Louinge sunn Sr Roger Towneshen at Londun geve these I pray you"), full of details about his sister's dowry: "My Mother her letter touching hir resolution concerning my Sisters portion."

———

110
Sir Harvey Bagot, bart. (1591–1660)
Autograph letter signed, to his father, Walter Bagot, with enclosed poetry
Oxford, May 14, 1609
Folger MS L.a.53 (1); L.a.58
Reproduced at 60%

It is rare today to find letters surviving with their enclosures, but the Folger's Bagot papers have yielded this example. In 1609, Harvey Bagot wrote from Trinity College, Oxford, to his father Walter Bagot. The letter, neatly written and in Latin, is highly formulaic and was evidently intended to show off the results of Harvey's university studies. Enclosed in the letter on a separate sheet was a verse, taking its starting point from two lines in Ovid's *Tristia*, dedicated from Harvey to his father, subscribed "your most obedient and studious son, Harveus Bagot." That the poem was inside the letter can be deduced from the impression of Harvey's personal seal (which featured his initials), which is clearly visible to the left of the verse. Despite the Latin content, Harvey addressed the letter in English so that the non-Latin-speaking bearer could deliver it accordingly.

109

111

Poem, "In reducem Ducem"

ca. 1627/28

Folger MS Add 806

The original folds and the stain from the wax seal of the outer letter are evidence that this 106-line poem was originally enclosed in a letter. A satirical account of the return of the king's favorite, George Villiers, the duke of Buckingham, from the infamous expedition to Rhe in November 1627, it circulated in multiple versions. This was typical of poems that were copied from variant sources and transmitted independently, rather than being the product of a single scriptorium. The Folger version begins: "And art returned great Duke, with all thie faults / thou great Comander of the All=go=naughts."

———————

112

Dorothy Constable

Autograph letter signed, to Lady Anne Ferrers

Edgeworth, May 4, 1633

Folger MS L.e.682

This letter, from Dorothy Constable to her sister, Lady Anne Ferrers, originally contained verses by Dorothy's daughter, written in her youth. Dorothy realizes that she will be seen as "a parshall and foolish mother" for sending these against her daughter's wishes, but she would rather have that than be thought "an vnkind sister."

     In this letter we also glimpse the difficulties of ascertaining where people are and the role that letters and their bearers play in conveying information. After a visit to Dorothy, Lady Anne returned home accompanied by Dorothy's son's servant, but the servant did not accompany her all the way, as he had been instructed. Now one Edward Littleton has worried Dorothy by informing her that Lady Anne did "not com home in easter week"; Dorothy is using Littleton to carry this letter. In the meantime, she waits for "m^r Boltons returne," since Mr. Bolton "might in forme vs bettor."

[superscription]

To my most deer and much
honored sister the Lady Anne
fferers at her hous at
Dunstall present thes
and my best wishis

[letter]

Deer Sister,

I much desier to heer of your safe ariuall at your owne home for
I understand by Mr Edward Litlton (whoam hath promised to
con=uay thes lines safely to your hands) that you wer not
com home in easter week. which makes me fear some disaster
might hapen and therfoer we long for m^r Boltons returne

that might in forme vs bettor. mi son was exseeding sory &
very angry with his man that he went no farther with you
for I a shuer you he (ment it) and com=manded him to waight
on you all the jurny and when he saw him com back at night
he would haue had him folloed you but he told him he brought
you beyand bedford & he should neuer ouer take you. but sence
we heard you lay in Bedford all night: Sweet sister I joy
much that I haue seen you and esteem it as a great fauor
both from my noble brother and your sellfe in that you wear
plesed to comply with my desiers. and giue me meeting. it hath
filld me full of contemplations and harty well wishis for your contents
and well faers. your sweet sosiety though shart hath made a great
impreshon of loue wher the carrackters of consanguinity wear so
deeply sett befoer. and I should euer be glad to giue testimony
of my affections one any occation that lieth with in my power
and your commands : now deer sister I think you may perseue
how preuelant your desiers ar with me. for I haue choes rather
to vndergoe the sensuer of a parshall and foolish mother. than an
vnkind sister. wherfoer sweet sister be plesed to keepe thes
verses from anys vew. for I ashuer you the cheef thing w*hich*
I and I think her frinds esteems them for is that thay wer
the frutes of her infansy. fer though ∧the∧ first of thes wer at
the age of 14 yett I haue many moer at the least 2 years
befoer that but I ∧se∧ she is so litle in loue with any she makes.
that she suppresis moer then I can possible saue from her: but
I confes my folly. the les she loues it the moer I delight
she should content her self to make moer: thus crauing a
fauerable construcitions of what erors you discouer ether in
her or me. reliing on your worthy disposistion which will be
an oblygation highle~estee~ estemed by

your affectionat sister

to sarue you

Dorothy Constable

Egworth this 4th of May

<u>1633</u>

[postscript in left
margin]

Sweet Sister present my saruis to S*ir* humphery
ferrers. I shall hartyly pray for both your
helths. good sister let me heer how you faer in
your helths. as often as you can. i haue sent you
the reseights allso, I pray remember my loue to my cosen lettes

113
John Greig
Autograph letter signed, to James Rattray, Laird of Craighall
April 12, 1677
Folger MS Add 1273 (140)

This letter from John Greig to the laird of Craighall commiserates with him on his father's death. But originally it contained some writing on the dead man, possibly poetry, since Greig refers to it as muse-inspired. Once again we confront the specter of bad handwriting: Greig admits that "myne is scarce legible" and suggests that the laird should have it transcribed "by some legible hand" if he feels it deserves to reach a wider audience—"if ye think it dare appear in the light."

> Laighwood 12 april 1677
>
> Much honored, On Sat*urta*y last I receaved ane letter sent be you (saving the Lords will) it being the first, came too shoone. Sir I am heavlilie sorie for the occasione for I am ane sharer in ye losse for as ye have lost ane loveing and deare father so I ane loving and kind friend yet Sir to sheu my respects & my oblidged dutie to him nou being dead as well as alive, I have roused up my dull and shalloue muse to trie what she could say in com*m*endation of her kind friend Such as it is I have sent here inclosed, & if ye think it dare appear in the light cause transcribe it by some legible hand. (for he see myne is scarce legible) & if not let it be buried in silence. I confesse it is not as I wold but as I could. Sir excuse my ignorance & fole and look upon me as Sir
> your well wisher, loving friend and servant to pouer
> John Greig

———

114
Christabella Rogers
Autograph verse, to Alice Fennell
ca. 1660?
Folger MS L.b.707

This letter consists of nothing but a verse in couplets defying the "tyranny" of Cupid. Presumably the creation of Christabella Rogers, it is presented by her to her cousin, Alice Fennell. The final line of the superscription "ddddd" is an emphatic instruction to "d" (deliver).

these
ffor my much
honoured Cusen
Al[i]ce Fennell
ddddd

[letter]
A songe made by Mrs Christabella Rogers
Cupid away for I defy
the power of all thy tyranny,
thy darts ar blunted and noe eyes
shall neuer make of me their prise
I am soe armd against thy will
it is not in thy power to kill
Noe louely face nor curled locks
shall euer make me feele those shocks
which some fond louers haue endured
for new resolues haue now quite curde
all those deep wounds which ons you made
and my disturbancis are layed
within the secrets of a hart
that will not thinke one former smart
anew relaps I feare it not
therefore leaue of each subtle plotte
against a soule that scorns to come
a captive to thy martyrdome
and by these Rithms Ide haue you know
that all in uayne you bend your bow
all you can get is but contempt
since frome loues passion ime exempt
you are a god but yet soe blind
that my strict thoughts youll never find
therfore Repayer to your fayer mother
and from her knowledge doe not smother
that enyme that you haue gaind
and let her see I am so chaind
to my obdurate will and pleasure
not one to fear or waite for leasure
till shee hath furnisht thee with darts
of power to perce all stony harts
Noe mine shall proue like adamant
atractiue by a full consent
to draw more harts yet not to thee
but that they may strait follow mee
to some enameled spash$_\wedge$ ^{ci}$_\wedge$as feild
to fix a battle not to yeeld
to thy weake power with crossed arm$_\wedge^{e}_\wedge$s
but they shall wake at thy alarmes
and with new uigour fight with thee
that thus wouldst take their libertie
arme arme all harts that will resist

for cupids entred in the lists
Rouze up my muse and with one word
distroy this boy which maks discord
in quiet soules that faine would bee
secured from his trecherie
challeng him boldly you will spie
the crafty winkeing of his eye
for weare he blinde as poets say
he neuer could our harts betray

[vertical on right side
of page]

Glossary

———

ADDRESS LEAF the outer fold of a folded sheet of paper, or the verso of a letter, on which the address or superscription is written (and where the endorsement, if any, is written)

AUTOGRAPH that which is written in a person's own handwriting; the author's own manuscript.

BEARER one who brings a letter, a verbal message, tidings, rumours, etc.

CARRIER a bearer of a message, letter, etc.

DUST-BOX a box from which "dust," i.e. fine sand or powder, is sprinkled on something (e.g. on writing, for the purpose now served by blotting-paper)

ENCLOSURE a document or letter enclosed within another.

ENDORSE to inscribe (a document) on the back *with* words indicating the nature of its contents, one's opinion of its value, some extension or limitation of its provisions, etc.

ENDORSEMENT a signature, memorandum, or remark usually written on the back of a document.

HAND the action of the hand in writing and its product; handwriting; style of writing; *esp.* as belonging to a particular person, country, period, profession, etc. The Elizabethan **SECRETARY** hand, a cursive script popular in England in the sixteenth and early-to-mid-seventeenth centuries, could be written at great speed and is notable for the single-lobed "a"; the flat-topped, open-tailed "g"; and the many variants of "r," "e," "s," and "h." The **ITALIC** hand, the hand used most frequently by women, has letter forms much closer to our own compared to the secretary hand. It was formed with fairly straight strokes and often distinguished by curved or "clubbed" heads on letters with ascenders (b, d, f, h, k, l). The **MIXED** hand, which became increasingly popular in the seventeenth century, combined attributes of secretary and italic hands, maximizing speed and legibility.

INKPOT a small pot for holding writing-ink.

INTERLINE to insert (a word or words) between the lines in a written document; also, loosely, between word and word.

PACKET a small pack, package, or parcel: in earliest use applied to a parcel of letters or dispatches, and esp. to the State parcel or "mail" of dispatches to and from foreign countries.

PARCHMENT the skin of the sheep or goat, and sometimes that of other animals, dressed and prepared for writing, painting, engraving, etc.

PEN KNIFE a small knife, usually carried in the pocket, used originally for making and mending quill pens.

POST from the beginning of the 16th c., applied to the system of men with horses stationed in places at suitable distances along the post-roads, the duty of each being to ride with, or forward with all speed to the next stage, the king's "packet," and at length the letters of other persons, as well as to furnish change of horses to "thorough-posts" or express messengers riding post.

POST-BOY a boy or man who rides post; a letter-carrier.

POST-HASTE haste or speed like that of one traveling "post"; great expedition in traveling.

POST-HORN a horn formerly used by a postman or the guard of a mail-coach, to announce arrival.

POST-HORSE a horse kept at a post-house or inn for the use of post-riders, or for hire for the conveyance of travelers.

POST-HOUSE an inn or other house where horses are kept for the use of travelers; a posting house.

POSTMASTER *orig.* a master of the posts; the officer who had the charge or direction of the post-messengers, whose office gradually developed into that of postmaster general. In the 17th and 18th c., the post-office servant at each of the stations or stages of a post-road, whose primary duty it was to carry the mails to the next stage, and subsequently, to receive and deliver or send out the letters for his own town or district; orig. called "post"; in 1668 *deputy postmaster*. The master of a posting station, who provides horses for posting; one who keeps a posting establishment (the several postmasters who carried the mails being the only persons licensed to let horses to travelers).

POST-OFFICE in early use, sometimes meaning the office of the master of the posts, or postmaster (general); in other instances it is difficult to separate it from the local center or head quarters of the department, the General Post Office in London or other capital. The name appears first under the Commonwealth, the earlier name having been *letter-office*.

POST-ROAD a road on which a series of post-houses or stations for post-horses is (or was) established; a road on which mails were carried.

POSTSCRIPT a paragraph written at the end of a letter, after the signature, containing an afterthought or additional matter.

POST-STAGE in 17th c., a stopping-place, station, or "stage" on a post-road, to which the king's packet or mail was carried from the previous "stage" and whence it was forwarded to the next; post-horses being kept in readiness for thus carrying the mail, and for the use of "thorough-posts" or express messengers, as also for the service of private persons traveling "post," who there took fresh horses.

POST-TOWN a town having a (head) post office, or one that is not merely a sub-office of another.

POUNCE a fine powder, as pulverized sandarac or cuttle-shell, used to prevent the ink from spreading in writing over an erasure or on unsized paper, and also to prepare the surface of parchment to receive writing. (a pounce pot is a small box with a perforated lid for sprinking pounce)

QUILL the feather of a large bird (usually a goose) formed into a pen by pointing and slitting the lower end of the barrel.

RECTO the front of a leaf of manuscript.

SAND-BOX a box with a perforated top for sprinkling sand as a blotter upon the wet ink of a manuscript.

SEAL a piece of wax or some other plastic or adhesive substance (originally, and still frequently, one bearing the impression of a signet), fixed on a folded letter or document, in such a way that an opening cannot be effected without breaking it. An engraved stamp of metal or other hard material used to make an impression upon wax, etc. affixed as a "seal" (also known as the seal matrix or die). A device or inscription engraved on a seal.

SEALING-WAX in early use, beeswax or a composition containing this, prepared for the purpose of receiving the impression of seals. It is usually coloured scarlet with vermilion, but black sealing wax is used for mourning, and green, blue, etc. for reasons of ornament.

SECRETARY one who is entrusted with private or secret matters; a confidant; one privy *to* a secret. One whose office it is to write for another; *spec.* one who is employed to conduct or assist with correspondence, to keep records, and (usually) to transact various other business, for another person or for a society, corporation, or public body. One who writes (on a particular occasion) for another. One skilled in letter-writing. In the titles of books on the art of letter-writing.

SIGNET a small seal, usually one fixed in a finger-ring. An impressed seal or stamp; *esp.* the stamp or impression of a signet.

SIGN-MANUAL an autograph signature (*esp.* that of the sovereign) serving to authenticate a document.

STANDISH a stand containing ink, pens and other writing materials and accessories; an inkstand; also, an inkpot.

SUBSCRIPTION a piece of writing at the end of a document, *e.g.* the concluding clause or formula of a letter with the writer's signature.

SUPERSCRIPTION the address or direction on the outer leaf of a letter.

VELLUM a fine kind of parchment prepared from the skins of calves (lambs or kids) and used especially for writing, painting, or binding

VERSO the back of a leaf in a manuscript.

WRITING BOX a small box for containing paper and other writing requisites. Also, a small portable writing-desk.

(definitions are adapted from the *Oxford English Dictionary*, except for "address leaf" and the secondary definitions of "hand")

Suggested Readings

Beale, Philip. *A History of the Post in England from the Romans to the Stuarts* (Aldershot: Ashgate, 1998).

Bergeron, David M. *King James & Letters of Homoerotic Desire* (Iowa City: University of Iowa Press, 1999).

Braunmuller, A. R. "Accounting for Absence: The Transcription of Space," in *New Ways of Looking at Old Texts: Papers of the Renaissance English Text Society, 1985–1991*, ed. W. Speed Hill (Binghamton NY: MRTS/RETS, 1993), 47–56.

Brayshay, Mark, Philip Harrison, and Brian Chalkley. "Knowledge, nationhood and governance: the speed of the Royal post in early-modern England," *Journal of Historical Geography* 24 (1998), 265–88.

Chartier, Roger, Alain Boureau and Cécile Dauphin eds. *Correspondence: Models of Letter-Writing From the Middle Ages to the Nineteenth Century*, trans. Christopher Woodall (Princeton: Princeton University Press, 1997).

Crofts, J. *Packhorse, Waggon and Post: Land Carriage and Communications under the Tudors and Stuarts* (London: Routledge and Kegan Paul, 1967).

Daybell, James. "Women's Letters and Letter-Writing in England, 1540–1603: An Introduction to the Issues of Authorship and Construction," *Shakespeare Studies* 27 (1999), 161–86.

Daybell, James, ed. *Early Modern Women's Letter Writing, 1450-1700* (London: Palgrave, 2001).

Daybell, James. *Privy and Powerful Communications: Tudor Women Letter Writers* (Oxford: Oxford University Press, forthcoming).

Donne, John. *John Donne's Marriage Letters*, eds M. Thomas Hester, Robert Parker Sorlien and Dennis Flynn (Washington, DC: Folger Shakespeare Library, forthcoming).

Gibson, Jonathan. "Letters," in *A Companion to English Renaissance Literature and Culture*, ed. Michael Hattaway (Oxford: Blackwell, 2000), 615–19.

Gibson, Jonathan. "Significant Space in Manuscript Letters," *The Seventeenth Century* 12 (1997), 1–9.

Goldberg, Jonathan. *Writing Matter: From the Hands of the English Renaissance* (Stanford: Stanford University Press, 1990).

Guillén, Claudio. "Notes Toward the Study of the Renaissance Letter," in *Renaissance Genres: Essays on Theory, History and Interpretation*, ed. Barbara Kiefer Lewalski (Cambridge MA: Harvard University Press, 1986), 70–101.

Hammer, Paul E.J., "The Uses of Scholarship: The Secretariat of Robert Devereux, Second Earl of Essex, c. 1581–1601," *English Historical Review* 109 (1994), 26–51.

Henderson, Judith Rice. "On Reading the Rhetoric of the Renaissance Letter," in *Renaissance-Rhetorik/Renaissance Rhetoric*, ed. Heinrich F. Plett (Berlin: Walter de Gruyter, 1993), 143–62.

Hornbeak, Katherine Gee. "The Complete Letter-Writer in English, 1568–1800," *Smith College Studies in Modern Languages* 15 (1934), 1–150.

Jardine, Lisa. *Erasmus Man of Letters: The Construction of Charisma in Print* (Princeton: Princeton University Press, 1993).

Lerer, Seth. *Courtly Letters in the Age of Henry VIII: Literary Culture and the Arts of Deceit* (Cambridge: Cambridge University Press, 1997).

Levy, F.J. "How Information Spread Among the Gentry, 1550–1640," *Journal of British Studies* 21 (1982), 11–34.

Magnusson, Lynne. *Shakespeare and Social Dialogue: Dramatic Language and Elizabethan Letters* (Cambridge: Cambridge University Press, 1999).

Magnusson, Lynne. "Widowhood and Linguistic Capital: The Rhetoric and Reception of Anne Bacon's Epistolary Advice," *ELR* 31 (2001), 3–33.

Magnusson, Lynne. "A Rhetoric of Requests: Genre and Linguistic Scripts in Elizabethan Women's Letters," in *Women and Politics in Early Modern England, 1450–1700*, ed. James Daybell (Aldershot: Ashgate, 2003), 51–66.

Murphy, James J. "*Ars dictaminis*: The Art of Letter-Writing" (ch. 5) in his *Rhetoric in the Middle Ages: A History of Rhetorical Theory from Saint Augustine to the Renaissance* (Berkeley: University of California Press, 1974), 194–268.

Robertson, Jean. *The Art of Letter Writing: An essay on the handbooks published in England during the sixteenth and seventeenth centuries* (Liverpool and London: University Press of Liverpool/Hodder & Stoughton, 1942).

Robinson, Howard. *The British Post Office: A History* (Princeton: Princeton University Press, 1948).

Schneider, Gary. *The Culture of Epistolarity: Vernacular Letters and Letter Writing in Early Modern England, 1500–1700* (Newark: University of Delaware Press, forthcoming).

Steen, Sara Jayne. *The Letters of Lady Arbella Stuart* (New York: Oxford University Press, 1994).

Steen, Sara Jayne. "Reading Beyond the Words: Material Letters and the Process of Interpretation." *Quidditas: Journal of the Rocky Mountain Medieval and Renaissance Association*, 22 (2001), 55–69.

Stewart, Alan. "The Early Modern Closet Discovered," *Representations* 50 (1995), 76–100.

Sutton, Peter C., et al. *Love Letters: Dutch Genre Paintings in the Age of Vermeer* (Greenwich, CT: Bruce Museum of Arts & Science; Dublin: National Gallery of Ireland, 2003).

Taylor, Nancy. *Cousins in Love: The Letters of Lydia DuGard, 1665-1672* (Tempe, AZ: Arizona Center for Medieval and Renaissance Studies in conjunction with the Renaissance English Text Society, 2003).

Van Houdt, T., J. Papy, G. Tournoy and C. Matheeussen, eds. *Self-Presentation and Social Identification: The Rhetoric and Pragmatics of Letter Writing in Early Modern Times* (Leuven: Brill, 2002).

Whigham, Frank. "The Rhetoric of Elizabethan Suitors' Letters," *PMLA* 96 (1981), 864–82.

Whyman, Susan E. *Sociability and Power in Late-Stuart England: The Cultural Worlds of the Verneys 1660–1720* (Oxford: Oxford University Press, 1999).

Wolfe, Heather. *Elizabeth Cary, Lady Falkland: Life and Letters* (Cambridge: RTM, 2001).

Woudhuysen, H. R. *Sir Philip Sidney and the Circulation of Manuscripts* (Oxford: Clarendon Press, 1986).

Index of senders and recipients*

———

———

* Letters are referred to by item number. Letters "sent" are in italic.

Design:
Studio A
Alexandria, Virginia

Printing:
Hagerstown Bookbinding and Printing
Hagerstown, Maryland

Paper:
Text: Crane's Choice Pearl White Digital, 28lb
Cover: Crane's Choice Pearl White Cover, 90lb

Type:
Minion

[postmasters' timestamps]
at dartford at tue in the after
none
Rochester at fyve
Syttyngbor*n* p*a*st 6.
Caunterbury past .8.